FROMMER'S

COMPREHENSIVE TRAVEL GUIDE

RIO '91-'92

by Michael Uhl

PRENTICE
HALL
PRESS

NEW YORK • LONDON • TORONTO • SYDNEY • TOKYO • SINGAPORE

FROMMER BOOKS

Published by Prentice Hall Press
A division of Simon & Schuster Inc.
15 Columbus Circle
New York, NY 10023

ISBN 0-13-334491-6
ISSN 0899-2762

Manufactured in the United States of America

CONTENTS

MAPS

A Disclaimer

Although every effort was made to ensure the accuracy of the prices and travel information appearing in this book, it should be kept in mind that prices do fluctuate in the course of time, and that information does change under the impact of the varied and volatile factors that affect the travel industry.

SENSUAL RIO: AN INTRODUCTION

1. THE LAND
2. RIO'S HISTORY

If ever we humans devise a universal language, our word for pleasure will undoubtedly be Rio. For no other settled stretch of earthly geography caters quite so uninhibitedly to the gratification of the senses as does this beachfront Eden of the South Atlantic. *Cariocas* (as Rio's residents are called) are unabashed hedonists. Their minds may worship elsewhere, but their bodies are surely pagan. One need not look beyond the blazing orb that shines so constantly over Rio's skies and beaches to guess the real object of the average Carioca's devotion. Indeed no social ideal is more cherished among them, rich and poor alike, than the "right" to spend—at a minimum—every weekend and holiday on some sandy beach washed by the pounding surf and bathed in the glimmer of a strong tropical sun.

Most days of course, Cariocas, like the rest of us, must work hard to get their living. But they also play hard, and often, at night; so much so that one could be excused for imagining that Cariocas have somehow evolved beyond the necessity of a good night's sleep, even during the work week. Many of Rio's top nightspots are open and animated seven days a week, year-round. So visitors will rarely be deprived of the opportunity for an evening of romance, music, and dance.

No activity among Rio's other sensual rituals, however, is more sacred than eating. The idea of a rushed meal, indifferently prepared and consumed with grim formality, would be an abomination to most Brazilians, particularly Cariocas who have honed the institution of "café society" into an existential artform. As for the quality of the Brazilian kitchen (Rio's very much included), few cultures, if any, can boast superiority.

The Carioca lifestyle was not created to satisfy the demands of tourism. Rio's unique culture of sensuality has long preceded the city's new-found popularity as a destination for the contemporary tourist. Effete European travelers discovered Rio's charms in the early 19th century. Even the somewhat stodgy Darwin, who stopped there in the 1830s, noted the rare grace and natural beauty of the city in the journal of his famous voyage. For many years thereafter, Rio remained the well-kept secret of adventurers and, later, of international jet-setters and some smattering of others who happened upon the city through commerce, study, or government service. Even today, tourism in Rio is only a thin overlay on what remains a thoroughly Brazilian city. Tourist facilities, moreover, are well integrated into the principal Carioca beach neighborhoods. Copacabana, for example, remains Rio's most popular tourist stop, as well as its densest—and still among its trendiest—neighborhood. Much appreciated Ipanema is even less touristy, but studded with fine shops, restaurants, and nightclubs. Hotels in these two neighborhoods in particular provide ideal bases from which to explore as many layers of the city's reality as desired, whether near or far. They are equally ideal places to come home to, where the services and conveniences that tourists depend on in a foreign culture are readily at hand.

1. The Land

Rio is a sprawling metropolis of approximately 10,000,000 inhabitants, and most of the city is of little interest to the casual vacationer. Tourist Rio is largely restricted to the **Zona Sul**—the city's southern neighborhoods—which begins at the mouth of the harbor in Guanabara Bay and continues along the shores of the Atlantic Ocean. The much larger **Zona Norte** is primarily suburban and, in places, terribly impoverished. Except at the fringes—close to Rio's downtown called the **Centro**—the northern zone is seldom visited by tourists. All the hotels, and most of the restaurants, shopping, nightlife, and sightseeing activities, are to be found in the Zona Sul. Rio's downtown has its day and nighttime attractions, but it is not where most tourists choose to stay when the alternatives include such beachside neighborhoods as Copacabana, Ipanema, and several other desirable locales on the outskirts of the city. Only the most intrepid are likely to wander beyond downtown to the edge of the Zona Norte, even though the attractions there include one or two fine museums, the zoo, the soccer stadium, and samba rehearsals for the clubs that perform in Rio's lavish pre-Lenten Carnival parade. Carnival, of course, is Rio's single most important yearly attraction. Thousands of international visitors flock to the city, where all normal business ceases for a week and the raucous partying in clubs and on the streets goes on around the clock. Hotel reservations for visits during Carnival time had best be made a year in advance. For the remainder of the year, despite numerous other events or activities of interest to special groups, Rio's tourist scene is dominated by the beach culture. And the vast majority of visitors from abroad come to soak up the sun, schmooze at poolside, experiment with new foods and drinks, shop for bargains in jewels and fashions, and, at night, listen or dance to the hot rhythms that have enhanced Brazil's musical reputation the world over.

Rio's natural beauty is unrivaled among the cities of the world, with nature's spectacular backdrop adding an omnipresent dimension. Rio may be enjoyed actively or passively according to taste. The curvaceous sweep of the city's shoreline is deeply satisfying to the mind's eye which so appreciates the shapes and forms of things. Several hotels, moreover, have rooftop restaurants or terraces with beach views that are memorable by day or night. The views from **Corcovado** and **Sugar Loaf Mountain** embrace the entire city at once, and are pure magic.

Most of Rio is built on a long, narrow strip of land that accompanies the undulating coast. Formed of the pulverized sediment deposited by tidal action over eons, this coastal swath today barely separates the ocean from the surrounding hills and mountains, several of which actually rise from the very edge of the water. The bald, volcanic cones closest to the sea, like Sugar Loaf Mountain, are among the city's most distinguishing landmarks. Slightly inland are the highlands, carpeted in lush vegetation, that reach almost to land's end and divide Rio into its two geographic zones. Straddling this boundary is the great **Tijuca Park,** an enormous green space penetrating to the very heart of the city. Tijuca Park is adorned by the peak of Corcovado, where the monumental statue of Christ spreads his arms over the city of which it has become the most recognizable symbol. Rio stretches over fifty miles along this narrow alluvial band, from midway up the bay at the beginning of the Zona Norte, around the harbor mouth occupied by the commercial center, and sharply south along the oceanfront embracing the chic beach communities of the Zona Sul. The human spectacle in Rio may change radically as you travel from neighborhood to neighborhood, but democratic Nature has spread its aesthetic bounty evenly within the city for the benefit of all.

2. Rio's History

A HISTORICAL SKETCH

Rio, as it appears today, did not really begin to take shape until well into the 20th century. By World War I, the communities of Copacabana and Ipanema were just emerging from their long-standing roles as fishing villages and summer communities. Development was concentrated in the downtown area, and it spread slowly inland and up and down the shores of the surrounding bayside, north to São Cristovão and Penha, and south to Glória, Flamengo, and Botafogo. Rio retained much of its colonial appearance until the mid-1900s when a spurt of planned expansion began to transform the city's diminutive Old World scale into the derivative grandeur of the empire period then fashionable on the Continent, where it marked the growth of European imperial ambitions. During those years, the helter-skelter layout of narrow stone lanes was replaced by wide boulevards designed for exclusive commercial use, and the eclectic communal covenant that had placed the mansions of the wealthy cheek by jowl with the hovels of the wretched was superseded by planned neighborhoods where residency was graded according to social position and income. The slums were cleared from the city center, and the *favelas*—the hillside ghettos which bear perennial witness to Brazil's third-world status—were pushed to the periphery of the city, where land speculation and development had been dormant.

Modern downtown Rio is today a city of skyscrapers, while the most prosperous of its beach communities and inland neighborhoods are densely packed with high-rise apartments. What remains of the city's colonial flavor—mostly churches, monasteries, and a few old government buildings and public squares—is preserved in the core of the city's oldest section, close to the waterfront between Praça XV (square) and the Praça Mauá. Other individual remnants of the colonial days are scattered throughout the city, offering momentary relief from the sea of modernity that surrounds them—added reminders that Rio, unlike so many of Brazil's historical cities, belongs not to the past, but to the present.

PORTUGUESE RULE

It was on a hill in the old downtown where the Portuguese established their first fortifications in 1560. They were spurred to finally settle the harbor they had discovered five decades earlier by the encroachment of the French, who had established a colony of their own on several islands in the Bay of Guanabara. In 1502, two years after Alvarez Cabral landed at Brazil with a fleet that was bound for India, Portuguese navigators were dispatched to explore and chart the coast of the new continent. Traveling to the south, they entered a harbor where the current was so swift that they imagined they had come upon a great river which they named Rio de Janeiro, having made the discovery on the first of January. During the ensuing years, the harbor was used for anchorage and resupplying by numerous explorers, but the Portuguese concentrated their own colonizing efforts on the northeastern coast of Bahia and Pernambuco, where they established sugar and tobacco plantations and were to soon dominate the world market in the production of those commodities. Until the French offered their challenge, Portugal had virtually ignored the south, except for the one prosperous settlement of São Vicente below Rio, in what is today Santos, the port city for São Paulo.

Mem de Sá, the Portuguese governor-general of Brazil who was based in the Bahian capital of Salvador, finally drove the French from Brazilian soil in 1567. From that time on, the city of Rio de Janeiro grew, slowly at first, until gold was discovered in nearby Minas Gerais in 1693. Then the port of Rio prospered as the shipping point for this new-found wealth that was to provide Europe with enough capital to finance the Industrial Revolution. The French returned in 1711 to sack the city, but Rio's residents ransomed their way to freedom. By 1763, Rio had recovered sufficiently to replace Salvador as the colonial capital of Brazil, a strategic move by the Portuguese to finally secure their boundaries with

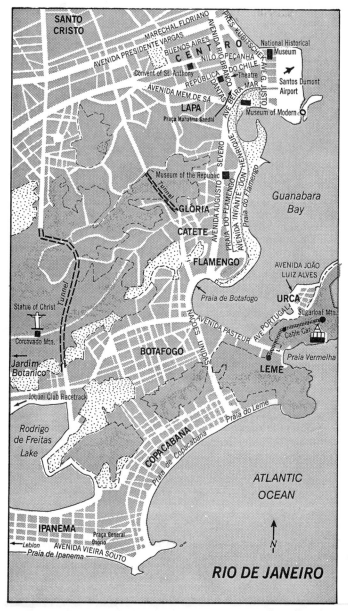

SANTO CRISTO

CENTRO

MARECHAL FLORIANO

AVENIDA PRESIDENTE VARGAS

BUENOS AIRES

NILO PEÇANHA

PREŜ. KUBITSCHEK

AVE. G. JUSTO

AVENIDA RIO BRANCO

REPÚBLICA

DANTAS

AVENIDA MEM. DE SÁ

Convent of St. Anthony

Theatre

AVE. BEIRA MAR

National Historical Museum

Santos Dumont Airport

LAPA

Praça Mahatma Gandhi

Museum of Modern

Museum of the Republic

GLÓRIA

Tunnel

SEVERO

AVENIDA AUGUSTO

PRAIA DO FLAMENGO

AVENIDA INFANTE DON HENRIQUE

Praia do Flamengo

CATETE

FLAMENGO

Guanabara Bay

AVENIDA JOÃO LUIZ ALVES

URCA

Praia de Botafogo

Sugarloaf Mtn.

Statue of Christ

Tunnel

AVENIDA PASTEUR

AVE. PORTUGAL

Cable Car

NAÇÕES UNIDAS

Corcovado Mtn.

Praia Vermelha

Jardim Botanico

BOTAFOGO

LEME

Joquei Club Racetrack

Rodrigo de Freitas Lake

Praia do Leme

COPACABANA

Praia de Copacabana

ATLANTIC OCEAN

IPANEMA

Praça General Osorio

Leblon

AVENIDA VIEIRA SOUTO

Praia de Ipanema

N

RIO DE JANEIRO

the Spanish to the south, as far as Argentina and the basin of the Rio de la Plata. The Passeio Público, Rio's oldest public park, and a busy downtown square called the Largo da Carioca, are two features in the contemporary city that survive from this period.

Rio had by now outgrown the confines of its hills by the harborside and began to spread into suburban lands that had hitherto formed the innermost circle of surrounding farms and plantations. By the beginning of the 19th century, neighborhoods like Laranjeiras, under the shadow of Corcovado, and coveside Botafogo, bordered at one end by Sugar Loaf Mountain, were where the city's most fashionable addresses could be found. Rio in those days enjoyed its privileged status in Brazil, its relative independence from the Crown in daily affairs, and its steady, if unspectacular, prosperity. But a major and unforeseen event was to undermine, with one dramatic stroke, the stolid self-satisfaction enjoyed by Rio's colonial population, and transform the city forever from a graceful provincial backwater into a capital of world power. In 1808, the Portuguese royal family was driven from Lisbon by the approaching troops of the Napoleonic army and transported under British sponsorship to their American colony in Brazil. João VI, then prince regent, who ruled on behalf of his demented mother, the Queen, arrived in Rio with an entourage of 15,000 noblemen and retainers; and for the next 13 years, the entire Portuguese Empire was ruled from the capital of its principal colony.

When Dom João returned to Portugal in 1821, he left his son, Pedro, who soon declared Brazil's independence and established the Brazilian Empire with himself as the first Emperor. During his father's residency, Rio quadrupled in size, and João introduced many administrative and judicial reforms and created institutions that had been absent from the colony, including Brazil's first newspaper, a state bank, a medical school, and the Botanical Gardens, which remain one of the monarch's most lasting contributions to the city. Rio survived the empire and became capital of the Brazilian Republic, belatedly established in 1889, and retaining its political primacy until 1960. In that year, the seat of government power was transferred to Brasília, the ultramodern planned city that was built over the short span of four years on an uninhabited plateau closer to the center of this vast country. Brazil remains relatively unsettled to this day. Rio is no longer the country's political center, nor even Brazil's largest city—outstripped some years back by dynamic, industrial São Paulo. But in the eyes of the world, and even for many of its own countrymen and women, Rio remains symbolically what it was in fact for two centuries—the first city of Brazil.

FAST FACTS RIO

This chapter contains practical information of a general nature that will make your stay in Rio more enjoyable and help you gain some insight into the more obvious social and cultural differences that distinguish Brazilian reality from your own.

AIRLINES: **VARIG Airlines** provides the greatest number of flights from the U.S. to Brazil, followed by **Pan American Airways.** Both airlines offer nonstop flights to Rio de Janeiro from New York, Miami, and Los Angeles.

VARIG also operates several flights to Rio weekly from Toronto and Montreal. The national airlines of various South American countries with flights originating in the U.S. also have stopovers in Rio. For a listing of these flights, consult your travel agent.

BABYSITTERS: The very best hotels offer babysitting services. You can expect to pay in the vicinity of $5 per hour, perhaps even more. Remember, you are hiring a bilingual babysitter, not a neighbor's teenaged daughter or son. Otherwise, you must pretty much resolve to have the kids with you, unless they're old enough to go to the pool or game room by themselves. For this reason, if you're planning to travel with children, you'd be best off selecting a self-contained resort, where there are likely to be both programs for children and babysitting when required. In Rio, the best bets, especially for parents traveling with small children, are the Sheraton, the Hotel Intercontinental, or the various apart-hotels (efficiencies) in Barra da Tijuca.

BANKS: Banking hours in Rio are from 10 a.m. to 4:30 p.m. weekdays. Major U.S. banks have branches in Rio: **Chase Manhattan,** Rua do Ouvidor 98 (tel. 216-6112); **Bank of Boston,** Avenida Rio Branco 110 (tel. 291-6123); **Citibank,** Rua da Assembléia 100 (tel. 276-3636). The **Banco do Brasil**—Brazil's largest bank—has branches throughout the city, including the International Airport, which is open around the clock.

CIGARETTES: American cigarettes were once fashionable in Brazil, but have all but disappeared from most counters where tobacco products are sold. Shops in all the better hotels sell American cigarettes, as do the top restaurants. Brazilian cigarettes appear to be of comparable quality, however, and are priced at around 50¢ a pack. There is little antismoking consciousness in Brazil, so non-smokers should prepare themselves for the assault. It would be most surprising, however, if some Brazilian smoker in your company should refuse to extinguish his cigarette when asked to do so politely. A total stranger will probably be less accommodating.

CLIMATE: Rio offers beach weather most of the year, with average temperatures around 80°F, climbing to 105°F on the hottest summer days, which in Brazil occur from December through February. Summer rains are frequent, but they often last for only an hour or two and bring welcome relief from the humidity. Bright, sunny days are very much the rule in Rio, but periods of rain lasting several days are also possible when the city is besieged by an ocean squall. Temperatures fall into the mid-60s in winter, with July being the "coldest" month. Travelers from the chilly north will find many winter days suitable for swimming and will be amused by the sight of Cariocas bundled up in their sweaters and windbreakers.

CLOTHING: The fashions of southern California and Rio have much in common, at least in spirit. Even formal clothes are loose-fitting. Brazilian women are very stylish and often wear makeup, coiffed hair, and high heels when dining out or attending social affairs. Men are equally fashionable but more informal, and rarely wear ties unless they are bankers or government bureaucrats. In fact, only one or two businessmen's clubs in downtown Rio require that male diners wear ties, while the fanciest French restaurants in Copacabana are filled with men in open-necked sport shirts and slacks—even jeans—at lunchtime. It isn't unusual to see people in shorts and T-shirts at the best restaurants off the beach during the day. And both women and men parade through the streets in the scantiest of swim wear in the beach neighborhoods, but no one wears bathing suits downtown. Both synthetic and natural fibers are popular in the fashion world, and women's clothes, in particular, are a real bargain for buyers with dollars. Be sure to pack a cold-water powdered soap like Woolite. Washing out your own clothes is the best antidote to potentially high hotel laundry bills.

CONSULATES: The American consulate is located downtown on Avenida Presidente Wilson 147 (tel. 292-7117). Canada's consulate is also in the Centro on Rua Dom Geraldo 35, third floor (tel. 233-9286). The British consulate is in Flamengo, on Praia de Flamengo 284, second floor (tel. 552-1422). The Australian consulate is in Botafogo on Rua Voluntário da Pátria 45, fifth floor (tel. 286-7922).

CREDIT CARDS: American Express, Diners Club, and VISA are most in evidence. Remember you will charge your purchase in *cruzados,* which, until recently, were computed at the official (*oficial*) rate of exchange, anywhere from 50% to 125% below the nonofficial rates known as the *paralelo* and the *turismo.* Today, credit-card purchases are computed at the *turismo* rate as it appears in the financial section of the daily newspapers on the day of your purchase, which means it is now practical to charge items and expenses in Brazil rather than pay cash, if you so desire. For a full discussion of the various rates of exchange—*oficial, paralelo,* and *turismo*—see "Currency" below.

CRIME: Street crime is a potential problem in Rio, as it is in many of the world's larger cities, especially those where great pockets of poverty exist. Generally speaking, however, luck and circumstance protect most of us from being victims of crime. But more important than sheer luck is how you choose to behave in unfamiliar conditions. When you travel, don't leave your common sense at home. Follow a few simple rules and you are unlikely to encounter any difficulty. Don't wear expensive jewelry or flash your bankroll on the street. Leave all valuables, including passport and airline tickets, in your hotel room, preferably under lock and key in the safe provided. Take nothing to the beach that you wouldn't mind losing. Do what the Brazilians do. Tuck the equivalent of a few dollars in the waistband or strap of your bathing suit. At night, travel by cab to and from your hotel and avoid areas—including the beach—that are dark and empty at night. Never needlessly call attention to yourself.

CURRENCY: The Brazilian currency is the **cruzeiro** This in turn was replaced by the **novo cruzado** in March 1989, when once again Brazil's currency was radically devalued for the second time in only three years as the result of the hyperinflation that plagues the nation's economy, and changed once again to the cruzeiro. There are three rates of exchange in Brazil: an official exchange rate, the *câmbio oficial;* a tourist exchange rate, *o dólar turismo;* and the semilegal "black-market rate," *o paralelo* (the parallel money market). All three rates are published daily in the economic sections (and sometimes on the front pages) of the major Brazilian newspapers, which dispels the notion that trading in the black market will involve you in some risky or nefarious dealings. The official exchange rate is increasingly limited to the practices of international trade, involving central banking services and the securing of letters of credit.

How, then, does the tourist trade at the more advantageous parallel rate? Don't worry, because as sure as the sun shines in Brazil, you will be approached by someone wishing to buy your **cash** dollars, probably as soon as you pass through Customs with your baggage in hand. It may be your tour guide or the person sent to transfer your group from the airport to the hotel. It may be the doorman or the bellboy, and most assuredly the porter behind the concierge desk. Assuming you know the current parallel rate (having glanced at the Brazilian daily during your incoming flight), you may still expect to exchange at three to four points below the rate listed in the paper. Why? Well, changing money is a sideline for many people in the service sector of the tourist business. In general, these small-scale money traders are not dealing with huge sums of money. They therefore attempt to negotiate the lowest possible rate in order to maximize their profit margin. You may be able to haggle for a point or two. The key to these negotiations, however, is knowing the current parallel rate.

It generally doesn't make sense to change more than $100 or $200 at a time. The parallel rate seldom drops, and you can do some serious sightseeing on that limited amount of money. The more money you exchange, however, the better rate you ought to find. If you are not comfortable changing money with your bellhop in the corridor of a five-star hotel, there are many businesses—travel agencies, boutiques, and the like—that trade in the parallel money market. Someone in the hotel or with your tour company will gladly indicate the address of a shop near your hotel. (They are probably getting a commission!) Go there with your cash or traveler's checks and your passport, and exchange your money in a suitable business environment. Traveler's checks, incidentally, trade at a point or two lower than cash, though who can argue with the good sense of traveling with as little hard currency as possible, unless you are traveling deep in the interior where traveler's checks and credit cards are just so much useless paper and plastic. The most important thing to remember when exchanging money at the parallel rate is that even if you receive a lower rate than that published in the newspaper, you are still getting a better deal than if you exchanged at the official rate.

The abbreviation for the cruzeiro is **$CR**. In the Brazilian reckoning of money, commas and periods are employed exactly *opposite* from North American usage. One thousand six hundred cruzeiros is written, $CR 1.600, while ten cruzeiros and fifty centavos appears as $CR 10,50.

CUSTOMS REQUIREMENTS: Besides clothing and personal belongings, tourists entering Brazil may bring one of each of the following items: a radio, a tape deck, a typewriter, film, and cameras—one video or movie camera, one still. You are further allowed to bring to Brazil items totaling $300 as gifts, including any liquor or cigarettes you purchase at the duty-free shop, and to return with $400 worth of Brazilian merchandise, not including certain craft items which are duty free. Under no circumstances should you try to enter Brazil with a portable or lap-top computer. Brazil and the U.S. are currently involved in an economic skirmish, where the former is trying to protect its nascent computer industry and the latter is demanding a piece of the Brazilian market for American computer products. Your personal computer could be caught in the cross fire and end up being confiscated.

DENTISTS: In the event that you require emergency dental treatment and are unable to obtain a suitable reference from your hotel or consulate, try **Clínica de Urgência,** Rua Marques de Abrantes 27, Flamengo (tel. 226-0083), or **Dentário Rollin,** Rua Cupertinho Durão 81 (tel. 259-2647).

DOCTORS: Luxury and first-class hotels generally have physicians on call. For any emergency medical care it would be wise to consult with a member of the diplomatic mission of your country of origin. The **Rio Health Collective,** Avenida Ataúlfo de Paiva 135, Suite 1415 (tel. 511-0949), offers travelers free references to English-speaking doctors in every area of medicine. Among the hospitals offering emergency care in Rio 24 hours a day are the **Hospital Miguel Couto,** Rua Bartolomeu Mitre, Leblon (tel. 274-2121) and the **Hospital Souza Aguiar,** Praça da República 610, Centro (tel. 296-4114). Telephone operators at these hospitals are not likely to speak English, however. Private clinics will more probably have staff and doctors who do speak English and other languages. One conveniently located clinic is the **Centro Médico Ipanema,** Rua Aníbal Mendonça 135, Ipanema (tel. 239-4647). Private ambulance services include the **Clinic Savior** (tel. 227-6187 or 227-5099) and **Pullman** (tel. 236-1011 or 257-4132).

DOCUMENTS FOR ENTRY: A visa is required for U.S. and Canadian citizens wishing to visit Brazil. Passports, valid for at least six months from the intended date of arrival, must carry a visa for Brazil. Tourist or transit visas, generally processed within one working day, are obtained from the nearest Brazilian consulate. One passport-size photograph, along with your round-trip ticket and a duly completed and signed application form, are required for the free visa, valid for 90 days (for tourists) or 10 days (transit). Visas are not required for British citizens who wish to enter Brazil for up to 90 days. They must have valid passports, however.

    Specialized Visa and Travel Consultants (SVTC), 60 E. 42nd St., New York, NY 10165 (tel. 212/867-4213, Fax. 212/983-5316), will secure your Brazilian visa for a fee of $30 (plus an additional $10 payable to the Brazilian consulate). Contact them initially for a visa application and to verify any changes in the fee structure or procedures, then fill in and return the application to SVTC by express mail along with your valid passport plus all necessary fees and photographs. Your passport containing the valid visa will then be promptly returned to you, also by express mail.

DRUGSTORES: Twenty-four-hour-a-day drugstores (*farmácias* or *drogarias*) operate in neighborhoods throughout Rio. Check for the most convenient location through your hotel staff. Prescription drugs—while this perhaps ought not to be the case—are fairly easy to obtain without the necessary paperwork. Brazilian medications are manufactured by the familiar multinational pharmaceutical companies, so the brand names will be recognizable.

ELECTRICITY: What we refer to as "house current"—110 volts—is rare in Brazil. Rio is said to be wired with 110, but my impression nonetheless is that there are a considerable number of 220-volt lines throughout the major hotels as well. Bathrooms in these hotels usually provide an alternate house current outlet suitable for electric shavers, but not for hairdryers. The top hotels often provide "hardwired" hairdryers as an extra feature in bathrooms. Bring the necessary 220-volt converter if you have any equipment you wish to run (slide projector, hairdryer, tape player, etc.), and always check with the hotel staff before plugging in anything. Adding to the confusion is the fact that outlets often accept plugs with rounded, as opposed to flattened, prongs. Some hotels provide necessary voltage transformers or plug adapters for guests. Be particularly careful in showers equipped with visible electric hot-water heaters (rare in Rio). People have been known to get electric shocks in such showers if the heaters are inadquately grounded.

ETIQUETTE: Generalizing about etiquette is a somewhat meaningless exercise. One could fairly suggest, though, that Brazilians are—or can be—more formal and more ceremonial than Americans. The Portuguese language itself retains both the formal mode of address (*o senhor, a senhora*) as well as the familiar form (*você* or *tu,* depending on the region). American brashness and straight talking can at times grate on Brazilians. The culture gap is based to some degree on Brazilian hypersensitivity to gradations of social class in their country, which have no functional counterpart in largely middle-class America. Needless to say, it is up to the individual traveler to be alert to any given situation and unravel the mysteries of cross-cultural differences.

FILM: Photographic film for most modern cameras is widely available throughout Brazil, as is tape for video cameras, especially in the larger cities. Film, however, is not one of the bargain items in Brazil, and can be priced at double the U.S. amount. Many travelers bring all the film they will need and store it in their hotel refrigerators to keep it fresh. Unless you are on an extended vacation, it is probably best to delay processing until you get home. Very rarely will you be restricted in the use of your camera, and then, generally only in museums and churches. If you are with a tour group, your guide will inform you where restrictions are in effect.

GAS: Gasoline is roughly twice as expensive in Rio as in the U.S. Many Brazilian cars today run on alcohol, a state-subsidized fuel which is slightly less expensive than gas. It is difficult finding either fuel on Sundays when most service stations are closed. Otherwise, gas stations are usually open from Monday through Saturday, from 8 a.m. to 6 p.m.

HAIRDRESSING: All luxury and first-class hotels have their own —sometimes unisex—hairdressers. Most visitors in Rio will not have to leave their hotels for a shampoo, a haircut, or styling. These facilities at the top hotels, like restaurants and bars, are generally open to the public, so you need not be a guest to enjoy their services. Standard barbershops seem to be well concealed in Rio, although hotel staff will be able to direct men who want to treat themselves to the luxury of a cheap and close shave done the old-fashioned way.

HITCHHIKING: While not illegal in Brazil, nobody does it nowadays. Over 20 years ago, however, I hitchhiked throughout central Brazil with pretty fair success.

HOLIDAYS: Principal holidays and festivals with their dates are as follows:

> **January 1:** New Year's Day—and the feast day of Iemanjá, goddess of the sea, accompanied by much public celebration.
>
> **February:** Carnival, the extended Mardi Gras celebration which brings Brazil to a standstill for at least five days before Ash Wednesday every year.
>
> **March/April:** Good Friday and Easter Sunday.
>
> **April 21:** Tiradentes Day, in honor of the Brazilian republican martyr.
>
> **May 1:** May Day.
>
> **June:** Corpus Christi.
>
> **June/July:** The Festas Juninas, important winter holidays on the feast days of Saints John, Peter, and Anthony.
>
> **September 7:** Independence Day.
>
> **October 12:** Our Lady of the Apparition.
>
> **November 2:** All Souls' Day.
>
> **November 15:** Proclamation (of the Republic) Day.
>
> **December 25:** Christmas.

Like North Americans in recent years, Brazilians have the habit of celebrating certain holidays not on the official dates, but on the Monday that falls closest to the official date. The *feriadão* (feh-ree-ah-*downg*), or long holiday weekend, is the result, meaning that you may find stores and banks unexpectedly closed if you have only consulted the "official" calender.

LANGUAGE: Brazilians speak Portuguese, the linguistic legacy of the country's original Portuguese colonizers. The Brazilian accent differs from that spoken in Portugal, much in the same way that American and British English differ. English is spoken by designated staff at the major hotels, specialized tour guides, and at airport information counters. Otherwise it would be fair to say that English —other than pidgin—is not widely spoken throughout Brazil, particularly as you travel any distance from the large urban centers.

LAUNDRY AND DRY CLEANING: Hotels normally offer two-day service and a special express service, which costs about 50% more. Hotel laundry service, while convenient, is nonetheless expensive. Travelers with a container of Woolite (in powder form in the event it opens in your suitcase) or some equivalent cold-water soap, and a summer wardrobe of wash-and-wear clothes will be able to avoid high-priced hotel laundry fees. The other option is to find the nearest *tinturaria* (dry cleaner) or *lavandaria* (laundry).

LIQUOR: Like most Americans, Brazilians tend not to be teetotalers. Their beers and wines (the great French burgundies duly excepted) rate with the world's best. **Cachaça,** a potent sugarcane brandy, is widely used in many cocktails and is favored by Americans. Bars open early and stay open late, very rarely closing before dawn on weekends. Drinking is generally inexpensive in Brazil, unless you insist on imported scotch, in which case you'll be charged a small fortune. Nearly quart-size bottles of beer, on the other hand, run about 50¢ to 75¢ a bottle. A good Brazilian wine can be had in most restaurants beginning at $6 . . . or less.

LOST AND FOUND: Lost or misplaced items are not necessarily gone forever in Brazil. Chances are, if you go back to the place where you last remember having the item in your possession—bars and restaurants in particular—it will be there waiting for you. Losses in cabs are more problematical, but you can have your hotel make inquiries at the local *delegacia* (police precinct). Report all lost traveler's checks and credit cards to the appropriate organization immediately.

NEWSPAPERS: The top newspapers are the *Folha de São Paulo, Jornal do Brasil,* and *O Globo.* The *Latin American Daily Post* is an English-language paper published out of São Paulo four days a week, with a Rio edition; it's good for entertainment, real estate, and business news. The very expensive *International Herald Tribune* is available generally only in Rio, São Paulo, and Salvador, as are the *Wall Street Journal, New York Times,* and *Miami Herald,* as well as *Time* and *Newsweek.*

OFFICE HOURS: White-collar business hours are normally from 9 a.m. to 6 p.m. Monday through Friday, with an hour off for lunch. Office lunch-hour periods are usually staggered from noon till 3 p.m. Longer hours and obligatory work on Saturday are the rule for most service and nonunion blue-collar jobs.

POSTAL SERVICE: The most convenient way to handle your outgoing mail is to purchase stamps from the reception desk in your hotel, and to have the staff mail your letters and postcards for you. In general, branches of the post office, **Correio** (co-hay-yu), in Rio are open from 8 a.m. to 6 p.m. weekdays, and until noon on Saturdays. The Copacabana branch, Avenida Nossa Senhora de Copacabana 540 is open from 8 a.m. to 8 p.m. weekdays, 8 a.m. to 6 p.m. Saturdays, and from 8 a.m. till noon on Sundays. The principal post office in Ipanema is located at Rua Prudente de Morais 147 on the Praça General Osório.

RADIO AND TELEVISION: Most hotel rooms in Rio have music piped in from a handful of local radio stations, with the Brazilian equivalent of elevator music. With your own radio, you ought to be able to pick up some of the best of Brazilian popular and country-style music from a wide variety of local stations. Some—but not all—luxury and first-class hotels have satellite dishes that pick up CNN newscasts throughout the day, and that big game or prize fight you thought you were going to miss. Brazilian TV is definitely worth tuning in on; the prime-time soaps and miniseries are a major export to Western European countries. Discreet female and male nudity often appears in both commercials and shows.

RELIGIOUS SERVICES: Brazil is primarily a Catholic country

—the most populous in the world, in fact—and every brand of Catholicism flourishes here from the most traditional to the most radical. Protestantism has made its inroads in Brazil over the years, and most denominations have houses of worship in Rio. There is also a religiously active Jewish community in the city. The other main religious movement in Brazil is the spiritism brought by the Africans, blended with the practices and beliefs of the original natives, and today widely practiced by Brazilians of all backgrounds and races. These religions—known as Macumba in Rio, and Candomblé and Umbanda elsewhere in Brazil—have also become something of a tourist attraction in recent years, in much the way voodoo, a related cult, has always been in countries like Cuba and Haiti.

REST ROOMS: Restaurants you are not eating in and hotels where you are not staying will nonetheless cheerfully allow you to use the facilities when necessary. There are otherwise few public toilets, and they are best to be avoided anyway, since they tend to be as filthy as the hotel and restaurant bathrooms are clean.

STORE HOURS: The shops in Rio are open from 9 a.m. to 6:30 p.m. Monday through Friday, and from 9 a.m. to 1 p.m. on Saturday. Shops close as late as 10 p.m. during the month of December. Shopping centers are generally open on Monday through Saturday from 10 a.m. till 10 p.m.

TAXES: There is no sales tax in Rio. What you see on the sticker —if there is one—is what you pay. Otherwise one bargains, and that of course is a science that some shoppers thrive on and others find a nuisance. Most hotels charge an across-the-board 10% service tax. So if the rate sheet indicates a charge of $70 a night, you're really paying $77. Please take note that every item appearing on your final hotel bill—long-distance phone calls, room service, laundry—is subject to this 10% tax. Restaurants also add 10% which serves as the tip. Depending on the nature of your airline ticket, you may have to pay a token airport tax between domestic destinations, and a $10 exit tax when returning home. Taxes and tariffs on items like U.S. cigarettes, imported liquor, and gasoline are high, often doubling the cost of imported goods.

TELEPHONES: Local phone calls from your hotel room are generally free. You might, on occasion, find a charge on your bill for a call you thought was local—say, to the airport—but was actually suburban and subject to a fee. Phone service is good over all in Rio, though payphones are a minor nightmare. The main problem is that you must use tokens, and inevitably there aren't any places around at which to buy them. Newsstands at airports—and supposedly elsewhere—sell phone tokens, called *fichas* (fee-shas). They come in a five-pack, and are inexpensive. If you're lucky, someone near the phone you want to use will know the nearest place to buy *fichas*. Feed in several tokens simultaneously to prevent being cut off after

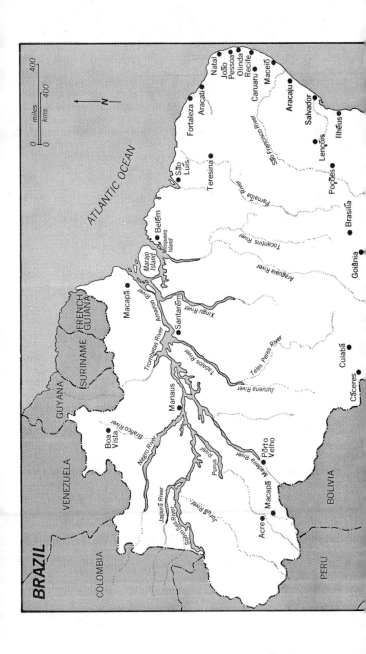

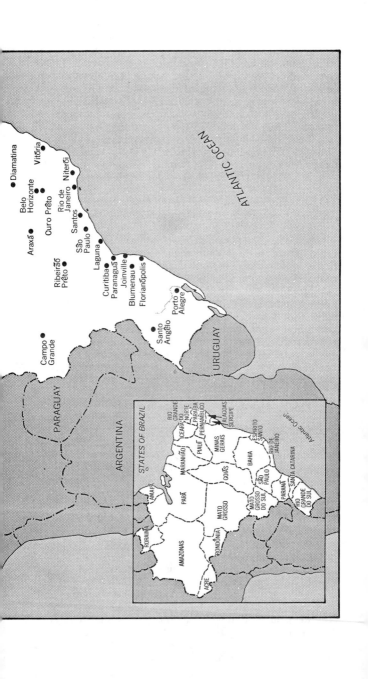

the first minute. Or better yet, stick to your hotel phone; it's a lot easier.

Telephone company offices, called TELERJ, are located throughout the city. Operator-assisted booths provide a more relaxed and private atmosphere for making both long-distance and local calls. The TELERJ at the International Airport is open 24 hours a day. In Copacabana, there is a TELERJ on Avenida Nossa Senhora de Copacabana 462, which is also open around the clock, and in Ipanema at Rua Visconde de Piraja 111, open from 6:30 a.m. till 11 p.m. To reach the international operator, who speaks English, dial 000 333. When calling the U.S. or Canada, you may dial direct using the code 001 plus the number. The area code for Rio de Janeiro is 021, and the country code for Brazil is 55.

TELEX: Your hotel will send your message, assuming they have a Telex machine, and the staff will notify you as soon as there is a reply.

TIME: There are three time zones in Brazil. Eastern and parts of central Brazil are three hours behind Greenwich Mean Time (London), or two hours ahead of U.S. Eastern Standard Time. West central Brazil and most of the Amazon basin are four hours behind GMT, while far western Brazil, primarily the state of Acre, is five hours behind GMT, therefore occupying the same time zone as New York City. Daylight Savings Time has been introduced throughout most of Brazil during the South American summer months of December through February. Not all cities, Belem for example, participate in this time change. Be aware of this potential confusion when making flight reservations during the periods of daylight saving in either hemisphere.

TIPPING: As with bargaining, there is no standard formula for tipping in Rio. How much or how little to tip is really up to you. Brazilians are, on the whole, light tippers. In a sense, there is no such thing as spare change in a country with Brazil's yearly rates of inflation—except for the very rich. Tourists, of course, are held to a higher standard, and generous tips are always appreciated—though they are by no means expected.

TOURIST ASSISTANCE: The city of Rio de Janeiro has installed a direct tourist assistance telephone line. Dial 1516 in any of the following situations:

- □ If you are lost in the city
- □ In case of personal injury or accident
- □ If documents or personal belongings are lost or stolen
- □ If you need to get in touch with your consulate

Remember, if you are calling from a public phone, you will need a token called a *ficha* (see "Telephones"). On the other hand, many hotels, restaurants, bars, and shops in Rio will allow you to use their phone for local calls.

GETTING TO KNOW RIO

1. GETTING INTO TOWN
2. ORIENTATION
3. GETTING AROUND RIO

You've just arrived in Rio, now what? If you are like most travelers, you'll want to go directly to your hotel to rest and freshen up. Fortunately, Rio's International Airport is an easy place to negotiate. First, you must have your visa verified and your passport stamped. The passport control official will also stamp and return a portion of your declaration slip, which you must hold on to and turn in when you leave the country. Next you will retrieve your luggage. Customs officials perform only random checking of tourist baggage, but even if you are chosen to open your bags, there won't be much of a delay. Before leaving the arrivals area, you may want to stop briefly in the duty-free stores for some last-minute shopping. Remember, imported liquor is one of the few items in Brazil that is not a bargain. So if you like to keep a bottle or two in your room, and you haven't already provisioned yourself, this is your last chance while in Brazil to get your favorite label at a reasonable price.

1. Getting Into Town

Most visitors from North America will arrive in Rio with a group or with a prepaid package secured through a travel agency back home. This being the case, you will very likely be met by a guide or driver the minute you emerge from the restricted zone into the airport's public spaces. Simply follow your tour leader, if you have one, or look for the person among the animated crowd of service personnel congregating by the exit gate who's holding a sign with your name on it, or whatever written signal you've been alerted to look for—the name of your hotel or package perhaps. Once your party or group is loaded into the waiting car or bus, you will be whisked away to your hotel. Since the airport is located deep in the

Zona Norte on the Ilha do Governador (Governor's Island), and you are undoubtedly headed for accommodations in the Zona Sul, the transfer will take anywhere from a half hour to an hour, depending on traffic and on the distance to the specific beach neighborhood that is your ultimate destination.

AIRPORT TRANSFERS

If your package or ticket does not include airport transfers, you have several transportation options for getting to your hotel: luxury car service, metered cab, or airport bus. You also have a few minutes to walk around the airport—one of the most modern in South America—buy a cup of coffee and a morning newspaper, and browse the gift shops and bookstore. If you have not arrived with cruzados in your pocket, now is the time to check the paper for the rate of exchange on the parallel market and to change at least an amount sufficient for some pocket money. If no one approaches you with an offer to change money (a circumstance that is, frankly, unimaginable), just ask any porter or cab driver where you might "change money" (the English in this case being almost universally understood), and he is likely to respond "how much?" Depending on the rate you agree on, you may want to change just enough to tide you over or a more substantial amount, if the price is right, so you don't have to waste any more time on this task, and you can get on with your vacation.

By Private Car

The most comfortable, and the most expensive, way to get to your hotel from the airport is by car service, in an air-conditioned sedan provided by one of two companies, **Cotramo** or **Transcopass,** whose counters may be found in the vicinity of the car rental agencies. You pay a fixed rate—in dollars if you like—calculated according to neighborhood zones; figure $15 to Copacabana and $20 to Ipanema.

By Taxi

Metered cabs are also available, but the drivers will not run on the flags; they will also insist on a fixed fare. This fare, however, will be cheaper than that of the car services, but the car—possibly a VW bug—may not be as comfortable. Furthermore, you may not be up to the haggling over price so soon after your arrival.

By Bus

A Greyhound-style bus, called the **frescão** (because it is air-conditioned), leaves for the Zona Sul approximately every half hour. While the bus costs only about a dollar and ultimately stops at or near most of the major hotels, it takes a long time. And you may not care to drag your suitcases that extra block or two after you've just spent the last half day in transit on an airplane. The route taken by the frescão will skirt closer to downtown than your private car or cab, and the ride can be an interesting first introduction to the city.

There is also a standard public bus—actually a series of buses

—from the airport to the city, and on to the beach neighborhoods. But this is even more of an adventure, which only the most intrepid will need to experience. Under the circumstances, the best bet is to treat yourself to the comfort and convenience of the car service.

2. Orientation

THE ZONA SUL

From the tourist perspective, as has already been noted in Chapter 1, the Zona Sul *is* Rio. I will, therefore, treat **Copacabana,** not downtown, as the city's geographic center. Seventy-five percent of Rio's tourist-quality hotels are located here and in **Leme**—the name of the vest-pocket neighborhood that occupies the northern end of Copacabana's famous strand. And besides sand, surf, and sun, Copacabana in particular offers a proliferation of fine restaurants, shops, and nightspots. Majestic **Avenida Atlântica,** with its delightful, wide sidewalks of white and black stones laid out in geometric mosaics, accompanies the beach the entire length of its sweeping curve, some five miles from one end to the other. The two neighborhoods of Copacabana and Leme are separated by the busy **Avenida Princesa Isabel,** which disappears into a mountain tunnel and carries endless streams of traffic to and from the centro. Of the two neighborhoods, Copacabana is by far the largest, though it is also relatively restricted in area—a long and narrow quarter rarely more than five blocks deep from the oceanfront to the nearby hills that form its natural inland boundaries. Promotional literature in Brazil inevitably characterizes Copacabana as the most densely populated neighborhood in the world, though this is hardly the dominant feeling one senses while exploring this residential bastion of elegance and affluence. To be sure, strings of high-rise apartments line the blocks and avenues, but they seldom exceed 12 stories in height, and—at least along swank Avenida Atlântica—the half-century-old relics in the deco style are architectural artifacts any city would be proud of. Leme, on the other hand, is truly tiny. It's one of Rio's most self-contained and charming beachside residential districts, nestled in a topographical cul-de-sac between the mountains and the sea, barely three blocks deep at its widest point.

Of equal importance to Copacabana, from the visitor's point of view, is **Ipanema** and its adjacent neighborhood of **Leblon.** These two neighborhoods also share a single beachfront, and they're divided by a tidal channel that flows to and from a natural lagoon—the **Lagoa Rodrigo Freitas**—located inland several blocks from the ocean and marking the boundary of yet another distinct residential district. From the air, the indented beaches of Copacabana/Leme and Ipanema/Leblon look like a pair of giant eyebrows, side by side, linked in the middle by an outcropping of land, where the tiny surfers' beach of **Arpoador** is to be found. And while Copacabana can boast a far greater number and variety of hotels, both along the beach and on its backstreets, Rio's most fashionable eating, shopping, and nightlife is concentrated on the streets of Ipanema, spilling generously into Leblon as well.

From these core neighborhoods, the Zona Sul fans out in three opposing directions: northerly toward downtown Rio; southerly along the Atlantic shore to the more remote beach areas; and inland, embracing the **Lagoa,** the forest, and the central hills. The Lagoa *bairro*—the Portuguese word for neighborhood (pronounced *bye*-who)—is primarily a very fashionable residential quarter, but along the lagoon's south shore are some of Rio's best clubs and restaurants as well. Beyond the Lagoa is the access road to **Corcovado**—Hunchback Peak—where, from the platform of the great statue of Christ the Redeemer, the combined view of cityscape and natural setting is one of the most breathtaking in the world. Spread along an arc around the hilly base of Corcovado are the chic and quiet interior neighborhoods of **Jardim Botânico, Laranjeiras,** and **Cosme Velho.** These areas are strictly residential, but very much attractions for those who enjoy a Sunday drive and an informal tour of private dwellings and winding roads. Westward from Corcovado is Rio's immense **Parque Nacional da Tijuca**—Tijuca National Park—worth a visit for its scenic beauty and uncultivated flora, even if only while traveling from one neighborhood to another.

Between the tunnel in Copacabana and the downtown section, are the bayside neighborhoods of **Botafogo, Flamengo,** and **Glória.** The bay beaches here are no longer considered suitable for bathing, though they remain in constant use by local residents who utilize them as outdoor public patios for sunning, exercise, and sports, like volleyball and soccer. Budget travelers in particular may find themselves staying in the handful of acceptable hotels in these barrios, which not only have their charm, but can also claim a variety of other attractions, from several specialty museums to a number of fine dining spots that overlook the harbor. If you turn right, when you emerge from the tunnel, you'll be going away from Botafogo and into **Urca,** a lovely waterfront neighborhood in its own right, but most famous for its dramatic cable car ride to the top of **Pão de Açúcar**—Sugar Loaf Mountain—Rio's other spectacular vantage point for viewing both city and bay.

Downtown Rio

Rio's *centro* is not for everyone. But for history buffs, patrons of high culture, and lovers of inner cities in general, a day trip or two downtown can be very rewarding. The major historical and art museums are located here, as well as the old Opera House—the **Teatro Municipal**—and the city's remaining colonial structures and plazas. Boat trips on the bay depart from the old waterfront (and from the marina in Botafogo too), and the daytime street life is animated by the throngs of vendors, shoppers, and city workers going about their daily rounds. At night there is the movie and singles scene in and around **Cinelândia,** and discoing in a few choice clubs. There are also a score of old restaurants and traditional greasy spoons called **pés sujos** (literally "dirty feet") that are worthy of attention. And, of course, the downtown **sambódromo**—the sambadome

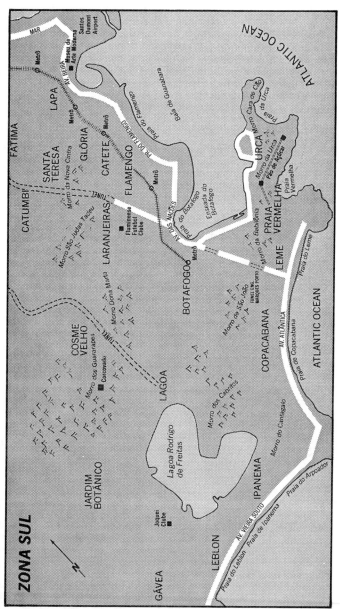

—is the venue for the annual Carioca madness that goes by the name of Carnival, where the samba schools and their casts of thousands parade in one of the world's greatest outdoor musical and theatrical spectacles. Rio's oldest hillside suburb, **Santa Teresa,** is only a short (but wild) trolley car ride from downtown, and it's one of the few neighborhoods in the city where the pre–20th century scale of life has been preserved.

Beach Neighborhoods

Returning to the beach neighborhoods, there are miles of strands that continue south beyond Ipanema and Leblon, the closest of which are **Vidigal** and **São Conrado,** where two of Rio's most luxurious resort hotels are located. Farther out is the 15 km (9 mile) long **Barra da Tijuca,** Rio's longest beach and an area that has undergone tremendous development over the past 20 years. Barra is where tens of thousands of Cariocas flock on the weekends to play on the sand, but the beaches are almost deserted during the week. Condominiums and residential hotels line Barra's principal oceanfront avenue, and South America's largest shopping mall is located only a few blocks off the beach. Beyond Barra are Rio's municipal outskirts, where the city's only remaining undeveloped beaches and summer communities, like **Recreio dos Bandeirantes,** are to be found. While remote from the center of action and difficult to reach except by car, these areas are also popular weekend retreats for those seeking some distance from the madding crowd.

THE ZONA NORTE

There are four or five reasons for tourists to visit the Zona Norte, but again the attractions here are not for everyone. A visitor going to the Zona Norte usually does so because he or she has a yen to get a step or two closer to some aspect of Brazilian culture that can not be found in the beach communities: a soccer game at **Maracanã Stadium;** a fullblown rehearsal of a samba school going through its pre-Carnival paces; the weekly **Fair of the Northeast** with its acres of food and merchandise stalls; or the **Quinta da Boa Vista,** the former royal palace of Dom Pedro I and his family, now a complex of museums and the site of Rio's zoo.

ENVIRONS

Several excellent day trips and weekend excursions may be made from Rio, the most popular of which are **Petrópolis,** the summer capital of Brazil's imperial family; **Búzios,** the popular weekend watering hole, about three hours up the coast; and **Parati,** a well-preserved historical town down the south coast, near the border of the state of São Paulo. These and several other out-of-town excursions will be treated in Chapter X of this guide.

---

3. Getting Around Rio

Rio is not the easiest city in the world for the tourist to get around in. Except for the excellent, but limited, subway system running between Botafogo and downtown (then on to the northern suburbs), the tourist is fairly dependent on taxis or hotel cars for traveling from place to place in Rio. By contrast, public buses are the preferred mode of transportation by *o povo,* "the people," a term Brazilians use when referring to the vast majority of people who, in this case, don't have cars and can't afford to take cabs. To be quite candid, you will seldom find middle- and upper-class Cariocas on the public buses. With a few exceptions, which will be listed below, they consider public buses unsafe. And tourists who ride the buses stand out even more than affluent Brazilians and make easy targets for muggers and pickpockets.

TAXIS

There are three varieties of cabs in Rio. Most plentiful are the **common metered cabs,** small cars painted yellow, which are hailed from the street or from official taxi queues at designated areas throughout the city. The meter has two flag settings, labeled 1 and 2. The no. 2 setting adds 20% to the fare and is used after 11 p.m., on Sundays and holidays, when outside the old city limits, or when climbing particularly steep inclines, like the access road to Corcovado. Meters are seldom calibrated to keep up with Brazil's galloping inflation. The meter reading, instead, is used as a base, and the true fare is calculated by reference to the *tabela,* an official table of updated equivalents that, by law, must be posted on the vehicle's rear window. Brazilians alighting from cabs at the end of their rides usually quote the meter figure aloud, and look closely over the driver's shoulder while he consults his own copy of the tabela. Thus do Cariocas themselves try to avoid being overcharged by Rio's notorious meter hacks, who have become particularly devious in their methods, being squeezed as they are between runaway inflation and the high cost of fuel. Even with the "tourist tax" exacted by many drivers, cab rides seldom exceed $3 to $5 for runs between neighborhoods.

The second type of cab in Rio is the **radio taxi,** which can be hailed on the street or summoned by phone. One reliable company is **Coopatur** (tel. 290-1009). The fare of a radio taxi seems to be roughly twice that of a metered cab, when their respective drivers are playing by the official rules. Radio-cab drivers will often try to hire themselves out to tourists for the entire time of their stay in Rio— an arrangement which, if the price is agreeable, can be beneficial for both parties.

Finally, there are the **luxury cabs,** like those dispatched from the airport or similar fleets that are attached to the city's top hotels. The fare of a hotel cab is generally four times that of a metered cab. The exorbitant price of the private cars makes the inevitable hassles with the metered-cab drivers all the more frustrating, since on occasion you can feel stranded between options, all of which are unacceptable.

BUSES

Adding to the frustration is the fact that, for most tourists, riding the public buses, even the air-conditioned frescãos, is not highly recommended. Most public buses—which are virtually free from the standpoint of a tourist's purse—are crowded, driven maniacally, and too often, since they are targets for roving bandits, dangerous. That being said, the odds of a safe bus ride are still overwhelmingly in your favor. And if you have the desire to really explore the city, the will to communicate using smiles and sign language, and a basic trust in people to help guide you when you're lost, buses can be the ideal form of transportation in Rio, taking you virtually anywhere in town for next to nothing. There are some lines, moreover, which need not be avoided at all. The open-sided *jardineira* buses that run along the ocean avenues from Leme to São Conrado are perfectly acceptable, especially if you're only using them for a short run—from Copacabana to Leme, for example, or from Ipanema to Leblon.

Bus stops are indicated by signs with the word *"Ônibus,"* but buses must still be flagged, since there are no automatic stops except at the beginnings and ends of the lines. You enter the bus through the rear door and exit from the front. It's advisable to carry small change when traveling by bus, since fare takers will often refuse large bills. Buses marked *"Metrô"* go to the subway station in Botafogo, while those indicating *"Castelo"* go directly downtown. The downtown terminal for the air-conditioned special buses is **Menezes Cortes,** located near Praça XV on Rua São Jose (tel. 224-7577). Here you can not only board a frescão back to the Zona Sul after a day in the Centro, but you can also catch buses bound for Petrópolis, Teresópolis, and other side-trip destinations within the state of Rio de Janeiro.

SUBWAYS, TRAINS, AND RIO'S LAST STREETCAR

The **subway** goes no deeper into the Zona Sul than its terminal station in Botafogo, but it's still the best means of public transportation for getting around in downtown Rio. To take advantage of this thoroughly clean and modern system, you must first get to the Botafogo station by cab or bus. From there, the many stops within the city will bring you within close range of numerous downtown destinations. Change from *linha* 1 (line 1) to *linha* 2 (line 2) at the *Estácio* station for the city's interurban bus terminal in São Cristovão or for the Maracanã soccer stadium. Another important line 1 stop in the Centro is *Cinelândia,* for the Teatro Municipal and the Sala Cecília Meirelles—venues for theater, opera, and classical music. This is also the closest stop to the in-town Santos Dumont Airport, where you get the air shuttle to São Paulo, or any number of air taxi services to resorts such as Búzios.

The *Carioca* stop places you near the terminal point of Rio's only remaining streetcar line, the **bonde,** which makes the dramatic ride over the *arcos,* the arched structure of an 18th-century aqueduct, to the historical hillside neighborhood of Santa Teresa. The bonde, which is ridden by thousands of commuters daily, is nevertheless the most dangerous of all of Rio's public transports. Despite the presence of special police, the open-sided trolleys are vulnerable to hit-and-run assaults by roving pickpockets.

Rio has several suburban **train** lines, but few carry passengers to far-flung interstate destinations. But there are still trains running to the relatively nearby cities of São Paulo and Belo Horizonte. The *Dom Pedro II* train station is located in the Centro off Praça Cristiano Ottoni (tel. 233-4090 or 233-3277).

CAR RENTALS

Before you decide to rent a car in Rio, spend some time riding around as a passenger in a taxi to get a feel for the Carioca style of driving, the rhythm of traffic, and the general layout of the city's roadways. Driving a car in Rio is a frenetic activity. There is little slow-lane driving, in fact, lane-driving discipline is practically non-existent. Cariocas love auto racing, and the sport is routinely emulated throughout the city streets, with tailgating, wild passing, and delayed braking being the acceptable rules of the road, not the exceptional deviations. Outside the city, where traffic is lighter, the pace is somewhat more relaxed, but you have to be on constant alert for the "other guy." Passing on blind curves, for example, is a common practice. Driving defensively is no mere public service slogan in Brazil, where motor vehicles rival infant malnutrition as a top yearly killer.

Cariocas, with their inimitable shoot-from-the-hip intensity, have nonetheless made their driving system work for them. And nowhere are the anarchic Cariocas more imaginative than in their capacity for finding parking spaces in a city virtually devoid of legal parking. The key word here is "legal." For two generations, Rio's drivers and constabulary have been locked in fierce struggle over parking regulations, with the drivers emerging victorious despite the best efforts of the traffic cops to impose good sense and order. Cariocas will park anywhere—driveways, sidewalks, even in the middle of the street. Pedestrians, furthermore, are always fair game in Rio. No one will slow down for you if you are crossing against the light, or even with the light in many cases. Traffic signals—especially after dark—are all but ignored, and even the sidewalks are not completely safe. Cars will suddenly emerge from building garages, most of which sound loud alarms for exiting vehicles, and drive half a block across the sidewalk—especially on wide Avenida Atlântica—for no apparent reason other than the whim of the driver. So when in Rio, always give way to approaching traffic, no matter where it finds you walking!

Now, if you still want to rent a car in Rio, you are probably best off limiting your patronage to **Hertz, Avis,** or **Budget.** Then, if something goes wrong—as is commonly the case with rental cars throughout South America—there will be someone accountable to whom you can forward your complaints. **Hertz** (tel. 398-3162) and **Avis** (tel. 398-3083) have locations at the International Airport. All three companies have offices in Copacabana. Their addresses are: **Hertz,** Avenida Princesa Isabel 334 (tel. 275-4996 or toll free in Brazil 011/800-8900); **Avis,** Avenida Princesa Isabel 150 (tel. 542-4249 or toll free in Brazil 011/800-8787); and **Budget,** Avenida Princesa Isabel 350 (tel. 275-3244). The Avenida Princesa Isabel is a principal access route in Copacabana between the Centro and the northeastern shore in one direction, and the city's southern beaches and southwestern shore in the other.

TOURIST INFORMATION

This guide, of course, is an indispensable reference to the life and attractions of Rio de Janeiro, as well as to some fascinating locales beyond the city limits. After reading it, accompanied by consultations with knowledgeable friends and travel professionals (agents and tour guides, that is), you should know pretty much what there is to see and do in the *Cidade Maravilhosa* (City of Marvels—a nickname derived from an old carnival hit tune) before you even get to Rio. These sources cannot, however, tell you who will be in concert at a particular jazz club during your stay or what the hottest—or even newest—discos, bars, and restaurants are at precisely that moment. There will be unforeseen and unavoidable gaps in this guide—unavoidable because information changes so rapidly in a dynamic metropolis like Rio—that may require you to find information elsewhere. Here are some useful suggestions on where to get that information.

The state of Rio de Janeiro and the city itself maintain promotional offices called *TurisRio* (formerly *Flumitur*) and *Riotur,* respectively. TurisRio has an **information center** with a highly enthusiastic and competent staff at Rio's International Airport. If you arrive in Rio without a hotel reservation, for example, they can help you find a room at a price you can afford. They can also give you basic transportation information: where to catch the airport bus; how to get to Petrópolis, Búzios, Paraty, or other destinations, popular or personal, within the Estado do Rio, the state of Rio, as most Brazilians call it. These are the very first people to take your questions to when you land in Rio.

Both **TurisRio** (tel. 1516 in Rio, or 021/252-4512 outside Rio) and **Riotur** (tel. 297-7117 or 242-8000) maintain offices downtown at Rua da Assembléia 10 on the seventh and eighth floors. And both agencies distribute printed materials on sightseeing and excursion options. Riotur also maintains branches in much-frequented locations like: *Pão de Açúcar* (Sugar Loaf Mountain), Avenida Pasteur 520 in Urca, near the entrance to the cable car (open from 9 a.m. to 7 p.m.); at the overlook on Corcovado Mountain; in the downtown bus station, *Estação Rodoviária Novo Rio,* Avenida Francisco Bicalho 1 (tel. 291-5151, *ramal,* or extension, 143), located in São Cristovão slightly to the north of the downtown area (open from 6 a.m. till midnight); the *Marina da Glória,* in Flamengo Park (tel. 205-6447), open from 9 a.m. to 5 p.m. English and other major Western languages are spoken at these locations. Riotur's 242-8000 number is a **multilingual information service** operating 24 hours a day. Another valuable number to have is 1516—the **Tourist Assistance Line** (see Chapter 2, "Fast Facts Rio," for more details), and **Brazil Nuts** (tel. 255–6692).

Maps are available, for a nominal fee, at the above-mentioned information centers, or they can be purchased at most local bookstores and newsstands, including those at the airport and bus station. For car travel, buy a copy of *Quatro Rodas,* a Brazilian road guide complete with a country map. *Quatro Rodas* also features individual city and state maps. Maps in Brazil tend to be attractive, but stylized and often incomplete. I've yet to find a really excellent map of Rio and would be indebted to any reader willing to pass along information about a source of good maps in Brazil. Please write Michael Uhl, c/o Prentice Hall Press, Travel Books, 15 Columbus Circle, New York, NY 10023.

The **principal sources of information** for most tourists, once settled in the city, are the desk staffs at their various hotels. The hotel *portaria* (concierge) is where you will deposit your key, pick up messages, and find out about local hot spots and tours. Keep in mind, however, that while the portaria staff can be an immediate and valuable source of information, and their services will cost you nothing, chances are your informant will receive a commission if you accept his or her recommendation. And while that recommendation may be quite sound, porters have been known to steer people away from certain choices in favor of others to guarantee their fees. The porters, by the way, will also be able to direct you to a nearby agency for changing money at the parallel rate.

You'll also be able to secure from the porter's desk—if a copy is not already in your room—the *Calendário Turístico,* a booklet published trimonthly and filled with ads and listings of local attractions and events. Riotur publishes the monthly *Rio Guide,* with up-to-date listings of restaurants, nightclubs, fairs, and cultural events.

Rio Firsthand

Being New Yorkers and seasoned travelers, we were both unimpressed by warnings of the dangers of a trip to Brazil. "New York City is just as dangerous as Rio, if not more so," we thought each time someone tried to dissuade us from spending our year-end vacation south of the border.

Still, it was not without trepidation that we began our Brazilian vacation. We took extra care to store wallets in front pockets and to leave watches and jewelry in the safe in our hotel room. And we walked around with little more cash than we needed to bring us back to our hotel each night.

Our Portuguese included little more than *Rio* and *de Janeiro,* but a working knowledge of Spanish guided us through most daily transactions. English was useful in limited situations, like changing money. Many hotels had English-speaking concierges.

The language barrier was further diminished by the fact that so many of Brazil's attractions need no translation. The beaches are beautiful in any language; if you want a beer while soaking up rays, just point to it at one of the many refreshment stands on the beach. An English-speaking guide helped us on our visit to Corcovado and the Tijuca rain forest, but we didn't really need him.

The majesty of the Christ the Redeemer statue, the rain forest greenery, and the views from high atop Rio's tallest mountain spoke for themselves.

Eating well wasn't a problem, either. In the *churrascarias,* or barbecue restaurants, the waiters came around with skewers full of food. By the time they arrived with the twentieth skewer of beef, chicken, ham, turkey, shrimp, lamb, or pork, we were too full to say no. Other restaurants usually featured translations on the menu, English-speaking waiters, or both.

It didn't matter. Regardless of what we ordered, the food was incredible, in both quality and cost. At one restaurant we had to sit at a table for four just to accommodate all the food the waiters brought us. In another, our after-dinner liqueurs, at $5 a shot, cost as much as our entire dinner.

We were a bit disappointed to find that our "beachfront" hotel, like all the other hotels in Rio, was actually across the street—a busy street at that, not unlike Chicago's Lake Shore Drive—from the beach. Still, like most of the rooms in the hotel, ours faced the ocean and provided brilliant views of the Atlantic. A Brazilian sunset viewed from the privacy of our balcony, as we sipped caipirinhas, made the inflated beachfront rate worth it.

The trips we took out of Rio were equally magnificent. A day-long tour of the islands around Rio was a cool way to spend an otherwise hot day. Our guide, William, spoke to us in at least four languages; by the time he got to English, we had already figured out what he was saying.

Almost the only problem we encountered was getting rid of our Brazilian money at the end of our trip. We bought more Brazilian coffee than we could carry, but at about 50¢ a pound, it barely made a dent in our cruzados. Bottles of cachaca (from which caipirinhas are made) lightened our wallets a bit, as did T-shirts and amethysts.

When we got home, we still had about $10 in cruzados left. No need to worry, though. If they're still worth anything, we'll be using them again soon.

John Rosenthal and Lisa Renaud
New York City

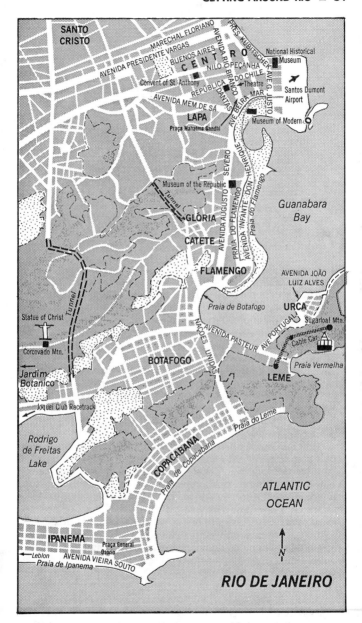

RIO DE JANEIRO

WHERE TO STAY

1. COPACABANA AND LEME HOTELS

2. IPANEMA AND LEBLON HOTELS

3. VIDIGAL AND SÃO CONRADO HOTELS

4. BARRA DA TIJUCA HOTELS

5. GLÓRIA AND FLAMENGO HOTELS

Rio's hotels rank with the best in the world. The deluxe hotels in particular offer the comforts, facilities, and service that contribute to Rio's reputation for hospitality and impeccable taste with a tropical twist. Furthermore, the visitor to Rio can be housed in one of the best rooms in town—with a glorious ocean view and across the street from some of the world's most privileged beaches—and pay half of what a hotel of comparable quality would cost in Western Europe or North America. Package and group discounts further reduce Rio's hotel rates to a level that many international travelers, who wouldn't dream of staying in such luxurious hotels elsewhere, have found irresistible in recent years.

RIO'S HOTEL SCENE

Rio is a beach town (in case you've missed the point!). The city's best hotels are all located in the beach neighborhoods of the Zona Sul, particularly in Copacabana, Leme, Ipanema, and Leblon. Slightly more remote, but compensatingly luxurious and self-contained, are two resort hotels in the beachside neighborhoods of Vidigal and São Conrado, the Sheraton and the Inter-Continental. It makes no sense to stay in one of the many hotels located in the Centro. There is virtually no residential life downtown. Streets there tend to be empty after dark, except in the immediate vicinity of the Teatro Municipál or other popular nightspots. On a given evening, you might want to go downtown to play, but all except the most confirmed inner-city buffs and students on a budget will want to wake up to the smell of salt water and the sound of the surf. The best super-budget lodgings for backpackers and students can probably be found in Flamengo, where back streets are appropriately threadbare and the location is advantageously close to both the Centro and Copacabana.

For over 15 years, Hans Stern, one of Rio's most successful jewelers, has collected data on how North American tourists organize their Brazilian vacations. He has concluded that 90% of all North Americans who come to Rio travel nowhere else in the country. Of this population, another 90%, according to Stern's estimate, arrive with a group or on a package tour. These groups and package arrangements to Rio are popular because what you get, practically speaking—low airfare, first-class beach hotel, prearranged tours and transfers—is often competitively priced with comparable tours to, say, Rome or Greece. The price of the package to Rio would cost you twice as much if you pieced it together yourself.

It is *not* wise to arrive in Rio without a hotel reservation. Since most visitors apparently wish to stay on the beach in Copacabana or Ipanema, and since there are precious few potential construction sites in these barrios for new seaside hotels—barring the unforeseen demolition or reconversion of an existing luxury apartment building—the number of available rooms is limited. During the peak season—in the summertime from Christmas until after Carnival, in the winter during the July school holiday, and on holiday or special-event weekends throughout the year—Rio's hotels easily fill to capacity. Even during the so-called off-season in Rio, if you arrive without a reservation, you are unlikely to secure a satisfactory room —for example, one in a prime location with a view of the beach. You may have to settle for a perfectly nice room but several blocks from the strand. This may not be the end of the world, but if your expectation of a Rio vacation includes a view of Copacabana's magnificent sweeping curve, you may be disappointed.

Every hotel reviewed in this guide includes breakfast in its daily rates. And breakfast can vary from a sumptuous buffet or room service with the works for no extra charge (on the deluxe level) to the hearty bread, cheese, and bananas of a budget establishment. Most hotels add a 10% service surcharge to their bills, which will apply to package clients only when they purchase extras like midnight room service, poolside drinks, restaurant meals they've signed for, and so forth.

Rio's hotel rooms tend to all contain some standard equipment. Bathrooms, for example, generally have bidets, a reminder of the Continental influence in Brazil. The mini-bar was almost certainly American inspired. Even the most underrated rooms contain these little refrigerators now, stocked with overpriced beverages and snacks. It's easy to beat the mini-bar monopoly, however. Do a little shopping of your own at the local food store. Buy what you want and then stock the refrigerator with your favorite items—which will cost a quarter of what the hotel wants to charge you. I'd suggest a few large bottles of mineral water, a six-pack of beer, wine, nuts and crackers, and several varieties of fresh fruit. Your room may also contain a small private strong box called a *cofre*. There is a daily fee for the safe's use at most hotels. The key may be obtained at the reception desk.

For the sake of simplicity and easy reference, the hotels in this guide will be presented by neighborhood, beginning with the deluxe listings, followed by first class, moderately priced, and budget hotels.

1. Copacabana and Leme Hotels

Copacabana's most expensive and desirable rooms are to be found in the handful of five-star hotels located on the Avenida Atlântica, opposite the beach. Next in price are the smaller and generally less elaborate four- and three-star hotels that also front the sea. Moderately priced hotels, some of which are considerably more modern and comfortable than their Avenida Atlântica counterparts, are found off the beach on side streets and back avenues. There are even, happily, a few hotels in Copacabana that can be categorized in the budget range.

DELUXE HOTELS

Like a fancy centerpiece, the **Copacabana Palace Hotel,** Avenida Atlântica 1702 (tel. 255-7070), stands near the midpoint of the beach. The seven-story building of carved stone has been combined with a more modern ten-story annex—which may soon be added to if a zoning battle is resolved in the hotel's favor. A circular drive leads past several elegant shops (jewelers, florist, bookstore) into a lobby which embodies a European club–like atmosphere. To one side of the hotel is the glassed-in and casual Pergula restaurant, behind which spreads one of Rio's largest swimming pools, with outdoor tables, chairs, and waiter service. Poolside life at the Copacabana Palace is an institution in itself. The hotel's more formal Bife de Ouro restaurant is one of Rio's finest, and prices are very reasonable.

Before the era of the high-rise five-star hotels, this was the best address in Rio; many travelers still hold to that opinion. Thanks to a recent multimillion-dollar facelift, the Riviera-style grand hotel is guaranteed a bright place in Rio's pantheon of hotels for years to come. The Copacabana Palace doesn't market to package tours, but the hotel does a brisk business with individuals, groups, and conventions. The well-heeled tend to favor this horizontal palazzo over the less formal atmosphere of the newer, fine hotels. And who is to gainsay their choice? A suite at the Copacabana Palace is still a way to treat yourself royally when staying in Rio.

Among the 222 rooms and suites, those along the front of the building are smallish but bright, furnished in mahogany. Armchairs and sofas are newly upholstered in fine floral-patterned fabrics, and baths are tiled, though also small. Singles begin at $115 and climb to $175, while doubles range from $130 to $192. The more pricey rooms front the sea. Suites, for $300 nightly, are sizable and luxuriously appointed, with a totally separate sitting room. Baths in the suites are mostly large and old-fashioned in white porcelain and tiles, with a pedestal sink and free-standing tub—both with fixtures of polished brass. All units have TV with cable reception, king-size or twin beds, and high ceilings; most are without balconies, but all are air conditioned. The Copacabana Palace offers numerous other amenities, such as parking, room service, and an in-house beauty salon.

The number one choice for visiting North Americans in Rio, however, is the stunning **Rio Palace,** Avenida Atlântica 4240 (tel. 521-3232). The staff actively pursues the American tourist market. That means you can almost be assured of plenty of company from fellow citizens of the States and Canada during your stay. Above all, the Rio Palace is one of the most comfortable and best-situated hotels in all of Rio de Janeiro. Two tall U-shaped towers in brown-hued tones of stone and glass occupy the farthest corner of Copacabana, opposite the beach's end which borders a historic site, a diminutive and still-active military fort. The hotel is also within five minutes' walking distance of Rio's other premier beach, Ipanema.

The terrace at poolside is probably one of the most popular spots in Rio to languish in the noonday heat, or to sip evening cocktails and toast the setting sun. Excellent food is served in the Atlantis restaurant, off the pool. And here, in the morning, a groaning breakfast buffet is set up with pastries, fruits, juices, meats, and cheeses, along with chafing dishes of bacon, sausage, and eggs. Coffee and milk are served piping hot directly at your table. As you look out beyond the terrace wall, you'll see the madcap scene of Rio's early-morning exercise mania unfolding on the beach below, as walkers, joggers, and bike riders share the wide, beach-long sidewalk with its famous mosaic pattern of undulating black lines against a sea of white. For dinner only, the superb Le Pré Catalan is the hotel's principal restaurant, contributing to the craft of haute cuisine, Rio-style, but under the supervision of a demanding and creative French chef.

All 418 rooms at the Rio Palace have sheltered balconies, half of which face an interior court and overlook a swimming pool; the other half give some eye-filling views of the surrounding sea. Rooms are large and offer every comfort in tasteful furnishings. Each room contains an elegant bath with shower and tub, a mini-bar, individually controlled air conditioning, and a color TV set featuring a CNN satellite channel and regularly scheduled English-language movies. Tariffs are $160 to $190 for singles, $180 to $210 for doubles with either twin or queen-sized beds. A favorite congregating place, day or night, is the lobby bar near the hotel entrance. The Horse's Neck Bar and the Palace Club, a private nightclub, are perennial nightlife favorites for guests and residents alike. Other services include indoor parking, a health club, and conference rooms, and an auditorium where shows feature international stars such as Frank Sinatra.

The posh **Meridien,** Avenida Atlântica 1020 (tel. 275-9922), occupies one corner of the intersection where Avenida Princesa Isabel leads to downtown Rio, at the boundary between Copacabana's red-light district and the staid, family neighborhood of Leme beach. The Meridien is Leme's only luxury hotel and is a favorite of European tourists. With its 37 floors of glass and steel, the Meridien is a portent of the architectural change bound to one day transform the skyline of the famous strand. The hotel has two fine restaurants: on the ground floor, the Café de la Paix, and on the roof, the St. Honoré, with its reputation for gourmet dishes and one of the city's great panoramic views. The lobby is all business, designed not for lingering but to funnel guests and visitors efficiently to various facilities, including a bar, shopping arcade, a small movie theater, computerized conference rooms, and the popular disco, Régine's, open daily only to guests and private members.

Modern in every way, the 497 rooms are decorated in bright pastel shades, with ultramodern furnishings. There are no balconies. The ample windows are sealed and equipped with blackout draperies. All rooms offer satellite color TV with movies, modern baths, safe-deposit boxes, and mini-bars. Singles range from $160 to $190, and doubles from $170 to $200.

One of the Meridien's best assets is its location in Leme. This section of the beach is pleasantly quiet, especially on weekdays. The surrounding neighborhood is just the perfect scale for getting to know well a single neighborhood in Rio during a relatively brief stay. Both on Avenida Atlântica and the parallel Avenida Gustavo Sampaio, a block from the ocean, are several attractive and excellent restaurants: the tiny Shirley's specializing in fish, and the touristy but tasty Máriu's *churrascaria,* where grilled meats are served *rodízio*-style—as much as you can eat for a fixed price. All the necessary neighborhood stores and services can be found among Leme's few back streets: a pharmacy, newsstand, stand-up corner bar, laundry and more. There always seems to be some movement in Leme on both its principal avenues, but even this street life, along with the light auto traffic, is on a diminutive scale appropriate to the limited size of this special little corner of the city.

The **Ouro Verde,** Avenida Atlântica 1456 (tel. 542-1887), is refined and efficient, a favorite of corporate travelers and journalists. Lacking a pool and other required amenities such as a hairdresser and sauna that would qualify the four-star hotel for official deluxe status, the Swiss-run Ouro Verde, nonetheless, has few peers in the city for quality of service and the overall tastefulness of its rooms and public spaces. The Ouro Verde Restaurant, located on the mezzanine overlooking the beach, is one of Rio's most popular, serving finely prepared meals on linen-covered tables made elegant by silver candlesticks, china, and crystal.

There are 66 rooms, all uniquely furnished, with fine period pieces in polished hardwood. Graceful watercolors decorate the walls. Embroidered towels embellish the modern combination baths. Rooms with covered verandas face the ocean, and all accommodations include TV, mini-bar, and air conditioning. Oceanfront rooms cost $125, double occupancy, $110 for singles; back rooms range from $100 to $110. A reservation well in advance is an absolute necessity.

The Ouro Verde is located beyond the Copacabana Palace in the direction of Leme, but is still close to the central stretch of the beach. A barrier of plants at the hotel's entrance separates a street-level bar from the distractions of the street. The small lobby stands at the bottom of an atrium, which rises all the way to the roof. The architectural details are rich in marble and highly polished hardwood mouldings and trim. An enclosed miniature garden at the rear of the lobby is the picture of a Portuguese *quintal,* an old-fashioned backyard. Off the lobby are formal sitting and reading rooms with club furnishings and tapestries. The clientele is all word-of-mouth; the hotel does not advertise, and does not accept groups.

Copacabana's Newest Deluxe Hotel

The **Rio Atlântica Suite Hotel,** Avenida Atlantica 2964 (tel. 255-6332), is the first deluxe hotel to open along the Copacabana beachfront in many years. With 228 suites and rooms spread over 18 floors, the marble and glass-faced Rio Atlântica would seem to squeeze snugly into a niche all its own on Rio's most famous strand, being half the size of its two elegant five-star competitors—the Rio Palace and the Meridien—and therefore presumably providing more intimate service and surroundings. As for the accommodations, the emphasis here is on suites; the hotel has attempted to broaden its appeal beyond tourists—who will not disdain the added space—to business executives in town on moderately extended stays.

When I visited the Rio Atlântica, the hotel was still six months from completion—but the spaciousness of the lobby and the presence of a rooftop pool also suggested that, despite its apartment-building scale, the hotel would possess some of the self-contained ambience of a genuine, full service resort that characterizes Rio's most luxurious establishments. Depending on how quickly the hotel catches on, the Rio Atlântica could offer quality digs at bargain prices for a year or two. The initial price strucure of $100, single, and $110, double, for rooms and from $130 to $140, single, and $140 to $150, double, for two-room suites makes this place a tempting choice. The sea-fronting $200 a night Oceanic Suite also promises to be an eye catcher.

UPPER-BRACKET HOTELS

The **Rio Othon Palace,** Avenida Atlântica 3264 (tel. 255-8812), toward the southern end of Copacabana beach, is first among of the Othon group, which boasts ten hotels in Rio, six along this same beach. You can't miss the 30-story brown-glass landmark that towers high above the other buildings along the strip. The tower is spaced between its neighbors in such a way that every one of the 606 rooms offers at least a partial water view. Call the Othon semi-deluxe. It has all the five-star amenities and caters heavily to package tour operators. Many Americans have very enjoyable stays at the Othon Palace.

The atmosphere is one of constant motion, and the public areas—the tiny pool, the rooftop bar—are somewhat worn in places. Unlike the other large beachfront hotels, the Othon Palace lacks transitional space between the sidewalk and the lobby, which subjects guests to hustlers right up to the entrance.

All the rooms have balconies, and they have been recently redecorated with tasteful streamlined furnishings. Bathrooms are lined in marble, and accommodations provide in-house video and multilingual TV channels. The rooftop Skylab bar opens to a sundeck with a small open-air pool. The Skylab is one of the hotel's most popular drawing cards, attracting a steady flow of local residents as well as guests. Small wonder, as the bar is aptly named. From here you get a superb close-up view of the hills behind Copacabana, where you can see quite dramatically how narrow a strip of land the neighborhood occupies between the coastal mountains and the sea. And you can also get a glimpse of life on the rising slopes, where even Copacabana's favelas are somewhat prosperous.

The Estância Restaurant on the third floor serves churrasco (a Brazilian barbecue of steaks and grilled meats) and offers a panoramic view of the beach. Breakfast is served in a lavish buffet-style in the Samambaia coffeeshop, also on the third floor. Other facilities include an "underground" disco in the basement, and a small health club on the roof. Singles start at $130, doubles at $155.

A neighbor of the Hotel Rio Palace on the southern end of Copacabana beach is the **Miramar Palace Hotel,** Avenida Atlântica 668 (tel. 247-6070). The beach ends here at a point that juts into the sea and forms a slight protective pocket from the relentless beating of the South Atlantic. A half dozen fishing boats are still hauled to the sand at this spot, an appealing anachronism in the otherwise seamless urbanity of Copacabana. The Miramar has surveyed this prospect for some time, and it has a venerable reputation. The large glassed-in bar at the edge of the sidewalk has long been a favorite rest stop for an afternoon of café leisure.

The lobby, reached through an entrance on a side street, is warm, but small and strictly functional, and the two smallish elevators are slow. But the Miramar is like a comfortable dowager, set in her ways, who sees little to be gained by speeding up the pace of life. A stylish staircase leads to a mezzanine and a better-than-average restaurant with a wide-angle window view of the beach scene across the avenue. The 150 rooms are quite comfortable, almost homey, not at all fancy in their decor. All the in-room basics and extras are here: full bath, TV, temperature control, and mini-bar. Still, one gets the feeling of a Copacabana from a bygone age, one not too distant perhaps, but past nonetheless. Even the service is somewhat premodern, with the staff exhibiting a kind of good-natured friendliness that can't be taught in hotel training seminars.

Other amenities include a tearoom (taking afternoon tea is fashionable in Rio), the rooftop *Ponto do Comando* bar with an open-air deck, and a third-floor coffeeshop above the restaurant that is visible from the lobby through a central atrium. Standard singles are $90 to $115 and doubles are $100 to $125, with beachfront rooms adding about 25% to the price. Off-season rates—for April through September—are $70 single and $80 double.

The **Luxor Regente,** Avenida Atlântica 3716 (tel. 287-4212), is the largest of the Luxor hotels in Rio, and is close to the Ipanema end of Copacabana Beach. Not only is the Regente favorably located, but it is also a very versatile hotel in the sense that it simultaneously appeals to and accommodates both individual travelers and—given its size of 263 rooms—groups as well. Groups are always coming and going at the Regente, but not every day, so that a nice balance in the public spaces is maintained between the waves of animation and peace and quiet.

Because of it labyrinthine interior—rooms are distributed among several towers and annexes—the intrinsic environment at the Regente is varied as well. I have stayed in both the older but attractive beachfront rooms with their old-fashioned verandas, and the more modern internal rooms tucked deep within the hotel and accessible by a separate bank of elevators. I prefer the former for the off-season, when the Regente is less crowded, and the latter for the high season, for the opposite reason. As to amenities, the small lobby seating area makes a very comfortable cocktail lounge, with a view of beach and street life that is both intimate and removed. Service at the hotel is superb—friendly and attentive—while facilities of note include the excellent Forno e Fogão restaurant (see separate review under Rio's Restaurants) and a large branch of the H. Stern jewelry store, staffed by a classy and non-pushy group of salespersons who seem as intent on educating potential buyers about gemstones as they are on selling them.

Another relatively new hotel along the Copacabana strand is the **International Rio,** Avenida Atlântica 1500 (tel. 295-2323), not far from the Hotel Ouro Verde and approaching the Leme end of the beach. The International Rio offers 177 rooms in what appears to be a first class tourist hotel, complete with rooftop pool, two bars, and a restaurant. Daily rates range from $123 to $146 for singles and from $134 to $165 for doubles.

Midway into Leme, the quiet end of the beach, is the **Leme Othon Palace,** Avenida Atlântica 656 (tel. 275-8080). This hotel probably occupies the best possible position along the 7 km (4¼-mile) strip, especially for those who like their beaches with more of a residential—as opposed to a recreational—flavor. Of the 193 rooms in this large rectangular block, approximately a third offer ocean views. Rooms are modern and adequately furnished, more with an eye toward durability than fashion. All rooms have covered balconies, plus full baths with separate tubs and showers, TV, air conditioning, and mini-bars.

Entrance to the lobby is on a side street. A second-floor restaurant is reliable for lunch, or as a fallback for the odd evening a guest might prefer to stay close to home. The Leme Pub offers live music, and a ground-floor coffeeshop recalls a saloon in Portugal, with its typical blue and white tiles. The Leme Palace has the experience and capacity to handle large groups reliably. Singles cost $93 to $103, and doubles run $121 to $134, depending on location.

A third Othon hotel, the **Lancaster,** Avenida Atlântica 1470 (tel. 541-1887), occupies one of Copacabana's several smart deco buildings (this one is a converted apartment house) that grace this famous ocean avenue. Narrow and small, the building's white façade sports a rack of curved balconies. Near the Ouro Verde and the Copacabana Palace, the Lancaster offers a suite-size room as its standard accommodation. Enter the lobby past a sunken sidewalk bar. Off the lobby is a small game room. The Lancaster restaurant is quite small, almost family scale, perfectly suitable for breakfast (included in the tariffs) and for other light meals.

The Lancaster's rooms are divided by partitions into a sitting area with TV, couch, table, and chairs, and a sleeping area with modern bath. Only rooms in the front of the hotel have balconies. Other rooms overlook an interior court and are a bit dreary for lack of light. These have sleeping areas that are slightly smaller than those on the avenue. The hotel's 70 rooms are priced according to location. Interior singles are $75 and doubles run $80, while deluxe front rooms range between $95 and $105. Special services include babysitting, free use of beach towels and umbrellas, and a car rental agency on the premises. Children under 8 stay in their parents' room free.

Luxor Continental, Rua Gustavo Sampaio 320 (tel. 275-5252). The Luxor chain has four hotels in Rio, three of which are in Copacabana or Leme. The Continental is not on the beach, but it occupies a prized location. This principal back street of Leme is a genuine neighborhood, complete with colorful street life, shops, and restaurants. The beach is only one block away. Recently redecorated, the 19-story hotel has adopted the color scheme of the other Luxor properties, making free use of vibrant and fiery shades of orange, red, and yellow.

The 123 rooms are smaller than average, and half the baths lack tubs, but all have bidets and some have phone extensions. Only the corner rooms offer narrow views of the beach through spaces in between neighboring buildings. Otherwise the hotel looks out onto back streets and nearby hills. There are TVs and stocked mini-bars in all rooms, which are also air-conditioned. The 320 Restaurant and Poty Bar are available for dining and drinks, to the accompaniment of live piano music. The Caramelo coffeeshop occupies the mezzanine and has its own entrance. Singles run $85, $100, and $115; and doubles, $95, $110, and $125.

The **Plaza Copacabana,** Avenida Princesa Isabel 263 (tel. 275-7722), located on the Copacabana side of the furiously busy eight-lane access road, is an 18-story four-star hotel about two blocks from the beach. Behind the lobby is a multilevel lounge with a restaurant overlooking an atrium that rises to an unusual domed ceiling. The 165 high-ceilinged rooms are comfortably furnished and include TV, mini-bar, and air conditioning. This hotel would provide convenient quarters for those whose interests or business took them frequently to the Centro while in Rio—from this location, the Botafogo Metro station is just a short cab or bus ride away. Perhaps because of its location, so near the tunnel and on the fringes of the Copacabana red-light district, the Plaza is not as expensive as the typical four-star hotel. Single rooms range in cost from $50 to $60, and doubles are $70 to $80. An added incentive is that the hotel does not add the usual 10% service charge.

At the **Olinda,** Avenida Atlântica 2230 (tel. 257-1890), café-style tables and chairs occupy the sidewalk at the hotel's entrance, surrounded by potted plants and hedges for privacy. The Olinda also has a small but old-fashioned lobby complete with overstuffed armchairs and table lamps. A three-star hotel fronting the sea at this central location along the Copacabana beach, the Olinda is some-what of a bargain. The 100-room hotel also has a restaurant and a beauty parlor. Rooms are airy and comfortable and cheerfully un-distinguished in décor. All contain what are the requisite amenities in every hotel rated by the Brazilian tourist board, including TV, mini-bar, and air conditioning. Rooms facing the beach begin to be competitive in price with the better hotels in the area. Staying here costs between $75 and $100 for a single, and $85 to $110 for a double.

The **Hotel California,** Avenida Atlântica 2612 (tel. 257-1900). This hotel with the felicitous name will remind some people of the popular song with the same title. A further distinguishing mark of the 12-story Mediterranean-style building is its location smack dab at the midpoint of the lengthy concave avenue. The closest the hotel comes to reflecting a West Coast image, however, is the bright side-walk bar located off the lobby entrance, with its striped slatted chairs and tables, and multicolored umbrellas. Otherwise, the 117-room hotel has a somewhat European atmosphere and caters to a repeat clientele of vacationers and business travelers alike.

The rooms are very pleasant, with comfortable furnishings and balconies. A few deluxe rooms facing the ocean feature huge veran-das with two entrances. Accommodations have large tiled baths with pedestal sinks and enormous tubs, plus the ubiquitous TV and mini-bar. All rooms are air-conditioned, but those in beachfront ac-commodations may get the same effect more naturally—especially on the upper floors—by channeling cool breezes off the ocean through an open balcony door. Some single rooms are quite small, and if they don't face the street, a bit dark as well. The Le Colonial restaurant specializes in both Brazilian and international meals. In addition to the marble-lined lobby, the other public spaces include a lounge, meeting rooms, and a pub with cigarbox-style paneling. The hotel, one of the Othon group, provides guests with umbrellas and towels for the beach. The prices parallel those of its companion hotel, the Olinda, with singles from $75 to $100, and doubles from $85 to $110.

Also centrally located along Copacabana's sweeping curve is the **Luxor Copacabana,** Avenida Atlântica 2554 (tel. 257-1940). This early version of a glass-and-steel structure is unusually thin and offers the unique feature of balconies with its side rooms and excel-lent views of the ocean. The reason for this architectural option is that the building next door sits back on the sidewalk considerably farther than the hotel, creating a welcome jog in the straight line of the long sidewalk promenade.

A variety of natural woods—particularly *jacarandá* or Brazil-ian rosewood—is used in the furnishings, bedboards, and finish trims. Natural plank floors stand out sharply against the bright pri-mary colors of the décor adding warmth and vitality. Lamps, ashtrays, and wall decorations are of modern design, as are the bath-room fixtures. Not all baths have tubs, but all have showers and bidets, as well as wall-phone extensions.

Front rooms have glassed-in balconies, furnished with tables and chairs—perfect for use as breakfast nooks. Corner suites that face the ocean are quite large and have spacious verandas filled with potted plants. There is excellent shopping in the boutiques on nearby side streets and behind the hotel on Avenida N.S. de Copacabana. The hotel's terrace is home to the Fogareiro bar and restaurant. The Luxor Copacabana's 123 rooms are divided into three categories—standard, superior, and deluxe—depending on size, location, and decorative appointments, and will cost you $108, $122 or $135 for a single, and $120, $135 or $150 for a double.

The **Copacabana Praia,** Rua Francisco Otaviano 30 (tel. 521-2727), was recently built right behind the Rio Palace, a short walking distance from both Copacabana and Ipanema beaches. This very small first-class hotel houses only 55 rooms, all of which face the front and have balconies. The staff is friendly and caters with equal grace to individual clients and small groups, many of which are from the States. Rooms are fully equipped with TVs, mini-bars, and individual thermostats. There is a small dip pool and sundeck on the roof, and a sauna as well. The Pícollo restaurant/bar serves international and local food. Singles begin at $65, doubles at $80.

The **Real Palace,** Rua Duvivier 70 (tel. 541-4387), was built in 1984 on this side street, two blocks from the beach. If the rooms are compared with, say, the Lancaster, they are much smaller, half as attractive, and almost twice the price. The 60 rooms have TVs suspended from the ceiling, hospital style, plus mini-bars and combination baths. At $150 for two, suites are the hotel's best bet. They are much more elegant and offer three times the space of the standard rooms. Suites have private saunas, showers with water massage, and two rooms—one with two large double beds, the other with leather armchairs and a couch, and a glass-topped table with four comfortable chairs. There is a small rooftop dip pool and a restaurant serving Spanish food. Singles are $90, doubles $100.

MEDIUM-PRICED HOTELS

The **Acapulco,** Rua Gustavo Sampaio 854 (tel. 275-0022), is a moderately priced alternative to the Meridien or the Leme Palace for those wishing to stay in Leme, who want to experience the vest-pocket atmosphere of a backstreet neighborhood and still be only a block from the beach. The deluxe double-occupancy rooms, costing $50 a night, are large with smallish beds and have balconies facing the street, where the rear of the towering Meridien dominates but does not darken the skyline. Even the smaller rooms off the front have a comfortable appearance and have good, functional baths, mini-bars, TVs, and air conditioning. Other features in this 123-room hostelry are parking facilities, a restaurant, and a coffeeshop. Singles are $35, doubles run $40 to $50, breakfast included. The Acapulco does not charge 10% for service, which adds to its genuine bargain status.

The **Rio Copa,** Avenida Princesa Isabel 370 (tel. 275-6644), is only a stone's throw from the tunnel leading to the center of the city, and three blocks from the beach. The hotel is relatively new, with double-glazed windows that effectively soundproof the rooms from the traffic below. Accommodations are spacious with Scandi-

navian furnishings, baths with showers, plus mini-bars and TVs.
The hotel is totally air-conditioned. The view above the muted din
of the street is of Copacabana's rooftops, and is wide and appealing.
Luxury doubles offer half again as much space as the standard
rooms, but the L-shaped design and narrow dimensions of the sitting area make the space impractical. Other hotel features include
executive meeting rooms, the Le Baron restaurant, Le Princesse bar,
and a coffeeshop open 24 hours a day. Rooms are priced at $55 for
singles, and $60 doubles.

Right before the tunnel on the Leme side are two private alley-
ways that are worthy of a quick peek if you find yourself walking in
or near this stretch of the avenue. Identify yourself as a curious tourist at the security gate, and the guard will probably allow you in.
You'll walk through the arch at the Edifício Winston (Avenida
Princesa Isabel 254) past the rows of charming houses to the end of
the alley and climb the stone stairs. The incline leads you up the
largely barren side of a hill on whose leeward face is the infamous
Favela de Babilonia, a shantytown of folkloric stature, once memo-
rialized in a poem by Elizabeth Bishop. The stairs rise several flights.
The view from the top is confined to nearby rooftops, but you will
also suddenly be within reach of the dense green vegetation that
covers the hills, much the way it must have been long before the New
World was colonized.

The **Debret,** Rua Almirante Gonçalves 5 (tel. 521-3332), is a
converted apartment building with 98 guest rooms that actually sits
on Avenida Atlântica but has its entrance on this side street. The hotel's intimate lobby, adorned with sculpture and paintings, invites
lingering. The rooms in the Debret are really a cut above Rio's other
three-star hotels in comfort and in the quality of furnishings, fixtures, and décor, which is formal and colonial. Front rooms
(actually in this case, side rooms) view the ocean. A new restaurant
has been added on the 12th floor. Room service is available 24
hours, and all rooms have TVs and mini-bars. You pay $55 for a sin-
gle room and $78 for a double.

The Debret is named for the romantic and naturalistic French
painter Jean-Baptiste Debret, whose paintings and graphics provide
a rich visual chronicle of early 19th-century life in Brazil. Debret
came with a team of French artists who were invited to Brazil by
Dom João VI, the prince regent who had fled Lisbon from
Napoleon's advancing armies in 1808. Debret lived in Brazil for
many years and helped to found the Brazilian Academy of Fine Arts.
His work emphasizes, in amazing detail, popular scenes from this
age, the dress and habits of masters, slaves, and Indians, as well as
depicting some important events in Brazilian history. Several
printed collections of his work exist and are worth scrutinizing in a
library or bookstore.

Several blocks in from seaside Avenida Atlântica, beyond Rua
Barata Ribeiro—Copacabana's third major avenue parallel to the
sea—is the **Copacabana Sol,** Rua Santa Clara 141 (tel. 257-1840).
Even here, the hotel is still only a five- to ten-minute walk from the
beach, and for the price, you may find the stroll worth the savings.
The surrounding neighborhood is filled with good, inexpensive res-

taurants, and the street life is relatively quiet, yet colorful, with open-air markets and many sidewalk vendors.

The hotel is new and quite attractive in appearance, and it provides features not usually required of a three-star hotel, including restaurant, bar, parking, and room service. Accommodations are large and well furnished, with TV, mini-bar, and air conditioning. The hotel has 70 rooms: singles range from $40 to $43, doubles run $42 to $45, and some very attractive suites go for a very reasonable rate of $60.

The **Bandeirantes Othon,** Rua Barata Ribeiro 548 (tel. 255-6252), with 96 guest rooms, is a relatively small hotel built more for commercial travelers than for tourists. This stretch of Rua Barata Ribeiro has less charm than the area around Rua Santa Clara farther to the north. The rooms are comfortable, however, and its location three blocks from Copacabana beach makes the hotel a fair choice for budget-conscious travelers who like modern surroundings. The Bandeirantes has a coffeeshop and bar, and offers limited parking as well as 24-hour room service. Singles range from $50 to $65, doubles $55 to $70.

Castro Alves, Avenida Nossa Senhora de Copacabana 552 (tel. 255-8815). Facing the Praça Serzedelo Correia, this small Othon hotel bears the name of Brazil's most beloved poet. Public plazas are rare in Copacabana, making this small park a welcome patch of green along this street of shops, apartments, and eating spots, one block from the water. There is a McDonald's on the next street, if that's your fancy. Next to the hotel, however, is a branch of La Mole, a chain of Italian restaurants with a reputation for good and inexpensive dishes. Hotel patrons also eat their buffet-style breakfast on the pleasant La Mole premises. The hotel has 76 rooms, all containing TVs and mini-bars. Other than room service, there are few other amenities provided by the hotel, where a single will cost you $46, and a double is $62.

The poet Castro Alves was Brazil's answer to Lord Byron, a total romantic given to the self-destructive melancholia and bohemian lifestyle made popular by the English poet of that mid-19th-century age. His passion for life is evident in his verse, though he died prematurely of consumption when only 24 years old. Alves was a great lover of his country's natural beauty, a confirmed republican, and one of the most committed voices of his time against slavery.

Located at the corner of Rua Paula Freitas, two-thirds of the way down the Copacabana strip, is the **Trocadero,** Avenida Atlântica 2064 (tel. 257-1834), part of the Othon group, and a favorite among traditional beach hotels for many years. While not cramped, the rooms aren't terribly spacious. Standard rooms facing the hotel's interior are actually larger than the deluxe front accommodations, which have good sea views, but no balconies. All rooms have old-fashioned baths with porcelain fixtures, plus TVs, mini-bars, and writing desks.

Redecorating is overdue throughout the entire hotel, as the public spaces are beginning to look a bit shabby. Yet one senses that the clientele might prefer this old-slipper ambience over the sometimes polyester slickness of more modern second-class hotels. Next to the lobby entrance is a sidewalk café behind a partition of shrubs, with access to an inside bar through a separate door. The Moenda restaurant is one of the few eateries left in Copacabana where real Brazilian food is served, including the aromatic *moqueca* fish stews of Bahia. Standards of service remain high at the Trocadero, which is similar to the Miramar in its personalized touch. Some of the hotel's 120 rooms—depending on location—can still be a bargain, given the beachfront location, with singles starting at $70 and doubles at $90.

The Copacabana Hotel Residência, Rua Barata Ribeiro 222 (tel. 255-7212). Travelers of the American highways have long been familiar with motels offering "efficiency" accommodations, which always include a refrigerator and stove, along with some pots, plates and eating utensils. The idea is that you can stop in an area of interest for several days, and—especially when traveling with the kids—economize on food by preparing your own meals.

The term for such units in Brazil is "Apart-Hotel"—generally two-room suites with bath and kitchenette. This one, the Copacabana Hotel Residência, is well located in a nice side-street quarter and is far more modern than the old roadside cabins reminiscent of family travel in the U.S. A sitting room with attached kitchenette and a separate bedroom add spacious comfort to normal single-room hotel accommodations. There is even a separate laundry sink for washing out clothes and bathing suits. In addition to parking facilities, the hotel has a small pool, an exercise room, and a sauna. The price, at $50 per night, $57 double, could make the hotel's location, three blocks from the beach, an acceptable sacrifice.

Half a block from the Rio Palace and its neighboring arcade of chic boutiques, is the **Riviera,** Avenida Atlântica 4122 (tel. 247-6060). The nicest rooms in the Riviera face the beach. The excellent location at this tranquil end of the strand compensates for the generally worn appearance of the lobby and other public spaces, and the sparseness of the room furnishings. The hotel however, has now commenced a full renovation. On the other hand, the guest rooms —all with combination baths, TVs, and mini-bars—are very moderately priced for a beachfront hotel starting at $50 for a single and ranging from $60 to $90 for a double, the latter price for a seafront room. The hotel also has room service, a restaurant, and a sidewalk bar.

The small **Praia Lido,** Avenida Nossa Senhora de Copacabana 202 (tel. 541-1347), is another option, for the budget-minded or an alternative for beach-area lodgings when the better hotels are booked. Near the Rua Duvivier cross street, the lobby to the 51-room hotel is found up a flight of stairs. An adequately furnished double room with basic amenities like bath, TV, mini-bar and air conditioning can be had for $44 a night. A small suite, with private sauna, is priced at a daily rate of $50.

The **Rishon,** Rua Francisco Sá 17 (tel. 247-6044), is located on a side street very close to Copacabana beach. This small hotel has large and comfortable rooms, with TV and mini-bar service. On the roof is a small dip pool and an ample sun deck. The hotel also provides room service and houses a restaurant/bar as well, where food prices are considerably less than those charged at beachfront hotels only a half block away. Singles range from $40 to $45, and doubles from $45 to $50.

THE BUDGET RANGE

The budget-range hotels in Copacabana tend to be simple backstreet affairs with a limited number of rooms. Always clean, they are the best bet for that small minority of North American travelers who come to Rio each year without prepackaged accommodations. While you will not experience the comforts of a resort with its many luxuries, large and small, you will likely get a step or two closer to the average Brazilian reality.

Half a block from Copacabana beach, the **Martinique,** Rua Sá Ferreira 30 (tel. 521-4552), is every bit as comfortable as many more highly rated hotels at half the price. The hotel is also located in the same desirable environs as the Rio Palace and the Miramar hotels, accessible by foot to both Ipanema and Copacabana. The beds are smaller than those I usually like in hotels and tend to prefer in my own home. For a large person, a small bed can be a big factor in choosing a hotel room where he or she expects to spend seven or eight nights. The hotel has a nice little lobby and a bar. Room service is also provided. Rooms cost between $30 and $38 for single or double. The Martinique also offers a mini-single for $25.

The **Excelsior,** Avenida Atlântica 1800 (tel. 257-1950), is a large beachfront hotel on the same block as the Copacabana Palace. Once undoubtedly a fashionable hotel, this Horsa group property is well broken in, but not without its charms. You enter from a side street into a spacious lobby, where on one end a pleasant bar overlooks the ocean. A stairway leads to the mezzanine restaurant, also with a wrap-around view of the beach scene, where a business buffet lunch is served daily.

The location and size of the 184-room Excelsior make the hotel popular for groups in the budget range. Rooms are larger than those in hotels constructed in more recent years. Furnishings are plain, but comfortable, and decorative prints brighten the walls. Tiled baths have large porcelain tubs. The good service and discount rates compensate for the somewhat dreary wood-paneled corridors. Staying at the Excelsior costs from $52 to $71 for a single and $58 to $79 for a double.

The **Hotel Diplomata** is on the Praça Demétrio Ribeiro at 103 (tel. 521-4443), set in from Avenida Princesa Isabel, across the street from the Suppertopf Restaurant. This is another very informal, small hotel with a good location for anyone who wants to be at the beach, but who also needs quick access to downtown. Like other hotels on this busy avenue, it is but a short cab ride to the Metro stop in Botafogo. Plain and simple, with no frills, the rooms nevertheless do have TVs and mini-bars. Singles are $35 and doubles run $45 to $50; pay in cash and receive a discount of up to 30%.

The **Biarritz,** Rua Aires Saldanha 54 (tel. 521-6542), is located on a narrow avenue that runs for around ten blocks between and parallel to Avenidas Atlântica and Nossa Senhora de Copacabana.

The Biarritz sits a short block from the beach, right behind the Othon Palace. The marble entrance and stately awning suggest more elegance than you will find inside. Beware also of the small beds. Otherwise, there are 29 modest but acceptable rooms and a public TV salon. Room service is also provided. The price for a double room is $38.

The **Copa Linda,** Avenida Nossa Senhora de Copacabana 956 (tel. 255-0938), is located in a building near the corner of the cross street Rua Bolívar on this busy commercial avenue. The reception desk is located on the building's second floor, up an unassuming flight of stairs. The 21 rooms are very small, very kitsch, very cheap —$18 for a double—and close to the beach.

The **Angrense,** Travessa Angrense 25 (tel. 255-0509), is located at the far end of a dead-end lane which is entered from the Avenida Nossa Senhora de Copacabana about 100 feet in from the Rua Santa Clara. This stripped-down boarding house is a suitable choice for unbearded youths and superannuated bohemians alike. Many of the 36 rooms have neither baths nor air conditioning, but cost less than $20 per night.

The **Grande Hotel Canada,** Avenida Nossa Senhora de Copacabana 687 (tel. 257-1864), is also near the busy Rua Santa Clara intersection. The rooms in this 72-room two-star hotel have been recently redecorated and are agreeably nondescript. Accommodations can be had for as little as $25 a night for a single and $27 for a double. Some of the better rooms are more expensive, up to $45 for a double. The hotel also has an "American" bar (a euphemism for a smallish alcove equipped with a traditional bar and stools). There is also a public TV room and room service.

Among Rio's two-star beach hotels, the **Toledo,** Rua Domingos Ferreira 71 (tel. 257-1990), is a cut above the average. This quiet street is half a block from the Avenida Atlântica, which it parallels. In all, there are 54 accommodations, some of which are unusually large. Single rooms are $35 and doubles are $39, a very good value considering the space and comfort. There are also several mini-rooms renting for as little as $15 a night. The hotel has a coffeeshop and bar.

Another choice in a quiet corner of the neighborhood, is the strangely named **Apa,** Rua República de Peru 305 (tel. 255-8112), a three-star hotel with two-star rates. And while the rooms are furnished in early Salvation Army, the beds are full-sized twins, a rare offering for a hotel in the bargain range. There are 54 relatively large rooms, all of which have TVs and mini-bars, priced from $24 for a single to $35 for a double. Services include parking, a coffeeshop, and round-the-clock room service. The Apa is about a five-minute walk from the Trocadero section of the beach.

2. Ipanema and Leblon Hotels

Rounding the point at Copacabana and running from the surfers' beach of Apoador to the cove's abrupt end at the base of a pair of mountain peaks called *Os Dois Irmãos* (The Two Brothers) are the beaches of Ipanema and Leblon. Both neighborhoods are more modern than Copacabana, having really come into their own only over the past 30 years.

The chart-busting pop song "The Girl From Ipanema," written by the late poet Vinicius de Morais and arranged by the musician Antônio Carlos Jobim, probably did as much to promote tourism in these neighborhoods as any other single factor. The avenues of principal interest are, in Ipanema, the oceanfront Avenida Vieira Souto, which turns into the Avenida Delfim Moreira on the Leblon end of the beach. Ipanema's main shopping thoroughfare is the Avenida Visconde de Pirajá, two blocks from the beach, along which are located some of the most fashionable boutiques, gemstone emporiums, and shoestores in the city. The Avenida Ataúlfo de Paiva is the main commercial street in Leblon, lined with the more day-to-day kinds of shops and services.

A DELUXE HOTEL

Not only is the **Caesar Park,** Avenida Vieira Souto 460 (tel. 287-3122), the best hotel along the fashionable beaches of Ipanema and Leblon, but it's one of the top deluxe establishments in the entire city. Service at the Caesar Park combines the cool efficiency one associates with European hotels with the easy-going informality so typical of Brazilians. Seen from the outside, the concrete, rectilinear structure is not architecturally impressive. But inside, attention to detail is the Caesar Park trademark. Everywhere, from the well-polished wood-paneled elevators to the walls in all public areas, there are decorative touches that are both pretty and beguiling to the eye, especially the selection of contemporary watercolors, prints, and posters.

This pampering carries over to the accommodations, which are light, spacious, filled with well-stuffed furnishings, and finished with the best of paints and fabrics in subtle tones. The elegant baths are equipped with such extras as terrycloth bathrobes, scales, hairdryers, bathing lotions, and even aftershave for men. Accommodations also include large-screen color TVs with satellite and closed-circuit video channels, mini-bars, and individual air-temperature controls.

The public spaces are even more attractive than the rooms. A rooftop pool, where breakfast is served daily, offers the best view of any hotel in Rio, a 360-degree panorama taking in Corcovado and the Lagoa basin, the beaches of Ipanema and Leblon, and the mist-shrouded Dois Irmãos and Pedra da Gávea (Lookout Rock) mountains. This latter peak is a launching pad for hang-glider enthusiasts, who on occasion land on the sand near the hotel, a jolting experience if you don't see the flyer's approach and the two of you are suddenly sharing the same beach towel.

One floor below the rooftop terrace is the justly respected Petronius restaurant, specializing in fine seafood dishes. Along the corridor which leads to Petronius is a series of giant tanks displaying tropical fish and crustaceans gathered from local waters. The Mariko

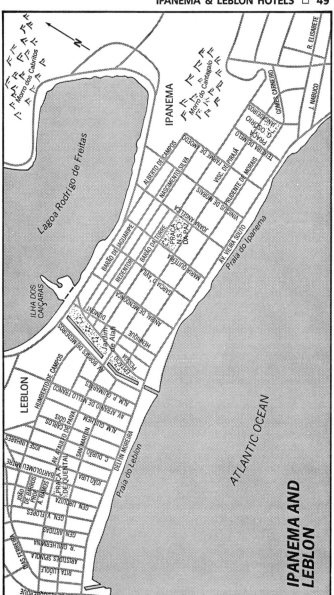

Sushi bar is also located on this floor. If your group or package offers the 221-room Caesar Park as an option, pay the premium and grab it. It will still be cheaper than paying the normal rates, which range from $185 to $220 for singles and $200 to $240 for doubles.

UPPER-BRACKET HOTELS

Located near the cross street Vinícius de Morais, named for the poet who wrote "The Girl From Ipanema," is the **Sol Ipanema,** Avenida Vieira Souto 320 (tel. 227-0060). The pub and café Garota de Ipanema, much frequented by Vinicius in his day, is still a popular daytime meeting place one block from the hotel.

The Sol Ipanema has 90 rooms on 15 floors, which are decorated in Brazilian earth tones with a generous use of rosewood throughout. Bahian tapestries with folkloric themes add texture to the general ambience. All rooms have TVs, air conditioning, and well-stocked mini-bars. As for the small dip pool and sundeck found on the roof, a bellhop was heard to comment that "No one comes up here." When asked why, he simply pointed to the gorgeous Ipanema beach down below and right across the street. Other features include a restaurant and bar, as well as parking facilities. Rates are $110 for a single and $120 for a double.

The **Praia Ipanema,** Avenida Vieira Souto 706 (tel. 239-9932), is under the same management as the Sol Ipanema. The 105 rooms are more stylishly decorated than at the companion hotel, with bold designer colors for walls and fabrics. Most rooms have token balconies which are too small for comfortable sitting. But they do add to the room's ocean view and allow the option of natural ventilation by leaving open the balcony door.

A dip pool on the roof is suitable for children, while a sundeck and bar provide a pleasant outdoor environment for evening cocktails. The La Mouette restaurant occupies the hotel's mezzanine with its own ground-level view of the local beach surroundings. Additional features are a lobby bar and an in-house hairdressing salon. Single rooms cost $100 to $125 nightly, and doubles cost between $115 and $140.

The **Everest Rio,** Rua Prudente de Morais 1117 (tel. 287-8282), is a 169-room hotel found on a tree-lined avenue one block from the water, directly behind the Caesar Park. While given a deluxe rating by the Brazilian tourist board, the Everest does not invite comparison with the city's finest hotels. The hotel's general appearance is streamlined and modern, but not luxurious. Rooms are spacious, with floor-to-ceiling windows and functional Scandinavian-style furnishings. All rooms are air-conditioned and contain combination baths, TVs, and mini-bars. The Everest offers special rates to business travelers who are in the city for more or less prolonged stays, and so there are often many longtime residents among the hotel's guests. The hotel does offer many first-class amenities, including a rooftop terrace 23 stories high with a splendid view from Corcovado to the sea. Other special features include a reasonably priced restaurant serving international fare, three bars located variously throughout the hotel, executive meeting rooms and convention facilities, a sauna, and a beauty parlor. The price range for single occupancy is $105 to $130, and doubles cost $125 to $155.

The **Marina Palace,** Avenida Delfim Moreira 630 (tel. 259-

5212), is the best hotel on the Leblon end of the beach. Leblon is even more residential than Ipanema, but among its numerous avenues and side streets are scattered many attractions in the form of shops, restaurants, clubs, and bars.

The Marina Palace also seems strikingly close to the mountain peaks of Gávea as they are seen from the rooftop pool area, which is spread with lounging chairs for sunbathing and also has a bar. The second-floor Bistro da Praia is quietly gaining in reputation among locals as a fine eating spot. The ocean view from the window seats is especially dramatic. The Marina Park's 163 bedrooms are adequate in every way, but lack the sparkle of other five-star hotels, and the large windows in the rooms are inexplicably sealed. TVs with satellite channels, mini-bars, and air conditioning are standard in all units, as are full-tiled baths. Other hotel amenities include meeting and banquet facilities, indoor parking, a coffeeshop, and a sauna. Rates are from $180 to $206 for singles, and $200 to $230 for doubles.

A smaller and less expensive version of the Marina Palace is the **Marina Rio**, Avenida Delfim Moreira 696 (tel. 239-8844), located a block farther down the beach. Both hotels are under the same management and guests at the Marina Rio may, for no extra charge, use all the facilities of its larger companion hotel. The accommodations of the Marina Rio are functional and roomy, also with sealed windows and without balconies. All 70 rooms, of course, are air-conditioned with TVs, mini-bars, and suitable baths. Hotel services are limited to a second-floor restaurant and a piano bar. Single rooms cost from $135 to $155 nightly, and doubles run from $150 to $170.

Baixo Leblon

Repeat visitors to Rio who want to be near the active beach life, yet also spend some time in a quiet part of town, are encouraged to look into the **Hotel Ritz,** Avenida Ataulfo de Paiva 1280 (tel. 239-2232). The Ritz is a residential hotel located in Baixo Leblon, one of Rio's most appealing neighborhoods and only minutes from Ipanema. Baixo—or Lower Leblon—is packed with some of Rio's best restaurants and nightspots, not to mention a slew of more informal sidewalk cafés and many shops—both plain and fancy. The Ritz offers 32 apartments, its deluxe version equipped with a large bedroom and spacious living room, plus a commodius veranda that stretches between and is accessible from both rooms. A small kitchenette, full bathroom, and a marble-topped dining table, seating four and set apart from the living-room area, round out the living space. The decor and furnishings are very modern but livable, and there isn't a hokey touch in the whole place. Facilities include a house restaurant and a small pool area that is almost conspiratorially intimate. Rates for the deluxe apartment described above are $65 for single occupancy, $70 for double; slightly smaller suites are priced from $50 for a single to $60 for a double.

MEDIUM-PRICED HOTELS

The **Arpoador Inn,** Rua Francisco Otaviano 177 (tel. 247-6090), is one of only two hotels in Rio where access to the beach does not involve crossing a heavily trafficked avenue. Located on a promenade overlooking Arpoador beach, this hotel of only 50 rooms has become a particular favorite among repeat visitors to Rio. The 15 oceanfronting rooms are especially desirable accommodations.

While by no means fancy—many rooms in fact providing only cot-sized beds—there is a cozy familiarity about this hotel that justifies use of the term "inn" in its name. Many guests spend time at the small coffeeshop restaurant on the premises, with its unusually close-up view of the beach and the sea. The Arpoador offers special discounts to "firms, diplomats and airline personnel." Advance reservations are an absolute necessity for ocean-view rooms, which cost $80 for doubles. Other rooms are priced at $55 for double occupancy.

The **Atlantis Copacabana,** Rua Bulhões de Cavalho 61 (tel. 521-1142), its name notwithstanding, is located closer to Ipanema than to Copacabana. The Atlantis is a brand-new hotel with 87 rooms and suites, in a very attractive building, located on a quiet street. Given a three-star rating, the hotel is really closer to a first-class establishment, considering its general appearance and many facilities. The room sizes are average, but well appointed with all the comforts. There is a rooftop sundeck with pool, and two bars, one an appealing spot off the lobby, and another a piano bar called the Gaivota (Seagull), where light meals are also served. Singles are priced between $43 and $50 and doubles range from $45 to $56.

Here is an apart-hotel option for Ipanema: the **Rio-Ipanema Hotel Residência,** Rua Visconde de Pirajá 66 (tel. 267-4015), which faces the neighborhood's principal square, the Praça General Osório. On the spacious grounds of this plaza, the Hippie Fair (or *Feirarte,* as it is officially called) is mounted every Sunday. The daily street life around the Praça General Osório is one of Rio's most colorful scenes. In addition to the many stands offering fruits and vegetables, both familiar and unfamiliar, there are multitudes of sidewalk vendors selling everything from household knickknacks to toiletry items. Among the most interesting displays are the strange assortment of roots, barks, and dried plants spread on wide patches of the sidewalk, and used for flavoring foods and for the preparation of medicinal teas and home remedies.

The ultramodern residence hotel overlooking this appealing hurly-burly scene offers two-room apartments with large verandas that front on the plaza for $65 per night double occupancy, or two-bedroom units at $85, with an additional 35% for each extra person.

THE BUDGET RANGE

Also around the corner from the Caesar Park is the **Ipanema Inn,** Rua Maria Quitéria 27 (tel. 287-6092), a 56-room hotel, owned by the same group as the Arpoador Inn several blocks away. The Ipanema Inn's front rooms offer a sliver of a view of the sea.

Given its side-street location, the higher the floor, the better the view. Like the Arpoador, the rooms here are simple in the tradition of a real beach hotel. With singles beginning at $35 a night and doubles at $38, the hotel is definitely a reasonable option for those who are budget-minded and want to avail themselves of the beach at the same time. TVs, in the rooms are optional, but all rooms do have mini-bars, telephones, and private baths. There are also a small bar and a souvenir shop in the hotel. The souvenirs include fossil fish amulets, lacquered piranhas, and Brazilian tarot cards.

Several doors in from the corner of Rua Vinícius de Morais, is the **Vermont,** Rua Visconde de Pirajá 254 (tel. 521-0057). This 54-room hotel is in the heart of Ipanema's most fashionable shopping district and two blocks from the beach. The atmosphere at the Vermont is spartan, but all the basics are there, including bathrooms, TVs, and mini-bars. The hotel also has a bar and offers room service. Singles are priced between $27 and $29, and doubles are $30 to $33.

The **Carlton,** Rua João Lira 68 (tel. 259-1932), is found on a tree-lined back street in Leblon. Leblon's general ambience is very sedate, and this mood is reflected in the Carlton, a beacon of shabby gentility in a sea of affluence. The 50 accommodations are roomy and comfortable. All rooms are air-conditioned and contain combination baths, TVs, and mini-bars. The hotel also has a coffeeshop restaurant and a bar. Rates begin at $35 for a single and $39 for a double.

3. Vidigal and São Conrado Hotels

These two areas stretch farther south on Rio's Atlantic Ocean beachfront. Vidigal was once a shantytown that has been transformed into a chic cliffside and canyon neighborhood for the urban well-to-do. In the early '60s São Conrado was still a remote, even primitive, beach. Today high-rises and condominiums dominate the skyline, but the beach is still among the most popular in the city.

DELUXE HOTELS

The **Rio-Sheraton,** Avenida Niemeyer 121 (tel. 274-1122), is Rio's only genuine resort hotel, set on an outcropping of rocks behind a small, private beach in Vidigal. This is the city's other hotel, where you can take a dip in the ocean without crossing a street. A sprawling complex, the hotel's public areas stretch from roadside to shoreline six stories down.

There are advantages and disadvantages involved in staying at the Sheraton. Unlike the other beach neighborhoods already described, there is no street life here among the hills and cliffs of Vidigal. You are dependent on transportation to get from here to anywhere else in the city. And transportation is of the usual varieties, with the usual associated problems: unsafe buses, hustling cab drivers, hassle-free but expensive hotel cars. The advantages are that once you are at the Sheraton, you don't necessarily have to go any where else—a boon to those travelers who crave the womb-like assurance of a truly self-contained resort.

Millions were spent in recent years to repair what had been the hotel's former reputation for shoddiness. The Sheraton now sparkles, and the rooms are warm and well decorated. The lobby is of cathedral proportions, but rectilinear and modern, sheathed in brown tinted glass. Full of movement, the lobby seems like a busy crossroads, with people coming to and from the arcade of shops, the One-Twenty-One bar, or one of the many service desks. Three flood-lit tennis courts and an equal number of freshwater pools are distributed on several levels of the spacious grounds. Also for the fitness-minded are a health club and sauna. Altogether, there are seven restaurants and bars within the Sheraton complex, including Valentino's, where fine Italian cuisine is served. The Casa da Cachaça is a bar specializing in cocktails made with Brazil's native sugarcane brandy, cachaça.

The Sheraton boasts 617 rooms, which are trimmed out in fine hardwood, and appointed with attractive rugs and wall hangings. The use of brass lamps and huge TVs recessed in bookshelves adds to the comfortable, den-like atmosphere. All rooms have tiled combination baths, and balconies with dramatic ocean views. The units in the five-story wings are much larger than those in the 26-floor main tower. Rates range from $145 to $165 for single rooms, and $165 to $195 for doubles.

The **Inter-Continental,** Avenida Prefeito Mendes de Morais 222 (tel. 322-2200), might just be Rio's most luxurious hotel, but it suffers from some of the same disadvantages as the Sheraton. The Inter (as the hotel is familiarly called by locals) occupies a favored spot in the moonscape of condominiums that is São Conrado. The spirit of orderly architectural harmony that guided the growth of Copacabana and Ipanema seemed to have vanished as development spread along the shore to São Conrado and Barra da Tijuca. The buildings glitter, but the streets are cold. The background, however, remains the unceasing natural beauty of the Rio mountains and seascapes.

In high-rise heaven, the planned environment is everything, and, in this regard, the Inter does not disappoint. The hotel's lobby is truly elegant, lined with stylish shops and plush banquettes in green leather. But the Inter's real focus centers on a geometrical arrangement of pools, lounging chairs, and outside eating areas. This is the most insulated and sensuous poolside in Rio. On those endless sunny days for which Rio is justly famous, the skies over the Inter are filled with the soaring antics of hang-glider pilots, who launch themselves from Lookout Rock, cheek-by-jowl with the hotel. Across the road is the lovely Pepino beach, somewhat abandoned on weekdays and destitute of services like roadside food stands and vendors, except on the weekends when it is a very popular and animated spot.

Accommodations within the hotel are spacious, with comfortable sitting areas and balconies. The decor is cool and stylish, with well-designed and original Brazilian furnishings and walls covered with textured paper. The baths are in stone and marble, fully equipped with robes and lotions, while the rooms all have individually controlled air conditioning, TVs, and mini-bars.

Liberally distributed throughout the hotel are numerous lounges, bars, and restaurants, including the Monseigneur, offering French cooking, and the new Alfredo di Lello's, for fresh pasta dishes. The Papillon discotheque is a favorite nightspot for the younger set, especially on weekends. A bar off the lobby has a satellite TV and features major U.S. sporting events. The Inter is extremely popular with American travel groups and is often included as an option in the most expensive packages. Charges for singles range from $160 to $180, and for doubles, from $180 to $190.

UPPER-BRACKET HOTELS

The **Nacional,** Avenida Niemeyer 769 (tel. 322-1000), is part of the Horsa group with hotels throughout Brazil. The building itself, a 26-story glass-and-steel cylindrical tower, was designed by Oscar Niemeyer, principal architect for the country's ultramodern capital, Brasília. The hotel has pretensions to luxury, but poor maintenance makes it more suitable for the convention trade, which the Nacional pursues over the conventional tourist down on a package and looking for splashy accommodations in a five-star resort. Major renovations, however, are now being undertaken to upgrade the Nacional.

The most striking feature of the pie-shaped rooms is the view. Niemeyer's design democratically distributes a dramatic slice of the natural surroundings to virtually all rooms. Accommodations are brightly decorated, but not up to the quality of other five-star hotels. All units have TVs, mini-bars, and are air-conditioned. The ground-level pool area is large and appealing. A private tunnel leads under the roadway to São Conrado beach. The hotel has several restaurants and bars, and a host of other guest and convention services. There are 520 rooms in the Nacional, and rates for singles are priced from $111 to $125, while doubles fetch from $125 to $140.

The **São Conrado Palace,** Avenida Niemeyer 776 (tel. 322-0911), is a hotel that will begin to figure more and more into the bargain-to-medium-priced tour packages. Jokingly referred to as the Favela Palace, the allusion has nothing to do with the hotel's location, at the foot of Rio's largest working-class hill town, that a lot of locals poke fun at. The population of the Rocinha favela is said to number some 600,000. But, while Rocinha may be no place to walk around in unaccompanied, it is a bona fide neighborhood—albeit mostly of the urban poor—not a den of thieves and desperados.

The São Conrado occupies a hollow among several clusters of lowland high-rises close to the shore. Still guests must ride a hotel shuttle bus the short distance to the São Conrado beach. The shuttle, which also makes runs to Copacabana and Ipanema, is furnished free of charge and operates on a regular schedule. Inside, the hotel is of genuine four-star quality, brand-new and generously spacious in both its rooms and its public areas. Accommodations are large and furnished with good, simple taste, similar to first-class wardrooms on cruise ships. Understated but well chosen prints personalize the quarters, which are equipped with balconies, baths with lots of elbow room, TVs, mini-bars, and air conditioning. Beyond the large, somewhat institutional lobby is a ground-level pool area that rivals that at most of the best hotels. Potted trees and umbrellas give the veranda a secluded air. Other features are a bar and a restaurant. In all there are 160 rooms, priced from $40 to $50 for a single and from $45 to $55 for a double.

---

4. Barra da Tijuca Hotels

Only 25 years ago, Barra da Tijuca, an extension even farther southward of Rio's magnificent shoreline, was virgin beach, surrounded by summer homes and squatters' shacks. Since the late 1970s, however, Barra has been the site of rapid development all along the 15-km (9-mile) long beach. Today, the strands are lined with mammoth high-rise buildings, mostly condos, built on the reclaimed swamplands that edged the sea. A long shallow lake separates development along the shore from that which is inland, where, in addition to more residential complexes, there are some of the largest supermarkets and shopping centers in South America. Surrounding the lake are the remaining marshlands, which serve as a habitat for wildlife. It is common to see large birds spread their wings against the morning sky and soar high above the protected marsh.

Barra tends to be popular with tourists from the southern cone of South America—Argentines, Uruguayans, Chileans—who come to sun in Rio during their winter or to shop for bargains all year round. So common is this latter experience that a favorite Carioca nickname for their Spanish-speaking neighbors is "Da me dos." In other words, since the merchandise in Rio is either rare or cheap by the tourist's standards, they are often overheard saying "da me dos" ("give me two"). Barra's hotels fill to capacity on at least two occasions during the year, Carnival and the Grand Prix Formula One race held in the spring at the nearby auto track.

Perhaps the visitors from the southern cone are quite happy staying out in Barra because they are not anywhere near as hampered by the language barrier and are thus able to get around town with a fair amount of ease. Most first-time North American visitors are not usually content to be in Barra. It's just too far from the action of Ipanema and Copacabana, a good half-hour cab ride away. Some tour packages offer very good deals, however, if you stay in Barra, where hotels are new but still relatively inexpensive. For those who already know Rio a little, Barra could be a very tempting base, especially if you have access to a car.

The **Tropical Barra,** Avenida Sernambetiba 500 (tel. 399-0660), is an attractive three-star hotel, frequently offered as a choice in the least-expensive package tours to Rio. The hotel sits across the boulevard from the beach, and its 86 accommodations are modern and comfortable. The Tropical Barra also offers such amenities as its own restaurant and bar. Single rooms start at $35; doubles, at $39.

Somewhat typical of the apart-hotels in Barra is the **Rio Hotel Residência,** Avenida Sernambetiba 6250 (tel. 385-5000). The Rio Hotel Residência caters to vacationing families and business visitors on extended stays. The 270 two-bedroom apartments include a sitting room and large balcony-terrace, plus full kitchen and bath. They rent for $150 per night, not accounting for discounts that might apply. Sports facilities include two squash courts, tennis and volleyball courts, and a large swimming pool. The hotel is further distinguished by the presence of the Le Petit Paris French-style restaurant, a nice addition to this somewhat suburban zone with its still considerable wide-open spaces.

Also prominent on the lodging landscape in Barra are the many **motels** frequented primarily by lovers for their assignations. Some are truly outlandish in the opulence of their decor, worthy of a visit as cultural artifacts if for no other reason. The most well-known of these is **VIP's,** located in Vidigal, set among the chic villas that are nestled in the folds of the mountains.

5. Glória and Flamengo Hotels

These are two contiguous neighborhoods along the entrance to Guanabara Bay on the Rio side. The beaches at the mouth of the bay are polluted and no longer suitable for swimming. Both Glória and Flamengo are close to downtown, however, and are serviced by the subway system. Some 30 years ago, these were still fashionable neighborhoods. Hollywood stars and heads of state all stayed at the Hotel Glória, and Flamengo, with its enormous apartments, was the residential area preferred by many of the city's most affluent citizens. Fickle fashion has moved the center of action farther down the beach, but both neighborhoods are bearing up well. In fact the grand old apartments are once more in great demand due to the shortage of good housing in the city's highly speculative real estate market.

As mentioned elsewhere, there are numerous hotels of the simplest variety throughout the back streets of Flamengo. If you are hunting for rock-bottom prices, it is preferable to stay in this residential area as opposed to downtown, which tends to empty after business hours.

The **Hotel Glória,** Praia do Russel 632 (tel. 205-7272), with its 700 rooms, is Brazil's largest hotel and is very popular with the tour operators who package the least-expensive trips to Rio. In the past, the Hotel Glória was on a par with the Copacabana Palace, attracting a jet-set clientele from all over the world. Today, with most tourists to the city wanting beachfront accommodations, the Glória has accepted its role as an alternative for those who want the amenities of a full-sized hotel and easy access to services at discount prices.

Set close to the sidewalk, the massive white stone building overlooks—approximately a quarter of a mile across a wide park—a section of the Flamengo beach and harbor. From here the historic downtown square, Praça XV, is about a 20-minute walk, though this is not recommended. The most direct route hugs the main thoroughfare, and often there are no sidewalks. On the other hand, subway access is rapid and direct. Rooms at the Glória are comfortable, but with no pretensions to luxury. The hotel's buildings curve around small but well-landscaped grounds, including a rock garden and an attractive pool area with surrounding patio. A second pool has been added, and the hotel's two restaurants have been recently reorganized and redecorated. There are several bars, a breakfast room, and a sauna, among other facilities. Rates are from $76 to $108 for a single, and $92 to $138 for a double, which are discounted considerably for group travelers.

Novo Mundo, Praia do Flamengo 20 (tel. 205-3355). This 40-year-old hotel, also facing Flamengo beach, has 200 air-conditioned rooms that are clean and well tended, all with baths, TVs, and mini-bars. The hotel has a restaurant, parking facilities, a barbershop, and an American bar. Singles start at $15 and doubles at $20.

RIO'S BEST BARGAIN ACCOMMODATIONS

There are several simple, inexpensive hotels of acceptable quality near the Glória Metro stop, among them the **Hotel Turístico,** Ladeira da Glória 30 (tel. 225-9388). Rooms here have small balconies and are priced in the $8 to $12 range. The nearby **Monte Castelo,** Rua Cândido Mendes 201 (tel. 222-1733), is even cheaper, with rooms costing from $5 to $7.

In Flamengo, is the ever popular **Hotel Flórida,** Rua Ferreira Viana 69 (tel. 245-8160), which has gained a quiet reputation over the years as one of Rio's best budget hotels. Rooms have polished parquet floors that recall the neighborhood's more elegant days, and contain good private bathrooms with plenty of hot water. Some rooms are equipped with air conditioning, and hotel facilities include a simple restaurant and safe-deposit boxes for your valuables. Rates are $10 to $15 per night. The nearby **Regina Hotel,** Rua Ferreira Viana 29 (tel. 225-7280), is also a good bet for a tidy room off the beaten track, although slightly more expensive at $16 to $20 a night.

RIO AND ITS RESTAURANTS

Food in Rio is fresh, varied, plentiful, and delicious. Culinary skills and food quality are consistently high in public eating establishments throughout Rio, whether you dine at the finest beachfront restaurants or in the simplest back-street cafés. And if tastiness and absence of indigestion are two reasonable criteria by which to judge restaurant food, visitors to Rio will find the Brazilian dining experience much to their satisfaction. Typically, Brazilian food is not fancy (except in fancy restaurants, of course) and certainly it is often far from delicate. But meals are well prepared and served in generous portions—with platters and stew pots groaning under the weight of their succulent meats or brimming over with a dozen varieties of fin and shell fish—and always accompanied by numerous and delightful side dishes.

RIO'S TWO-MEAL DIET
Eating in Rio requires having to pace yourself in between meals. The breakfasts served by most tourist-quality hotels (included in the price of your room) can be lavish, so tempting to many that any idea of a formal, sit-down lunch at midday is quickly abandoned. The two-meal diet—breakfast and dinner—is a common response among international tourists to the abundance of food served at each meal. Another useful strategy to consider is the single-meal-for-two option. Say two or three people go to an average-priced restaurant for lunch. The ambience is comfortable,

tables covered in white starched linen, and the waiters, while not formal, are well trained and helpful. You order one serving of breast of chicken, sautéed in some sauce of the cook's invention. The platter arrives with enough meat, rice pilaf, mashed potatoes—usually two starchy foods, good news for carbohydrate fans—and everyone fills his or her plate. You order separately a large hearts-of-palm salad and whatever other side dishes you might want, plus beer or freshly squeezed fruit juice, and finally coffee, and the bill comes to about $3 apiece.

Haute cuisine, on the other hand, is not the forte of the Brazilian kitchen. Brazil's French restaurants have flourish and style, but there is seldom a genuine delicacy in their dishes. But the point in Brazil is not to seek food you could easily find in New York or France. Instead, turn your imagination in the direction of the best in home-cooking. Then imagine eating this fare twice a day in a great variety of seafoods, pastas, poultry, or meat, with side dishes of rice, beans, potatoes, and greens, not to mention a whole lot of delicious foods you've never heard of. That's Brazilian cooking, with its emphasis on heartiness and taste, and it is likely to keep your palate in a state close to ecstasy during your stay in Brazil. *Bom apetite,* as the Brazilians say!

INTRODUCING BRAZILIAN FOOD

The meals you will be offered in Rio fall roughly into two categories: traditional dishes and international dishes. One traditional dish, feijoada—a meat and black-bean stew—is routinely eaten every Saturday throughout the country by rich and poor alike. Thus two styles of feijoada have emerged, a fancy buffet style with all the ingredients (including prime cuts of beef and pork) served separately, popular with hotels, and a more home-style feijoada served stewlike from a single cauldron, preferred by the more traditional restaurants. The standard accompaniments of feijoada are white rice, **feijão** (black beans), **couve** (shredded kale), orange slices, and **farinha** (manioc flour). International dishes, on the other hand, are those which bear familiar names, like *veal Milanese* or *beef Stroganoff,* made especially appetizing because they are prepared by some typically competent Brazilian cook, and because any number of side dishes from simple rice and beans to exotic *farofa* can add the inimitable ingredients that make any Brazilian meal truly Brazilian.

Farofa is totally unique to Brazil. Flour ground from the manioc root is fried in oil. Bits and pieces of many things, from egg to vegetables or meat, may be added to the pan, and the dish arrives at the table looking like a sawdust pilaf. Despite farofa's pedestrian appearance, its taste is positively addictive, especially when used to soak up juice from black beans.

Regional Food

Several excellent restaurants in Rio serve *comida bahiana,* the cuisine of Bahia, with its heavy African influence. *Vatapa, xim xim de galinha* and *moquecas* are the centerpieces of Bahian cooking. **Vatapa,** a side dish, is a kind of mush made from bread dough, cashew nuts, and dried shrimp, a delicacy when prepared with care.

Xim xim (pronounced approximately "shing shing," the final letter, however, being a nasal vowel, not a consonant) is a dish of diced chicken and other savories, which can include fish or shrimp, nuts and vegetables, blended with coconut milk. **Moquecas** are seafood stews, and all three dishes are spicy and cooked in the strongly flavored **dendé,** or palm oil.

Churrasco

Brazil is a great cattle-producing and meat-eating nation. And **churrasco,** the Brazilian version of the barbecue, is proportionately grand, a feast way beyond the scale of that dear ritual we all love to perform on the backyard grill. When dining out, Brazilians eat their grilled meats at establishments called **churrascarias,** some of which serve their fare **rodízio-**style, where waiters circulate endlessly from table to table filling your plate with ten or more different types and cuts of meat or fowl, and where only considerations of health and good manners set limits on the amount you may consume. In many churrascarias, $10 can go a long way.

More Tips on Brazilian Food and Drink

No discussion of typical Brazilian food would be complete without mention of **canja,** an excellent chicken soup, as hearty and healthful as any you will ever taste. And fruits. Without exaggeration, there are a hundred varieties of edible fruits that are either native to Brazil or were adapted to its fertile soil. Alas, to sample them all you'd have to travel throughout the entire country. Rio, however, offers a fair share of the varieties.

Buffet breakfasts at the top hotels offer a selection of fresh fruits daily, including **pineapple,** several types of **melon** and **bananas,** and **mango.** The more exotic fruits, like **caju** (the fruit that bears a single cashew nut to each peach-sized orb), **tamarind,** and **breadfruit,** along with dozens of new varieties that you will discover, can be purchased from vendors at open markets on the streets. If you express enough curiosity at any given stand, the vendor is very likely to offer a slice for you to taste. Practically any bar, lunch counter, or restaurant you stop at will include freshly squeezed orange juice on its menu. A dozen other varieties of fruit juices, pure or in combination, can be had at juice bars which are popular throughout Rio.

The bounty in fruit throughout Brazil is only matched by the abundant catches from the seas of **frutos do mar**—shellfish, fin fish, shrimp, crab, lobster, and octopus. This marine cornucopia is harvested, seemingly without end, from the omnipresent ocean along the coast and from the many inland river systems.

The Couvert

The **couvert** is a common feature of most restaurant meals in Rio. The term means "cover" and refers to the standard selection of appetizers—bread and butter; some pâté; a crûdité of radishes, carrots, and celery; plus a half-dozen marble-size, hard-boiled quails' eggs—brought to your table automatically. The couvert, which generally costs a dollar or two at moderately priced restaurants, is optional, and may be refused.

Brazilian Beverages

In addition to the many varieties of freshly squeezed fruit juices, Brazil produces a popular soft drink, **guaraná,** made from a berry of the same name which grows only in the rain forest. Other international brand soft drinks such as Pepsi, Coke, and Fanta are widely available. **Mineral water,** plain or carbonated, is a common sight at Brazilian meals, as tap water tends to be avoided for direct consumption. Ask for *agua mineral,* either *com gaz* or *sem* (with or without fizz).

The most popular alcoholic beverages are **beer** for most occasions, wine at meals, and a cocktail called a *caipirinha,* made from **cachaça** (a potent sugarcane brandy), crushed fresh limes, and sugar over ice. Brazilian brewers can hold their own with any of the great beer makers worldwide. Brand names like Antarctica and Brahma are most popular. A .75-liter (18-oz.) bottle of Brazilian beer costs roughly 60¢ in most bars and cafés. Brazil also has a flourishing **wine** industry, which, like the breweries, is located in the south, heavily populated by descendants of German and Italian settlers. In restaurants, Brazilian domestic wines are comparable in price to their California equivalents purchased retail. Imported wines, French in particular, are steeply priced, as are imported whiskies—some brands of scotch fetch in the vicinity of $10 per drink.

The better grades of cachaça can also be drunk pure, like cognac. Sippers of whisky might find this inexpensive drink an adequate substitute, though *pinga,* as the drink is also called, which can be quite smooth, has none of whisky's smoky taste. The welcoming drink your package offers—if you travel to Rio with a package—will most certainly be a **caipirinha.** Once discovered, many drinkers will ask for nothing else for cocktails. Caipirinhas are also *de rigeur*—only for those who enjoy alcoholic beverages of course—when eating the Brazilian national dish, feijoada. That is, until the end of the meal, when the other national drink, coffee, is served.

Brazil is, and has been for some time, a major world producer of **coffee** beans. Brazilians drink their *cafezinhos* (little coffees) frequently throughout the day, in demitasse cups and usually quite sweet. For those who like black unsweetened coffee, ask for *café sem açúcar* (the *em* in *sem* is a nasal vowel, but if you say *"sang,"* you will be understood; the *ç* in *açúcar* is pronounced like an *s*—ah-*sue*-kah). Coffee with milk can be hard to come by after breakfast, the only time during the day when Brazilians drink their own version of café au lait, *café com leite* (*leite* is pronounced lay-chee). Otherwise, coffee is served constantly, everywhere throughout the city, at stand-up counters, in jewelry stores to browsers, at meetings of any sort, and on the street by vendors. Great boxes of Brazilian coffee, in beans or ground, can be purchased in the airport duty-free shops before returning home, as can bottles of cachaça.

RIO'S RESTAURANT SCENE

While still a bargain for most North American visitors, Rio is one of Brazil's most expensive cities. Happily, restaurant food in the Cidade Maravilhosa remains one of its best bargains, offering good quality at every price level. Eating *bom e barato* (well and cheap) is, after all, a national Brazilian pastime that few visiting travelers will disdain. Most entrees in the average good restaurant—the exception is almost inevitably a fancy lobster or shrimp dish—seldom go higher than $10, with most costing a good deal less. You have to go out of your way to spend more than $15 per person for an excellent restaurant meal in Rio, including beverages, dessert, and service. Indeed, for $15 a day, a budget-minded visitor avoiding the more pricey and fashionable restaurants can eat and drink quite well in Rio. A service charge of 10% is included with all restaurant bills. Some diners leave a few small bills on the table to sweeten the tip for the waiter (who only shares in the official gratuity with the rest of the staff), but this practice is completely discretionary.

Fancy Food, Local Drinks. Rio has its share of fancy and expensive restaurants. These tend to offer French-style cooking and service, and to be located in the best hotels. But even if your taste runs to gourmet meals, or you just want to splurge, the bill will seem modest when compared with a comparable eatery in other major world cities. The trick to dining economically in Brazil, even in the ritziest of places, is to stay away from imported beverages, which can cost you two to three times more than you are used to paying at even the most expensive bars and restaurants back home.

Snacks. With the generous breakfasts included in the price of your room at virtually all the hotels mentioned in this guide, many travelers will feel the need for only a light snack at lunch time. Rio abounds in small cafés, fast-food emporia (both of the home-grown and multinational variety), juice bars, and traditional lunch counters. You can eat very well in Brazil at these simple establishments. Many of these snackbars will be described in more detail at the end of this section.

As with hotels, restaurants will be listed by neighborhood and price range.

1. Copacabana and Leme Restaurants

There are restaurants of every category densely packed within the borders of this great district. Dress is never formal, even where the service is ceremonial. Neither jacket nor tie is required for men dining in Rio, except in one or two business restaurants downtown. The Copacabana area is particularly informal, with people constantly dropping into the many restaurants on the way to or from the beach.

THE UPPER BRACKET

Spoken of in Rio with a praise bordering on reverence, the **Ouro Verde,** Avenida Atlântica 1456 (tel. 542-1887), has no trouble living up to its exhalted reputation as one of Rio's finest traditional French restaurants. Climb the stairs from the lobby of the Ouro Verde hotel to the mezzanine. The relatively small room displays elegantly set tables, each with silver candlestick, silver salt shakers, and pewter pepper mill to complement the starched-linen covers and the fine settings of crystal and china. A few select tables line the front wall beside large windows that admit welcome ocean breezes along with a wide view of Copacabana beach.

The food and impeccable service soon direct your attention away from the seating arrangements and the view. Daily at lunch there is a cold buffet with a choice of some dozen platters, including salad niçoise, various pâtés, smoked meats and cold cuts, vegetables and greens. The price: $10. Typical specialties served at both lunch and dinner are shrimp sautéed in whisky for $12, shredded veal in cream sauce with hash browns for $5.50, and rolled beefsteak, filled with diced, sautéed onions, and sweet pickle, smothered in a deep brown gravy for $7.50. For dessert there are many delicate pastries, fresh fruit with whipped cream, and a moist bread-based concoction with raisins called "diplomatic pudding" and, of course, crepes Suzette. Open daily from noon to midnight.

The **Le Pré Catalan,** Avenida Atlântica 4240 (tel. 521-3232), is a fine French restaurant serving nouvelle cuisine for lunch and dinner. Though it's ensconced directly on the premises of the Rio Palace hotel, you need not enter the hotel to get to the restaurant, which is serviced by a separate elevator right before the main entrance to the lobby. Elegant decor, imaginative cuisine, and service with a flourish combine to maintain the restaurant's reputation as one of Rio's finest. Supervision of the fare is in the hands of a highly regarded French chef, who maintains very consistent standards of quality in the preparation of many complex and subtle dishes.

Two people dining at Le Pré Catalan can fully indulge their culinary passions, eating several courses, drinking both cocktails and wine, and still escape for only slightly more than $100 between them. You may also dine quite satisfactorily for less, or try the fixed-price lunch menu, a bargain at around $12, including dessert but not beverage. The cushioned banquettes and large tables encourage an abundant meal, consumed at a civilized pace. Part of the enjoyment involves allowing ample time to take in the surrounding mise-en-scène among animated fellow diners and to observe the staff in its perpetual state of formal attentiveness. Periodically, at the signal from a captain, waiters lift, in unison, the silver covers from the principal dishes when they arrive at a given table.

For dinner you may also order from a fixed-price menu confiance, which includes appetizer, entree, and dessert for around $25, or choose from a wide selection of à la carte suggestions. For a first course, you might have slices of duck or rabbit, each in its own delicate sauce, followed by an even more elaborate and succulent entree of lobster, large shrimp, or a prime cut of lamb or beef. A soufflé or a plate of mixed pastries and a strong cup of aromatic Bra-

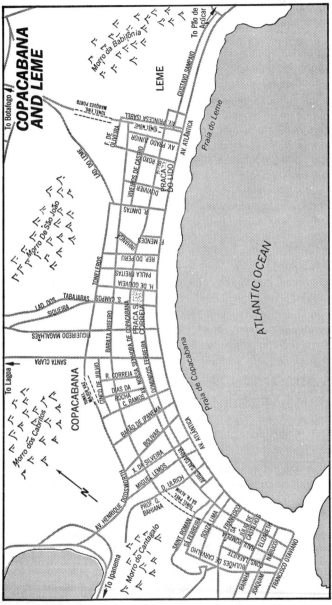

zilian coffee will round out the meal—in all, a memorable culinary experience. Reservations are necessary, especially if you want to eat Lunch is served from noon until 3 p.m. on weekdays only; dinner from 7:30 p.m. until 1 a.m. or later, depending on the evening.

Le Saint Honoré, Avenida Atlântica 1020 (tel. 275-9922), is located at the opposite end of Copacabana beach, in the equally swank Hotel Meridien. In contrast to Le Pré Catalan, which is draped and mirrored like a French salon, the Le Saint Honoré is wrapped in windows, and occupies the top floor of its hotel, 37 floors high. By day the restaurant is bathed in natural light, and at night the grand panorama of curvaceous Copacabana beach and its surrounding mountains is projected on the glass against a starlit sky and a shimmering sea.

Delicate seafood dishes are a specialty of the St. Honoré's kitchen. But whatever you sample in this fine restaurant—from the delectable hors d'oeuvres to something suitably rich from the dessert tray—you will be satisfied with both the quality and the value. Entrees begin at $15. Lunch is also served at the St. Honoré, and at $12 for selections from the set menu, you can't go wrong. Open for lunch from noon to 3 p.m., and for dinner from 8 p.m. until midnight. On Saturdays, only dinner is served; the restaurant is closed on Sundays.

For over 40 years, **Le Bec Fin,** Avenida Nossa Senhora de Copacabana 178 (tel. 542-4079), has been one of Rio's shining culinary institutions. With only nine tables, the restaurant's atmosphere is intimate but not cramped, and the decor subdued and comfortable. Service is civilized and deliberately slow. As in all good French restaurants, the emphasis is on the food. Entrees range from $10 to $25; lobster and duck are house specialties, with many traditional dishes, including steak au poive and steak Diane, always available as well. Le Bec Fin is open daily for dinner only from 8 p.m. to 2 a.m.; reservations are essential.

MEDIUM-PRICED RESTAURANTS

The price range for meals in this category is fairly broad, starting as low as $6 for simple fish dishes and going no higher than $20 for the most expensive repasts.

Overlooking the street through gauzy curtains and narrow blinds at ground level in the Copacabana Palace is an unheralded but excellent steakhouse, the **Bife de Ouro,** Avenida Atlântica 1702 (tel. 255-7070). There are curved banquettes and large potted plants to screen the views from table to table. On the walls are the large canvases of artist Jorge Guinle Filho, explosions of powerful colors that are very true to their tropical inspiration.

This unusually pleasant interior does not overshadow the good food, however, which also happens to be very reasonably priced. Appetizers, including creamed soups and smoked fish are between $2 and $6; fish dishes range from $8 to $15; and no beef or steak dish is more than $10. Figs flambé over ice cream and coffee brewed at your table add the final touches to an epicurean meal. The service at the Bife de Ouro is just right, attentive but not solicitous. The lunch and dinner menus are the same. Open for lunch from noon to 4 p.m., and for dinner from 7 p.m. to midnight. The other restaurant at the Copacabana Palace is the Pergula, a more informal, day-room environment for lunch and light meals, overlooking both the street and the hotel's magnificent pool area.

Well into Leme is **Máriu's,** Avenida Atlântica 290 (tel. 542-2393), the only churrascaria along this oceanside avenue. The restaurant occupies the first two floors of a modern building and overlooks the beach through a façade of plate glass. Inside, Máriu's serves its barbecued fare either round robin or rodízio style, the cuts including sirloin, lamb, loin of pork, sausages, and smoked ham. You can eat as much as you want, but leave some room for the many side dishes of salads, french fries, farofa, cold asparagus, and hearts of palm. It's beachfront location makes Máriu's a more expensive choice than the average churrascaria, but for $15 a person, depending on your bar bill, meat-eaters can eat and drink divinely. Open daily from 11 a.m. to 2 a.m.

Shirley's at Rua Gustavo Sampaio 610 (tel. 275-1398) is the epitome of neighborhood restaurants. Tucked into the space of a small storefront, the restaurant only has a dozen tables. Thus, the perpetual line for seating underscores the popularity of this primarily Spanish-style seafood establishment. A typical fish plate here costs between $7 and $10, while lobster dishes run about $17. Open daily from noon to 1 a.m. No credit cards.

Suppentopf, Avenida Princesa Isabel 350 (tel. 275-1896), is a German restaurant set back in an arcade not far from the tunnel entrance that leads from Copacabana to downtown Rio. The attractive rathskeller atmosphere is conducive to what one does in a typical German beer garden: drink lager and eat dishes like schnitzel and sauerkraut—the food in this case being largely of Bavarian origin. Entrees cost between $5 and $15. Open from noon to 3 a.m. No credit cards.

The **Café de la Paix,** Avenida Atlântica 1020 (tel. 275-9922), is the Meridien Hotel's casual restaurant. Because this is also the Meridien's breakfast room, the early morning crowd is generally made up of the hotel's guests, though the café is a favorite choice for power breakfasts among local business people as well. The street entrance opens directly onto Avenida Atlântica, opposite Leme beach, and the café's brasserie ambience makes for a pleasant and suitable setting for casual meals at any time of day. Reasonably priced casseroles reminiscent of French country fare are the house specialty, and include a seafood stew for $11, coq au vin for $10, pot au feu for $7.75, and a lamb stew for $10. Open daily from 6 a.m. till midnight.

A Marisqueira, Rua Barata Ribeiro 232 (tel. 237-3920). Offering a menu of over two-dozen fish dishes, this Portuguese-style seafood restaurant is on one of Copacabana's most congenial backstreets. For soup lovers or those who only want to eat lightly, try the *caldo verde,* that wonderful and traditional Portuguese soup made from purée of potato and filled with crispy kale and slices of country sausage. Here, $7 to $8 entrees are the rule. There is also a branch of A Marisqueira in Ipanema, at Rua Gomes Carneiro 90 (tel. 267-9944). Open daily from 11 a.m. to 1 a.m.

Not far from the venerable Hotel Miramar is the **Pomme d'Or,** Rua Sa Ferreira 22 (tel. 521-2548), a favorite among local residents who are fond of French cooking at reasonable prices. The restaurant occupies a large, attractive space and offers a list of daily specials from $7 to $12, while the most expensive dish on the menu, lobster, is $20. Open daily from noon to 2 a.m.

The **Enotria,** Rua Constante Ramos 115 (tel. 237-6705), is several blocks in from the beach, near the corner of Avenida Barata Ribeiro. This tiny and newly renovated two-story restaurant serves some of the best Italian food in Rio. Loveseats and armchairs add a touch of the salon to the Enotria's ambience. All pastas and breads are prepared daily in the Enotria's kitchen. At the attached gourmet shop next door, you can buy take-out for those midnight snacks back in the hotel. The Enotria offers daily specials from a fixed-price hand-written menu as well as à la carte selections. Some dishes include tortelli di porri (cheese filled tortellini), giamberoni ai pinoli (shrimp in cognac with pignoli nuts), and for dessert, pera a la Cardinali (chilled stewed pears, with ice cream and strawberry mousse). Prices for entrees range between $8 and $20. The Enotria is open only for dinner, and reservations are suggested. Closed Sundays and no credit cards are accepted.

Another neighborhood institution, the churrascaria **Jardim,** Rua República de Peru 225 (tel. 236-3263), has been a reliable steak house for many years. If anything, the restaurant has just gotten more and more informal with age, giving less and less attention to decor. The result is refreshingly provincial and confirms the notion that the consumption of barbecued meat does not require fancy surroundings. The word *jardim* means garden, and there is a small open-air sitting area that is particularly pleasant at night. Service here is à la carte, not rodízio. For a selection of meats, which are cooked within view over charcoal pits, try the mixed grill. Prices from $8 to $15 reflect both the quality of the meats as well as the status of the restaurant. Open daily from 11 a.m. to 1:30 a.m.

Atlantis, Avenida Atlântica 4240 (tel. 521-3232). Adjacent to the pool on the terrace of the Rio Palace Hotel, the Atlantis functions as an all-purpose quality restaurant for both lunch and dinner. Guests of the hotel also use the Atlantis as a breakfast room in the morning. With a wide-ranging menu, the restaurant can serve practically anything from sandwiches to full-sized meals in a variety of environments: inside the restaurant itself, on the terrace overlooking Copacabana beach, or at poolside tables. On Saturday the Atlantis features a formal feijoada, and on Sunday, a brunch. Many meals are in the $6 to $12 range, including a fixed-price luncheon menu. Open from 6 a.m. to 1 a.m.

The **Forno e Fogão,** Avenida Atlântica 3716 (tel. 287-4212), is the house restaurant of the Hotel Luxor Regente, recommended for its very tasty yet moderately priced dishes. Often when a hotel like the Regente caters to not only tourists but a sizable number of business travelers, there is a strong motivation to keep up the standards of its kitchen. Any business traveler will tell you that not every lunch or dinner has to be a splurge or a culinary event. Sometimes you just want a normal meal without a lot of fanfare, but you always want the food to be a cut above average. People on vacation sometimes feel this way, too. I mention this because I have eaten two business lunches at the Forno e Fogão, and both were excellent. And if I were staying in the vicinity of the Regente in Copacabana for five or six days, I would seriously consider taking at least one meal here. The Supremo de Frango, a generous portion of breaded chicken in a cheese and tomato sauce, priced at $7.50, was particularly good, as was the cultured trout at about $10. Open daily from noon to midnight for lunch and dinner.

BUDGET-RANGE CHOICES

The **Arosa,** Rua Santa Clara 110 (tel. 262-7638), is a classic—a clean, well-lighted place, once an abundant species of restaurant throughout Copacabana, now sadly all but extinct. So thank your stars for the Arosa. It's the kind of place you could dine at regularly, in between those weekly binges at more pricey restaurants. The interior is paneled in light-toned woodwork, and the spacing among the tables is very generous. The menu features meat, chicken, and seafood dishes, with most entrees falling in the $3 to $5 range. A delicious pan-fried filet of fish with a pilaf of white rice costs $4. Open daily from 11 a.m. till midnight.

A Polonesa, Rua Hilário de Gouveia 116 (tel. 237-7378), is located between Avenida Nossa Senhora de Copacabana and Avenida Barata Ribeiro, offering pirogis, stuffed cabbage, and borscht right here in Rio. These Eastern European flavors provide a nice change of pace for dinner or weekend lunch. Open Tuesday to Friday from 6 p.m. to 1 a.m., and on Saturday and Sunday from noon to 2 a.m. Soups cost between $1.25 and $2, while entrees are priced from $4 to $5.

Boninos, Avenida Nossa Senhora de Copacabana at Rua Bolívar (tel. 262-7638), is an old-fashioned tea room and restaurant. The back room here is a pleasant air-conditioned salon, ideal for a quick afternoon pick-me-up. In front is a lunch counter serving ice-cream sundaes as well as coffee, tea, and diverse snacks and pastries. Most items on the menu are priced between $2 and $3, while shrimp platters run up to $10. Open from noon until midnight.

Da boca pra dentro, Rua Almirante Gonçalves 50. This is a typical-looking hole-in-the-wall lunch counter like many others of similar appearance found throughout the streets of Copacabana. Except in this case the quick and easy snacks are vegetarian salads and sandwiches. Very inexpensive, from 50¢ to $1.50.

Some Favorite Leme Hangouts

The **Fiorentina,** Avenida Atlântica 454 (tel. 541-2441), an inexpensive Italian café-restaurant near Máriu's, has long been a favorite watering hole of Rio's artistic and theatrical community. In fact my own introduction to the place was in the company of several Amazonian actors based in Rio and active in experimental theater. What is so special about the Fiorentina is that it is probably the only remaining beachfront café in Cobacabana/Leme that those traveling on a budget can afford to eat in. Many of the pasta, meat, and fish dishes are in the $3.50 to $5 range, and the joint is a hot spot on many weeknights, but especially on weekends, when it often remains open till 6 a.m. Open daily from 11:30 a.m.

The **Nogueira Restaurante,** Rua Ministro Viveiros de Castro

15 (tel. 275-9848), cooks *tudo na brasa* (everything on the grill), making this corner café, with the busy Avenida Princesa Isabel on its Copacabana side, the Brazilian equivalent of an American bar and grill. Late nighters love this place, and I am told that most nights (mornings?) it's hard to find an empty table around 4 a.m. The menu features about 70 dishes—mostly seafood, meat, and fowl—with most dishes big enough for two. The average bill comes to around $7 per person, assuming you don't share or have a few beers. Another night-owl special, **El Cid,** Rua Ministro Viveiros de Castro 15B (tel. 275-4597), is half the size but just as colorful and located right next door, offering essentially the same fare. Both establishments are open daily from around 11 a.m. till 6 a.m.

A popular daytime hangout for the Leme beach and neighborhood crowd is located on the opposite side of Avenida Princesa Isabel, on the corner of Avenida Nossa Senora de Cobacabana, called the **Taberna do Leme.** The Taberna is really just a bar, with the usual fast food, *salgadinhos,* and the clientele spills out onto the sidewalk—some women but mostly bare-chested men with a draft beer in hand, clustered in groups, chatting away. There is something appealing about this informal scene that makes you want to glue yourself right into the picture.

Speaking of *salgadinhos,* those doughy delights filled with everything from chicken to shrimp to hard boiled eggs, an exemplary species of them can be found at the Ipanema end of the beach in Copacabana, at the **Pastelaria Miguel de Lemos,** Rua Miguel de Lemos 18E (tel. 521-0295). Try the fresh-squeezed orange juice and a coxinha de galinha, fresh from the oven. Coxinha is a chewy pastry filled with a kind of spicy ratatouille of chicken, and costs little more than a dollar.

Botequims, juice bars, pizza parlors, and fast-food establishments abound among the side streets of Copacabana. A **botequim** is usually a bar with a small counter where patrons stand for a quick nip of pinga (cachaça), a beer or soft drink, or a cup of cafezinho. Depending on its size, the botequim may also have a grill for turning out a *mixto* sandwich (grilled cheese and ham) or some similar eat-on-the-run specialty.

The **juice bars** are less common than botequims but never more than a few blocks from any given point in the neighborhood. Having a *vitamina* (an instant dose of vitamins) in the form of a squeezed or blended fruit drink is an old Cariocas tradition—especially the morning after a binge on the town without the benefit of much sleep. A great variety of fruits is usually in season at all times of year.

Several chains of **pizzarias** (really simple Italian restaurants) are located throughout the city. A branch of Bella Blu is on Rua Siqueira Campos 107. Pizza Pino's is on Rua Constante Ramos 32, and the Bella Roma can be found on Avenida Atlântica 928. Pizza, spaghetti and meatballs, lasagna, and so forth. Open throughout the day, from 10 a.m. until midnight, and later on weekends.

For fast food, a **Bob's** or a **Gordon's**—and now a **McDonald's**—is always somewhere in the vicinity. Mostly hamburgers, fries, and shakes. What else?

But there is some novelty in Brazilian junk food, for those who may be curious. The little meat pies called o *pastel* and the shrimp-filled *empadinha* are widely available at most fast-food outlets and at lunch counters, one variety of which are the **galetos,** the inexpensive barbecued-chicken counters that usually offer a variety of grilled meats as well.

2. Ipanema and Leblon Restaurants

The adjacent neighborhoods of Ipanema and Leblon combine to form Rio's premier restaurant district, where people go to see and be seen, and where gourmands maintain their perpetual vigil for the latest in new wave culinary artistry. Most restaurants in the district, moreover, are not super-chic, but fall into the medium-price category. After all, city folk who dine out frequently like to eat well and to be presented with a wide variety of choices; they don't want to pay a fortune for every meal they consume. As a rule in Rio, the fancy restaurants tend to be scattered throughout the city, while the highest concentration of good, convivial, and reliable eateries are to be found in Ipanema and Leblon.

THE UPPER BRACKET

The **Esplanada Grill,** Rua Barão da Torre 600 (tel. 239-6028), is currently one of Rio's most fashionable dining spots. On Fridays the Esplanada is crowded from lunchtime till late into the night, with a clientele whose manner signifies that the place is definitely "in." The restaurant's decor is a mixture of high tech and traditional, but by no means flashy or obvious. You must look closely to see the unusual combinations: the highly stylized concrete wall columns, for instance, are inlaid with fine polished hardwood. This and other details suggest an architectural vision of some freshness.

But the Esplanada is essentially a steakhouse, and the quality of the food is what brings people back again and again, once the thrill of rubbing elbows with the "in" crowd wears thin. The meats are indeed superb, combining buttery tenderness with exquisite flavor. According to Cardoso, the Esplanada's manager, the owners raise their own beef cattle, on the flat plains of the South American pampas; they don't serve the *boi de Minas*—that is, cattle bred in the nearby hilly state of Minas Gerais. Whatever its pedigree, the picanha bordon, at $12—and about the most expensive cut on the menu—is delicious. Twenty-five other cuts and combinations are available and priced from $7.50 to $12. The Esplanada's menu also features a half-dozen elaborate salads ($3 to $6) for noncarnivores. Open Monday through Friday from noon to 4 p.m. and 7 p.m. to 2 a.m.; open 24 hours Saturday and Sunday.

The **Petronius,** Avenida Vieira Souto 460 (tel. 287-3122), is the pride of the Caesar Park hotel. The Petronius is a picture of swank in its decor and of romance in its mood—cream-colored banquettes separated by panels of etched glass, a white grand piano on a raised platform between an alcove bar and the dining area, the formal air and attire of the staff, and the starlit Ipanema night seen through a wall of windows high above the beach.

The Petronius specializes in seafood served in a manner that only French cuisine could inspire. The fish in pastry or the soufflé of codfish (unbelievably good) are samples of the imaginative presentations that emerge from the kitchen. The Petronius may have the further distinction of being the only restaurant in Rio that serves its martinis with pimiento-stuffed green olives. As for dessert, the little goblets of chocolate filled with liquor and topped with whipped cream require no additional commentary. An excellent and expensive restaurant. Expect to spend between $40 and $50 per person for a no-holds-barred bout of feasting. Open for dinner only, from 6 p.m. to 1 a.m.

On a side street not far from the Caesar Palace is **Tiffany's,** Rua Prudente de Morais 729 (tel. 247-0580). On those two days annually when the day and night are of equal length—on the two equinoxes, that is—this very chic and very "in" restaurant sees fit to change its menu. The production of nouvelle cuisine as featured at Tiffany's is an endless series of performances. The chef at Tiffany's must be a relentless student of world cookery, and certainly his menu recognizes no national boundaries. His creations are inspired by both East and West. They are also expensive, around $30 a person, but that will likely include drinks or wine.

Tiffany's seems to function as a tavern for a very smart set of local gentry who come to exchange the news of the day with their peers, and perhaps further a pet interest or two. But the atmosphere is by no means closed and the house treats all its guests admirably. Particularly attractive are the intimate dining alcoves, with their touches of fresh flowers and fine works of art. There is a pianist to entertain nightly in the downstairs bar. For drinks, Tiffany's opens daily at 5 p.m.; for dinner, served upstairs in this two-story house, service begins after 7:30 p.m. and continues until closing at around 2 a.m. Reservations are suggested.

MEDIUM-PRICED RESTAURANTS

Back to the Caesar Park for the hotel's rooftop restaurant, the **Tibérius,** Avenida Vieira Souto 460 (tel. 287-2122). As Shecky Green might comment, "With a view like that, how bad can the food be?" Not only Rio's best rooftop view, but good standard Brazilian fare from appetizer to entree. Lunch will cost somewhere in the $10 to $15 range. Open daily from 7 a.m., when breakfast service begins there for hotel guests, until 11:30 p.m.

Le Streghe, Rua Prudente de Morais 129 (tel. 287-1369). The name means witch in Italian, an allusion to the artful brewing up of new wave cuisine Italian style, the trademark of Le Streghe. To satisfy himself that a given dish embodies a particular taste from Italy, the owner will sometimes amuse Customs officials with suitcases filled with cheeses or herbs on his return from visits to his old homeland. Le Streghe is one in a trio of nightspots under the same roof, a former private house across from Ipanema's main square, the Praça General Osorio. In addition to the restaurant, there is a popular piano bar and the Calígola discotheque.

The food is very good, as the kitchen turns out some delicious variations using familiar basics like veal and pasta. Noshing before the meal can mean sampling the prosciutto or eating delicate breaded crab legs. Prices are quite reasonable given the quality of the meals: veal dishes run about $8 to $10, pastas are between $4 and $5, and the shellfish dishes are priced somewhat higher, up to $20 for such plates as green pasta with seafood sauce. Open for dinner from 7:30 p.m. till 2 a.m. Reservations are recommended.

Guests staying in hotels at the Rio Palace end of Copacabana can easily walk the several blocks to the **Grottammare,** Rua Gomes Carneiro 132 (tel. 287-1596), a popular Italian seafood restaurant. Simply head down Rua Francisco Sá which, after several blocks, turns into the Rua Gomes Carneiro as soon as you have crossed the Avenida Bulhões de Cavalho. The restaurant specializes in salads, pasta dishes, and grilled fish—whatever species turn up daily in the nets of the fishermen who supply the Grottammare. Seafood dishes are priced between $8 and $15, while pastas and salads generally cost between $5 and $6. Open every night for dinner from 6 p.m. until the last customer leaves in the early morning, and on Sunday at noon for lunch, as well.

Finally, someone has opened a restaurant where one can enjoy the Brazilian national dish, feijoada, any day of the week, not just at the traditional Saturday lunch. Located at the very beginning of Ipanema, and somewhat obscured from the street by a newspaper stand, is the **Casa da Feijoada,** Rua Prudente de Morais 10 (tel. 267-4994). Owner Leonardo Braga, who spent three years in California, decided that the black bean, a former staple of the local diet, should make its comeback in Rio. The full blown feijoada feast includes soup (caldo verde or black bean), salad, batida cocktail, and the usual array of pork and beef cuts served with white rice, fried manioc, *couve* greens, orange slices, and farofa—all for $6.50. Those who fancy other regional Brazilian foods will also probably find what they have in mind on the house menu: everything from Tutu a Mineira to Caldeirada de Pescador, the latter a mariscada to rival the finest. The restaurant will also deliver meals within its general vicinity (which may include some of the hotels at the posto 6 end of Copacabana), and is open daily from noon to midnight; on weekends from noon till 1 a.m.

Albérico's, Avenida Vieira Souto 236 (tel. 267-3793), is Ipanema's most animated beachfront café. When the weather is hot, on any given night of the year, and a cool breeze blows in from the Atlantic, hordes of young people gather at Albérico's sidewalk tables—sometimes in parties of 20 or more. The restaurant also has a second-story dining area, where serious diners can escape the downstairs revelry and enjoy a tranquil meal, surrounded by open windows. Full seafood dinners are available, but most patrons are satisfied with the snacks, light meals, and free flow of *chopp*—draft beer. Open daily from 11:30 a.m. to 2 a.m., until 4 a.m. Saturday and Sunday.

The **Via Farme,** Rua Farme de Amoedo 47 (tel. 227-0743), is located a block or so from both the beach and the popular Garota de Ipanema bar. Here, according to the slogan with which the restaurant emblazons its menu, you will find "La Vera Cuccina Italiana—Genuine Italian Cooking." The Via Farme's popularity since opening four years ago attests to the veracity of that claim. Diners may choose from a varied menu that includes traditional meat, fish, and pasta dishes as well as pizza. Meals are priced between $3.50 and $15. Open daily from noon until 2 a.m. or later, depending on business.

A short walk from the Caesar Park Hotel is this attractive Italian restaurant with traditional checkered tablecloths, the **Porto di Mare,** Rua Maria Quiteria 46 (tel. 247-9506). If candles in empty straw-wrapped bottles of chianti were added to the table settings, the ambience would be just like that of an intimate Italian restaurant in New York's Greenwich Village during the '60s. Pasta dishes average $2.50, while fish plates are $6 and up. Open daily from 11:30 a.m. until 2 a.m.

The **Mediterrâneo,** Rua Prudente de Morais 1810 (tel. 259-4121). This festive-looking eatery with a definite flavor of the Mediterranean shore occupies the first and second floors of a corner house. Divided rooms and balconies provide separate areas for intimate dining amid nautical bric-a-brac and polished woodwork. It's generally crowded, so reservation or not, you'll probably have to wait a few minutes for a table. For a filling and satisfactory meal, try the spaghetti Mediterrâneo, a concoction of pasta and fresh seafood, including giant shrimp, mussels, fish, and squid. With a couple of draft beers or a carafe of red wine to wash it all down, the meal will cost you about $13, including service. Mussel and fish dishes run between $6 and $10, while lobster can cost as much as $20. Open from noon until 2 a.m. daily.

The **Mistura Fina,** Rua Garcia d'Ávila 15 (tel. 259-9394), is ideal as a supper club or for an evening of music and drinks. A popular dish in the downstairs restaurant is the flank steak with potatoes gratiné for about $6, or steamed clams in orange sauce for around $12. The restaurant is open daily from noon till 3 a.m. The Mistura Up, offering live music (a pianist or a small group playing light jazz), opens at 6 p.m. and—at least on weekends—doesn't close until dawn.

The **Lord Jim,** Rua Paul Redfern 63 (tel. 259-3047), is on the last street in Ipanema before crossing into Leblon. The British lion holds forth in this genuine public house re-created in the tropics. Boisterous and rowdy in a good-natured way, the weekend crowds exercise their Anglo-Saxon nostalgia for pub life to the tune of endless rounds of good English bitters, kidney pie, and a rousing game of darts. 'Ey what? Lord Jim's is the crossroads and meeting ground for Rio's English colony and therefore a favorite attraction for many visitors to Rio from the diverse countries of the English-speaking world. In addition to the traditional English fare—roast beef, Yorkshire pudding, fish and chips—tea is served daily from 4 until 6:30 p.m. Closed Monday, both pub and restaurant are open between 4 p.m. and 1 a.m. Tuesday through Saturday, and for lunch on Sunday, from 11 a.m. until the normal closing hour.

Saborearte, Avenida Bartolomeo Mitre 297 (tel. 511-1345), in Leblon, is more new wave than nouvelle, as the emphasis here is on the novelty of food combinations, deriving only remotely from any tradition of French cooking. All the dishes are therefore unusual—some quite tasty, others less successful. Such are the risks in all experimental arts, whether in the theater or in the kitchen. The menu, furthermore, changes frequently, and is likely to be completely different by the time this guide comes into circulation. A few of the more interesting selections at the time of writing were the boi de manço appetizer of sun-dried beef, a Brazilian version of prosciutto, very tender and with a sweeter taste. The cream of manioc and cheese soup was excellent—a truly new taste. The trout lightly baked in its own juices was quite delicate. With beer, dessert, and tip, the cost was about $15 per person. Open daily for dinner from 8 p.m. until 1:30 a.m., and for lunch on Sunday after midday.

Antônio's, Avenida Bartolomeo Mitre 297 (tel. 294-2699), is directly next door to Saborearte, at the virtual midpoint along the avenue. Antônio's is a long-standing hangout for the "in" crowd. The cooking is French and the atmosphere very appealing. Most meals are in the $8 to $10 range. Open daily from noon till 3 a.m.

Un, Deux, Trois, Avenida Bartolomeo Mitre 123 (tel. 239-0198), another Leblon favorite, is a good choice for both dinner and dancing. The restaurant, however, is separate from the nightclub, and separate reservations are required for both establishments. The fare is standard Brazilian, most often indicated by the term "comida international" (international cuisine) in restaurants throughout the city, and ranges from $7 to $15 per entree. The nightclub features dance-band music and supper-club environment. Open daily for dinner from 7 p.m. until 2 a.m., and for lunch on the weekends after noon. There is a reasonably priced feijoada served every Saturday. The nightclub remains open until the wee hours on the weekends.

On the Leblon stretch of the beach at the corner of Rua Rainha Guilhermina, the **Caneco 70,** Avenida Delfim Morais 1026 (tel. 249-1180), offers the advantages of being both an outdoor café and a popular restaurant. A large open space, it is an ideal lunch and beverage spot in between sessions in the sun. Or, for a genuinely downhome–style feijoada, come here on Saturday, when another national dish is also served—*cozido,* a beef-and-vegetable stew originating in the northeast. Both dishes cost about $6, and as the waiter explains, "Um da pra dois" (One serving is enough for two). For a more private meal, the second-floor terrace is suggested. Open daily from 10 a.m. until 4 a.m.

Gula, Gula, in the Marina Palace hotel, Avenida Delfim Moreira 630 (tel. 259-5212), is attractively situated on the mezzanine of the hotel and looks out over the beachfront through a wall of windows. The tables are covered in tea-service pink, and the daily specials, including steak, shrimp, and fish platters, are priced economically from $5.50 to $10. Open daily from noon to midnight.

BAIXO LEBLON

Baixo Leblon refers to a place of imprecise boundaries at the far end of Leblon beneath the mountain peaks that block the neighborhood's westward expansion. The little cul-de-sac community here has several poles: the end of Leblon beach, the triangle where its two principal thoroughfares meet—Atualfo de Paiva and Dias Ferreira

—and the quiet streets around the Praça Atahaulpa. The area combines both long-established residents and a new, younger crowd, with popular cafés and some of Rio's finest restaurants existing side by side.

On the popular front is a unique cocktail bar called the **Academia da Cachaça,** Rua Conde Bernadotte 26, Loja C, across from the Casa Sendas supermarket and near the intersection with Rua José Linhares. (Conde Bernadotte is a small diagonal street about four blocks away from the beach, from the vicinity of the Marina Palace Hotel.) The specialty at the Academia, a pleasingly ostentatious little place incongruously set in a small shopping mall, is *cachaça*—or *pinga,* as the sugar cane distillate is more commonly called. In all, about 50 varieties of the potent libation from various *pinga* producing regions are offered on the bar's drink menu, priced between 60¢ and $1.50 a shot. Twelve blends of *caipirinha* cocktails —including kiwi and *caju* (the cashew fruit)—are also offered. On the snack menu are many *pesticos* (appetizers) in the $1.50 to $5 range, from nuts and raisins to lobster bits, fried manioc to meatballs. Open daily from 5 p.m. to midnight.

Backtracking and continuing west on Avenida Ataulfo de Paiva, there are several attractive outdoor cafés in the vicinity of the Praça Antero Quintal, including the **Café Look,** at Avenida Ataulfo 900 (tel. 259-0594), just opposite the plaza and open from noon to 4 a.m. daily. Featured here are many blue-plate specials, with meat dishes averaging $3.75, fish $4.25, and pasta $2. Similar in style, appearance, and menu is the **Luna Bar,** just up the block.

Turning the corner on Ataulfo de Paiva, where Rua Dias Ferreira comes in on an angle, you will encounter another cluster of oft-frequented neighborhood restaurants in Baixo Leblon, including **La Mole,** Rua Dias Ferreira 147 (tel. 294-0699). La Mole calls itself *o lugar da gente*—the "people's choice"—and one correspondent of a large-circulation U.S. daily newspaper who lives in the neighborhood swears by the place. La Mole has branches in four other locations throughout the city, and specializes in Italian dishes priced in the $3 to $5 range. Open 11 a.m. to 2 a.m. daily.

Immediately next door is the **Arataca,** Rua Dias Ferreira 135 (tel. 274-1444), a restaurant featuring exotic regional dishes from the Amazon. *Tucunaré, pirarucu,* and *surubim* ($6.50) are among the Amazon River fish on the menu, along with the signature dish of Para State: a spicy duck dish of Indian origin called *pato no tucupi* ($6.75). The house cocktail is the *batida de cupuaçu* ($1.30), a blend of vodka, or cachaça, with one of the Amazon region's many tasty fruits. Open daily from 11 a.m. to 2 a.m. Arataca also has a second branch in Copacabana.

The **Bozó** is another find on Rua Dias Ferreira, located at no. 50 (tel. 294-1260), completely different from the two neighboring establishments mentioned above. The Bozó has a cave-like atmosphere, in contrast to the bright open-air style of its rivals. Behind the entrance façade which mixes wood paneling with a large display window filled with liquor bottles, lies a quiet and orderly interior, invisible from the street, that resembles the dining room of a modest private club. On the menu is *comida típica,* or typical Brazilian fare; favorite dishes from Minas and Bahia like *lombinho tropeiro,* (pork loin with beans and farofa at $3.50); and *moqueca de badejo,* a sea bass stew costing $4.50. The Bozó is open daily from noon till 4 a.m., and delivers carry-out meals as well. Next to the Bozó is another noteworthy café, the **Farol do Leblon.**

Baixo Leblon's Upscale Eateries

One of Rio's most unique and charming steakhouses is the **Buffalo Grill,** Rua Rita Lufolf 47 (tel. 274-4848), where an elfish maitre d' named Garrincha pampers a select clientele with the most tender cuts of meat, prepared to perfection using skills and years of accumulated experience that have made him a semilegendary figure in the world of Rio's churrascarias. The restaurant is also the only one in Rio to serve genuine buffalo steaks—not our North American bison, but the Asian species. Now, this may not sound like much of a distinction: Is buffalo that different from beef, you might legitimately wonder? Well, to my taste it is, somewhat sweeter, agreeably gamey, and very tender. I recommend the *picanha* cut over the filet, because the former is served with a strip of tasty fat that blends well with the meat. I found the filet a bit too rich. An order of *picanha* for two costs $22 and includes a variety of trimmings. Other types of grilled meats are also offered, such as beef, lamb, and chicken. And filet mignon dishes head the list with nearly a dozen different preparations, all around $8.50, from *steak au poive* to Filet Tom—named after frequent patron, composer Tom Jobin, who prefers his steak smothered in *béarnaise* sauce and accompanied by new potatoes with tiny onions. The Buffalo Grill, incidently, occupies both floors of a corner building, with a separate piano bar downstairs, and the restaurant upstairs, an elegant space where tables next to the windows face both streets. Open daily from noon to 2 a.m.; the bar—with its own menu of canapes and appetizers—stays open slightly later on weekends.

The **Antiquárius,** Rua Aristides Espinola 19 (tel. 294-1049), is perhaps the best Portuguese restaurant in Rio. It specializes in *bacalhau* (codfish), that denizen of northern Atlantic waters with its grotesque visage and flaky, delicate meat. For perhaps two centuries before the Plymouth colony took root in Massachusetts Bay, fishermen from Brittany, the Azores, and the coast of France and England plied the waters off Maine and Nova Scotia and filled their boats with this one fish prized above all others in Europe at that time. No country today upholds the tradition of codfish cookery more than Portugal. But the fish must be imported to Brazil, and so its cost is always more than steak and sometimes priced with shrimp and lobster. Maine lobstermen, who often discard this unwanted interloper from their traps, would be surprised to learn how much a good codfish will fetch in Brazil. The Antiquárius offers many codfish dishes, including the standard Portuguese concoction, many times more appetizing than its basic ingredients of bacalhau, scrambled eggs, and potatoes would imply. The cost is about $12. Other daily specials, primarily seafood, are listed at $8, $10, and $15. Open daily from noon till 2 a.m. It's popular, tiny, and crowded, so reservations are a necessity.

Two other dining choices near the very end of this delightful neighborhood, and under the very shadow of Vidigal Mountain, which hovers above, deserve mention. The **Florentino,** Avenida General San Martín 1227 (tel. 274-6841), open from noon to 2 a.m., is always packed at the dinner hour, and is spoken of fondly by Rio's culinary cognoscenti. The menu is international, leaning toward classical Italian fare, and entrees are priced from roughly $10 to $15. Nearby is Leblon's answer to Ipanema's Lord Jim, the **Piccadilly Pub,** Avenida General San Martín 1241 (tel. 259-7605). The Piccadilly, with its bar downstairs and restaurant on the second floor, where nouvelle cuisine is served, keeps pub-type hours; open daily from 6:30 p.m. till 1 a.m.

Around the corner from the Antiquárius is the Avenida General San Martín, where a number of restaurants are located between Rua Rita Ludoff and Rua General Artigas, including the **Helsingor,** Avenida General San Martín 983 (tel. 294-0347). The real treat at this Danish restaurant is the Sunday smörgåsbord, a buffet of cold meats, fish and vegetable salads, cheeses and pâté, bread and, of course, Scandinavian crackers. The Helsingor also fills the gap in the Rio restaurant scene for a first-class sandwich-and-salad restaurant. Prices on the varied menu range from $4 to $10. Open Tuesday through Saturday, for dinner only, from 6 p.m. until 1 a.m., and on Sunday for lunch and dinner from noon until closing. No credit cards accepted.

The third large avenue in from the beach is the Avenida Ataulfo de Paiva, recommended for its street life, a variety of shops and services, and a number of snack shops and restaurants, like the **Real Astória** at no. 1235 (tel. 294-0047). The Real Astória offers Spanish specialties in the $5 to $8 range, and looks like an attractive place to eat. It's open daily from 11:30 a.m. to midnight.

JAPANESE AND CHINESE RESTAURANTS

There are several Japanese restaurants in the Ipanema/Leblon area. Two reliable choices are:

Tatsumi, Rua Dias Ferreira 256 (tel. 274-1342), which features sushi, sashimi, and saki on this very pleasant residential back street in Leblon. For $10, you can fill yourself to blissful satisfaction, if raw fish and tempura are to your taste. And that includes dessert, plus a few rounds of flavorful Japanese beer and saki. Open weekdays for dinner from 7 p.m. until 1 a.m., and on weekends for both lunch and dinner, from 2 p.m. until the last customer pays his bill.

The **Mariko Sushi Bar,** Avenida Vieira Souto 460 (tel. 287-3122), is the top-of-the-line sushi bar at the Caesar Park hotel. The chef at the Mariko, who speaks little Portuguese was brought directly from Japan, a noteworthy fact only because Brazil has the largest Japanese community in the world outside the mother country itself. Nothing but the best, however, for the expensive and elegant Mariko. Prices are in the $10 to $20 range. Open for lunch and dinner daily.

READER'S SUGGESTION: Donella Novak writes that she was "able to find an excellent Chinese restaurant in Ipanema, the Restaurante Ming" (tel. 267-5860), Rua Visconde de Pirajá 112, "where dinner for two costs approximately $20."

BARGAIN FOOD IN IPANEMA AND LEBLON

Typical of the excellent lunch counters found throughout the city are the **Chaika** and the **Padaria Ipanema,** both on the Rua Visconde de Pirajá, near the Praça da Paz square. You may just want to pick up one of those delicious loaves of bread you've been eating at breakfast in your hotel for a picnic on the beach. Or you may want to take a quick lunch break from a shopping spree in the nearby boutiques. In that case, either at the counter or in a booth, the perfect snack to satisfy both your palate and your schedule is a plate full of tasty, inexpensive *salgadinhos*. These are the little pies and pastries filled with cheese, chicken, minced meat, egg, or shrimp that cost between 25¢ and 50¢ each.

Don't forget the **Garota de Ipanema** outdoor café on nearby Rua Vinícius de Morais, the very popular daytime hangout for a beefsteak sandwich, a cooling freshly squeezed cup of orange juice or a well-chilled glass of draft beer. Other Ipanema options for informal and inexpensive eating are the **Pizza Palace,** Rua Barão da Torre 340; the **Rio Nápoli,** Rua Teixeira de Melo 53; and **Bonis,** a fast-food emporium on the corner of Rua Henrique Dumont and Rua Visconde de Pirajá.

There is a vegetarian restaurant in Ipanema, the **Natural** on Rua Barão da Torre 117 (tel. 267-7799).

In Leblon, both **Bela Blu,** Rua General Urquiza 107 and **La Mole,** Rua Dias Ferreira 33, have branches of their pizzerias.

---

3. São Conrado and Barra da Tijuca Restaurants

IN AND AROUND SÃO CONRADO

There are a number of fine restaurants that make a spin out to São Conrado worth the effort. For those staying at one of the São Conrado hotels, these restaurants are the perfect option for evenings when you don't feel like hopping a cab to Ipanema or Copacabana.

Guimas II, Estrada da Gávea 899 (tel. 322-5791), is the clone of a very popular, artsy dive located in Gávea, not far from the Jockey Club racetrack. The "new" Guimas, however, is no true carbon copy; the name and menu are the same, but the setting—among the swank boutiques of the São Conrado Fashion Mall—is super chic, whereas the original has overtones of a Bohemian café. Despite the exact duplication of the menu, though, these two establishments ought to be thought of as completely different restaurants, so radically different are they in ambience and style. A dish I would recommend at either place is the *pato da fazenda*—braised duck ($9.25)—or the trout in garlic sauce ($6).

A Special Churrascaria

The **Oasis,** Praça de São Conrado (tel. 322-3144), is not far
from the Inter-Continental Hotel, on the same road that goes to
Barra da Tijuca. You won't find a better barbecue house in Rio than
the Oasis, where the meat is served rodízio style. Proof of this statement is the fact that the Oasis is a favorite of the Cariocas
themselves. Like most churrascarias, the restaurant is large, plain,
and simple—the white tablecloths are the one concession to décor.

To begin the rodízio ritual at the Oasis, the tables are covered
with side dishes: fried bananas, potato salad, hearts of palm, tomatoes, lettuce, chips, fried manioc, farofa, and various condiments
and sauces. The meats start arriving immediately, carried on skewers by waiters who are moving constantly from table to table. The
agility of the waiters is their craft as they carve the juicy slices with
unerring dexterity directly onto your plate. Try to convince the
waiters (against the tide of their generous impulses) that you really
do want tiny slices on the first round. That way you can try everything that interests you and select more carefully from the endless
offerings that follow, until you say "uncle" and call for your bill.
Among the alcoholic beverages, good Brazilian beer is the proper
accompaniment, with perhaps a shot of pinga (cachaça) as an apéritif. Mineral water—both with and without carbonation—aids the
digestion, say Brazilians, who always have a bottle or two open on
their tables. They should know. For about $10 a person, you can
have as good a churrasco blow-out at the Oasis as anywhere in Rio.
There is a companion Oasis located downtown on Rua Gonçalves
Dias 56 (tel. 252-5521). In São Conrado, hours are 11 a.m. until
midnight daily. And in the Centro, weekdays only, from 11 a.m.
until 4 p.m.

Neal's, Estrada da Barra da Tijuca 6250 (tel. 399-3922), is
Rio's American restaurant. Actually Neal (the owner), lately of New
York City, has two establishments with the same name, one in
Botafogo at Rua Sorocaba 695 (tel. 266-6577) and this one, with a
Barra da Tijuca address, though it's very close to the São Conrado
end of this neighborhood. By cab from Copacabana through the
Dois Irmãos tunnel, the ride takes about 20 minutes. The brand-
new Neal's is a structure open on four sides, ultramodern, and yet,
with its textures and abundance of vegetation, the perfect tropical
temple for a Saturday night out. Rock music, videotapes, and American chow, with that inevitable Brazilian flavor, attract large crowds
on the weekends to the large tables for the platters—hamburgers,
ribs, ample salads, etc., priced between $8 and $15. Open daily for
lunch and dinner, from noon to 1 a.m. weekdays, later on weekends.

The **Monseigneur,** Hotel Inter-Continental at Avenida
Prefeito Mendes de Morais 222 (tel. 322-2200), is an upper-bracket
French restaurant. While it may not be strictly required, men might
feel more comfortable in a jacket and tie as a complement to the formal air of the restaurant's décor and service. The setting is warm and
posh, and tables richly set. For the originality and quality of its food,
the Monseigneur has few rivals among the city's fine French restau-

rants. The duck and veal are prepared very well in rich, tasty sauces. The desserts, such as warm chocolate bonbons filled with ice cream, are equally excellent. For a moderate binge you will spend about $40 per person at the Monseigneur, including beverage. Women, by the way, are presented with a long-stemmed rose as they leave the establishment. Open daily from 7 p.m. to 1 a.m.

Also at the Inter-Continental is **Alfredo di Roma** (tel. 322-2200). This is a classy pasta house with its roots in Italy at the original Alfredo's, where the fettuccine dish by the same name was said to have been created. Naturally, all the pasta is made fresh on the premises. The restaurant is bright and overlooks the hotel's pool terrace and the peaks of the Pedra da Gávia mountain. Pasta dishes of numerous varieties predominate on the menu, which also offers a selection of chicken, veal, and seafood choices as well. You'll spend $15 to $20 per person for a full meal, including drinks. Open for lunch daily from noon until 3 p.m. and for dinner from 7:30 until 11:30 p.m.

The **El Pescador,** Praça São Conrado 20 (tel. 322-0851), is a very reputable seafood restaurant, another eating option for guests staying at the hotels in São Conrado. The restaurant's dining terrace is recommended, weather permitting. *Frutos do mar* (fruits of the sea) from local waters are served in a great variety of ways, but you can also dine on typical Spanish dishes and mixed barbecue grill. Portions at the El Pescador are especially generous. Most prices are between $7 and $15. Open from noon to midnight daily, it's located in the same complex as the popular discotheque, Zoom.

BARRA AND BEYOND

The most developed segment of Barra Beach is that which is closest to São Conrado. After the first 6 km (3½ miles) or so, the remainder of the 20-km (12-mile) beach becomes more and more sparsely settled. This initial stretch of Barra, however, is a landscape of high-rise complexes, usually centered on a fair chunk of real estate, and often separated by an equally generous space from its neighboring buildings. Across the Avenida Serambetiba is the beach. On the edge of the sand, many roadside stands cater to weekend bathers with snacks and beverages, but there is no sidewalk life. It is the land of shopping malls—some of the largest in the world—magical commercial hamlets offering entertainment as well as access to hundreds of shops. There is still something of an urban-frontier look about Barra. Scattered among these condo fortresses, however, are a handful of very good restaurants, to the relief of both beachside residents and the seasonal tourists, who are blessed with the option of dining well locally without having to always commute to Ipanema or other older parts of the city.

Le Petit Paris, Avenida Serambetiba 6250 (tel. 385-5776), is a fine French restaurant attached to the Rio Hotel Residência, Barra's newest apart-hotel. You may eat voluminously here for $20 per person from a first-rate menu of appetizers and entrees. The chef's special veal and the shrimp encased in pastry were lovely, especially in the context of an endless flow of appetizers, breads, drinks, and wine. Open for dinner Tuesday through Saturday from 8 p.m. until 1 a.m., and on Sunday for lunch, after midday, as well as dinner.

The **Rodeio,** Avenida Alvorada 2150 (tel. 325-6113), is a churrascaria that does not serve its fare rodízio style. Knowledgeable diners, though, still consider it to be the best barbecue restaurant in Rio. Avenida Alvorada is a principal thoroughfare in Barra, running perpendicular to the beach. The Rodeio is not cheap—about $20 per person with beverage for some fine cuts of meat plus the usual barbecue house trimmings. Nearby is the mall-colossus, Barra Shopping, and the equally cavernous Carré Four supermarket. Open weekdays from noon to 3 p.m. and 7 p.m. to 1:30 a.m., on weekends from noon to 1:30 a.m.

The **Ettore,** Avenida Serambetiba, is tucked among a string of shops in a tiny mall off the oceanfront avenue on the upper stretch of the beach. The Ettore is not hard to find, since the mall in question is the only one along the strip. The restaurant is what one American, a resident of Barra calls "a very suitable Italian restaurant"; the kind of place rural residents are grateful for when they don't have the energy to drive back into town for dinner. Prices range from $5 to $12.

Beyond Barra is yet another string of beaches continuing down the so-called *Costa Verde* (Green Coast) for a dozen miles or so until reaching Rio's suburban city limits. First comes Recreio dos Bandeirantes, a favorite retreat for weekenders, those with vacation homes, and for day-trippers too, who come out to enjoy the unblemished beach. The lone restaurant across from the 6-km (3½-mile) long beach is the **Ancora,** open daily from 9 a.m. until midnight. Prainha comes next, refuge of the middle class, as well as a favorite spot for surfers. Finally there is Grumari, end of the line, virtually deserted on weekdays, and home to the rustic beach bar, the **Vista Alegre,** a roadside favorite with a great view down the coast, if you happen to find yourself in the vicinity.

About an hour's drive from Rio's Zona Sul, some 50 km (31 miles), is the **Pedra da Guaratiba beach,** well beyond Barra da Tijuca in the direction of Angra dos Reis. Two restaurants in this region have become famous in recent years, attracting a steady stream of weekend gourmets.

The first is **Cândido's,** Rua Barros de Alarcão 352 (tel. 395-2007). Simple in appearance, Cândido's has retained for a decade its reputation as one of the finest seafood restaurants in or around Rio. The *Santolas,* a variety of crab imported from Chile that is considered a great delicacy, are priced at about $40 per kilo. The lobster stew, a Bahian-style moqueca, costs $15, while the crab moqueca is $5. Also available are a variety of shrimp and fish dishes in the $8 to $12 range. Open Tuesday through Friday for lunch and early dinner from 11:30 a.m. until 7 p.m.; on weekends, to 11 p.m.

The **Quatro Sete Meia,** Rua Barros de Alarcão 476 (tel. 395-2716), is a Canadian-Brazilian co-production which also features seafood moquecas, but is much smaller than its nearby rival, Cândido's. The 476 (which is what *quatro sete meia* means) has seatings for meals, and reservations are therefore quite imperative. The open-air terrace offers a fine view of a coastline very active with fishing craft. Expect to spend $20 to $25 per person at this rustic gourmet haven by the sea. Open Friday through Sunday from 1 to 11 p.m.

A READER WRITES: "You should know about a new restaurant in Pedra de Guaratiba; **Taba do Guará,** Rua Belchior da Fonseca 399 (tel. 395-0842). The restaurant was opened in June 1989 by its owner and head chef, José Ricardo de Oliveira, a native of the village, formerly employed in the dining rooms and kitchen of neighboring Quatro Sete Meia. Taba do Guará specializes in *moquecas* and other typical Brazilian seafood dishes and also features excellent *massa* (pasta) and *carne* (meat) plates. Some guests claim it is now the best restaurant in the village, where prices, however, continue to be more modest than those of its rivals. The restaurant is open seven days a week for lunch, and on Fridays, Saturdays, and Sundays for dinner as well." (James W. Partridge, Berkeley, CA).

Reader James W. Partridge writes further that "Pedra can be reached from the beach avenues of Copacabana and Ipanema by a beautiful drive along the spectacular highway through São Conrado and Barra da Tijuca, up and over a little mountain and into the quiet countryside beyond. The Santa Cruz bus from Castelo (downtown) also runs on the same beach avenues. It is easy to understand why so many people visit Pedra for a relaxing change from Copacabana and Ipanema."

About 20 km (12 miles) before reaching Pedra da Guaratiba, is the fishing town of **Barra da Guaratiba,** where some 30 restaurants have sprung up in recent years as local outlets for the abundant daily catch from the surrounding waters. First among equals is **Tia Palmina,** Caminho de Souza 18 (tel. 310-1169), sitting at the top of an incline with a private parking lot, offering a single fixed meal for all patrons at about $10 for adults and half price for children 8 or under. A typical meal might include, for beginners, fried shrimp, *pasteis de camarão* (small shrimp turnovers), and mussels. Entrees could be fried filet of fish and a baked dish of marinated fish, plus *bobo de camarão* (a shrimp paste), vatapá, pirão (a kind of grits made from manioc flour), rice, and octopus farofa. For dessert, a cavalcade of fresh fruits along with varied sweets of coconut, melon, banana, and jack fruit *(jaca)*.

Two other choices for Barra da Guaratiba come to me by word of mouth. The **Legal Cantinho da Tia Penha,** roughly translated as Aunt Penha's Groovy Little Corner, and The **Barraca da Baiana.** At Tia Penha's, lines form on the weekend—patrons are given numbered tickets to maintain the rule of first come, first served—and diners come to savor the risotto of cuttlefish ($3 a plate) or the moqueca of octopus ($5 a serving). The Barraca da Baiana (really a roadside stand) specializes in pasteis, those incomparable turnovers in light pastry, filled, in this case, with delights from the sea.

4. Lagoa and Jardim Botânico Restaurants

An immense lagoon, the *Lagoa Rodrigo de Freitas,* occupies much of the center ground between the barrios of Copacabana and Ipanema. On the margins of Lagoa, as the district is always referred to in conversation, are some of Rio's most exclusive houses and apartment buildings—and a number of its better bars and restaurants as well. The restaurants listed here tend to be of the upper-bracket variety.

Antonino, Avenida Epitácio Pessoa 1244 (tel. 267-6791), is quiet elegance by the shaded banks of a lagoon. At night, the glass façade at Antonino's always seems bathed in shimmering sepia tones, adding an evocative element of timelessness to the experience of dining there. Even the solemn formality of the waiters seems an anachronism, albeit a pleasant one. From the font of this genteel sensibility, Antonino's has managed to maintain the consistently high standards of its kitchen. Here you will eat the familiar dishes, including spring lamb or *badejo* (sea bass), cooked to perfection. With appetizer, dessert, and beverage, the bill comes to about $40 per person. Open daily from noon to 2 a.m.

The back room at **Castelo da Lagoa,** Avenida Epitácio Pessoa 1560 (tel. 287-3514), is a clubhouse for one of Rio's best-known society journalists and his circle, primarily actors and actresses. The restaurant's décor is even a little flashy, Hollywood-style, but the prices are reasonable and the food reliable. The vichyssoise, followed by grilled *langostino* (a kind of saltwater crayfish), makes for a tasty lunch, especially if you have time to linger in the tranquil atmosphere of a table in the outdoor patio. A full lunch or dinner can be had for between $20 and $25 per person. At dinner, the restaurant tends to fill up, and the movement of customers is constant between the restaurant and the attached Chico's Bar, one of the most popular bars for singles and couples in Rio, where there is always a solid jazz group. The restaurant is open daily from 11 a.m. until 5 a.m. the next morning.

Guimas, Rua José Roberto Macedo Soares 05 (tel. 259-7996), is one of the hottest small restaurants in Rio, with only a dozen tables or so. It is almost impossible to get a seat without waiting for an hour. The ambience is bistro-like with contemporary graphics and posters announcing recent art exhibitions or plays filling the walls. Each table is equipped with a cup of crayons for doodling on the white paper tablecover. Guimas serves the latest in Brazilian nouvelle cuisine in relatively large portions. Typical are the linguine with smoked whitefish, and the spicy scalloped chicken served with beets. With drinks, dessert, coffee, and tip, expect to spend about $13 a head. Guimas, despite its popularity, is not a household word among Rio's cab drivers. It's not far from the Jardim Botânico end of the Lagoa. Ask your driver to call ahead for directions, if possible (he can call from the porter's desk if you're leaving for the restaurant from your hotel). The cab ride from Copacabana ought to be in the $3 to $4 range. Open for dinner only, 7 p.m. until 1:30 a.m. daily.

Jardim Botânico

Jardim Botânico designates a neighborhood as well as a vast public garden. It's a quiet residential quarter nestled against the hilly interior of the Zona Sul, and not necessarily a center of gastronomy. One little family-style eatery here, though, is worth attention. At the **Couve Flor,** Rua Pacheco Leão 724 (tel. 239-

2191), you pay by the serving, selecting from a variety of hot dishes —the lasagna ($2) seems very popular—and cold salad platters displayed in a deli case. First you find a table, then order at the counter and the waitress serves your meal. It's a great place to mix and match flavors—for example, I combined traditional black beans and rice with a fancy pasta and tuna salad, and then had a big dish of strawberry ice milk for dessert. Including fresh-squeezed orange juice, my bill came to about $4. To get to the Couve Flor, take a cab or a bus to the street just beyond the botanical gardens—Pacheco Leao, if you are coming from the direction of Copacabana or Ipanema/Leblon. Turn left, then continue for about a quarter of a mile.

Also on the Jardim Botânico end of the Lagoa, near Botafogo, is **Troisgros,** Rua Custodio Serrão 62 (tel. 226-4542), a restaurant operated by a French chef who was formerly with Le Pré Catalan at the Rio Palace hotel. The chef personally supervises the creation of all meals, and so his menu is limited and includes a set plate from appetizer to dessert, which changes from day to day. This *menu confiance* is priced at about $15 per person. Expect to spend about $35 per diner, including drinks, wine, and tip. Open Monday through Saturday for dinner from 7:30 p.m. to midnight.

---

5. Flamengo and Botafogo Restaurants

Flamengo and Botafogo were the fashionable beachfront neighborhoods dating from before the turn of the century until the '50s. As desirable residential areas, they have undergone a revival in recent years as well, due to the high rents demanded for much smaller apartments in other districts. There are a fair number of fine restaurants to be found in both these barrios, often hidden on some unassuming back street, but also overlooking the *Baia da Guanabara* (Guanabara Bay). The nearby strands along the bay have long been replaced by the ocean beaches from Leme onward as desired swimming and tanning spots.

Clube Gourmet, Rua General Polidório 186 (tel. 295-3494); another chef-owned upper-bracket eatery, has an unimposing exterior on a narrow back street in Botafogo across from an old cemetery. Inside, the converted town house is smartly decorated and informal —so informal that the restaurant was deliberately designed so that patrons wishing to dine outdoors on the patio must first cross through the kitchen. Typical of the dishes is the veal Margherita, flavored with tomato and cheese, and leg of lamb, delicately spiced and cooked in white wine. A soufflé of *maracujá* (a mango-like fruit) is popular for dessert. The menu is prix fixe, and a full meal will cost about $40 per person, wine included. Open for lunch every day except Saturday from noon to 3 p.m., and for dinner daily from 8:30 p.m. to 1 a.m.

Maria Tereza Weiss, Rua Visconde de Silva 152 (tel. 286-3866), features typical Brazilian food, and is located in a large old manse on a winding tree-lined road in the heart of Botafogo. Senhora Weiss is the author of several standard cookbooks on Brazilian fare, and many of her personal creations grace the menu. This, at least, is one restaurant in the city where you can order black beans with any meal. The tasty turtle bean has inexplicably disappeared from the menus of many regular day-to-day restaurants. This would be an ideal choice for a Saturday feijoada. Entrees range in price from $7 to $15. Open from noon to 1 a.m. every day except Monday.

The **Sol e Mar,** Avenida Repórter Néstor Moreira 11 (tel. 295-1947), can be found on the same dock where the Bâteau Mouche excursion boats are boarded. These are the day-trip cruises that sightsee among the islands of Guanabara Bay. The Sol e Mar (Sun and Sea) is a Spanish-style seafood restaurant, very expensive for full dining. A large deck sticks out over the bay and offers one of the best close-up views of Pão de Açúcar from sea level in Rio. This is a most peaceful spot to enjoy a drink or a light meal either before or after a night on the town. There is light music and dancing, nightly, at the Bâteau Mouche Bar, located behind the restaurant. The Sol e Mar is open daily from 11 a.m. until 3 a.m.

Laurent, Rua Dona Mariana 209 (tel. 266-3131). Formerly the head chef at the St. Honoré, the owner opened his own fine restaurant in 1986 here in the heart of Botafogo. Once a large and lovely private house, the many rooms add intrigue and intimacy to the dining experience. The food is superb, with special attention given to soups and salads. With a drink or wine, plus one of the rich tarts or other pastries for dessert, expect to spend approximately $30 to $35 per diner. Open Monday through Saturday from 8 p.m. to midnight. Reservations suggested on weekends.

The **Barracuda,** Marina de Glória (tel. 265-3997), is nestled on dockside among the moorings of pleasure cruisers and yachts bordering the neighborhoods of Flamengo and Glória. You actually have to drive onto the wharf through a guarded gate to get to the restaurant. Dining is inside and there is no particular view of any note, but the decor is appropriately nautical. The Barracuda is one of the only seafood restaurants in town where you can order a mixed seafood barbecue served on a skewer. The apple salad is also an unusual and welcome accompaniment. A lunch of seafood for two, including appetizers and a couple of rounds of caipirinhas to wash it all down, will cost perhaps $40 in all. Reservations for lunch are suggested, as the restaurant's proximity to downtown makes it a favorite spot for business luncheons. Open daily from noon to midnight, though it closes an hour or so earlier on Sunday nights.

Café Lamas, Rua Marquês de Abrantes 18 (tel. 205-0799), located on a side street in Flamengo, is one of Rio's oldest restaurants, though no longer at its original site. The interior is reminiscent of the popular cafés found in cities throughout Europe, which no doubt served as prototype for a style of public eatery that, although once common in Rio, is now disappearing. The Lamas keeps café hours, making it a convenient choice for afternoon lingering or early-morning meals—breakfast or supper, depending on whether you've just gotten up or haven't been to bed yet. The food is standard café fare, and very reasonable, in the $3 to $7 range, with a varied menu including the usual snacks, meat, chicken, and fish dishes. Open daily from 6:30 a.m. to 4 a.m.

---

6. Centro Restaurants

The restaurant scene downtown, from the tourist's point of view, is actually somewhat of a novelty. The whole Centro—as one might well imagine of a busy urban downtown—is packed with places to eat, catering primarily to the lunchtime needs of the thousands who work there. The variety in eating establishments runs the gamut from simple *galetos* (barbecued-chicken counters) to a handful of fine clubs and restaurants, including the only restaurants in Rio where men are required to wear jacket and tie. Since downtown Rio virtually empties after business hours, most restaurants there don't serve dinner. Indeed many are closed over the weekends. Those places that remain open at night and on Saturday and Sunday usually provide other attractions, in some cases their unique location or historical significance.

DOWNTOWN'S BEST

The **Café do Teatro,** Avenida Rio Branco, occupies the basement of the *Teatro Municipal,* Rio's grand old Opera House. The restaurant's Doric columns and walls of mosaic tiles make you wonder if perhaps you haven't stumbled onto the stage setting for one of the classical productions. The food is also classically international, as the Café do Teatro is under the stewardship of the same group that owns and operates Antonino's in Lagoa. It's open only for lunch on weekdays from noon until 3:30 p.m.; the *prix-fixe* menu at about $12, with beverage and dessert, is a reasonably economical choice. Please take note that no credit cards are accepted.

The **English Bar,** Rua do Comércio 11 (tel. 224-2539), is a popular choice among business people who work downtown and who want to eat well without traveling to the more fashionable areas. Prime rib of roast beef is a favorite meal here, but the menu is fully international, offering French, Spanish, and Portuguese specialties as well. Entrees are in the $8 to $15 range, and a full meal can easily cost you $25 per person. Open weekdays only from noon till 4 p.m. for lunch, and until 8 p.m. for cocktails.

La Tour, Rua Santa Luzia 651 (tel. 240-5795). A revolving carousel of a restaurant 34 stories above it all, La Tour makes one full turn every hour. Yes, it *is* a bit of a tourist trap—the food is nothing special and too expensive at that—so have something simple like grilled filet of fresh fish. But the view is stunning, a wholly different perspective on Corcovado and Pão de Açúcar, than that from the various perches in Copacabana or Ipanema, plus a panorama of Guanabara Bay as well. For any full dinner or lunch from the international menu, expect to pay $20 a head. Open noon to midnight daily.

THE MEDIUM RANGE

Café Nice, Avenida Rio Branco 277 (tel. 240-0490), is a stone's throw from the American consulate and Pan Am offices, both of which are on nearby Avenida Presidente Wilson. The Café Nice is found below ground level, down a flight of stairs in an office building on this the second largest of Rio's two major boulevards (the first is Avenida Presidente Vargas). Café Nice serves two distinct functions: during the day it's a popular spot for business lunches, but at night it's transformed into an equally popular singles bar and disco with live music, sometimes rock, sometimes samba. Meals are priced in the $4 to $12 range, and drinks (domestic drinks that is) are inexpensive.

At one point some years back, the **Alba Mar,** Praça Marechal Âncora 184 (tel. 240-8378), was about to be closed. A dozen waiters decided to pool their resources and buy the place, forming a partnership that still endures. The restaurant has been operating since 1933 in the last remaining cast-iron and leaded-glass building—an octagonal tower—of what was once the dockside municipal market. The Alba Mar is only a short walk from the Praça XV and should be considered as a lunchtime option during a visit to this historic square. Careful on the walk. There are few sidewalks once you get close to the water's edge, and the traffic is relentless. Eating at the Alba Mar will not necessarily be the culinary high point of your stay in Rio. But the view of the waterfront and the bay from the third-floor windows will more than compensate for the simple seafood fare. Typical entrees run between $5 and $15. Open from 11:30 a.m. until 10 p.m.; closed Sundays.

The **Colombo,** Rua Gonçalves Dias 32 (tel. 231-9650), is a genuine fin-de-siécle café, opened in 1894, and an unchanging Carioca landmark in a city that has shed its skin a dozen times since this café was built. It's a favorite spot for munching salgadinhos or pastries with a steaming cup of cafezinho and an ideal setting for an afternoon spot of tea. Fortunately the art nouveau décor is made of stone and crystal or you might be tempted to eat that too. The second-story gallery encircles an oval opening above the café's ground floor, and is an ideal setting for a downtown luncheon. The Colombo's prices are only slightly higher than other typical cafés, which means it remains an economical choice. Open Monday through Friday only, from 6:30 a.m. until 8:30 p.m.

The **Bar Luís,** Rua da Carioca 39 (tel. 262-6900), is another traditional and informal lunch spot, a favorite of journalists and editors who work in the nearby offices of publishers and periodicals. Founded in 1887, Bar Luís is even more venerable than the Colombo, though the atmosphere is more saloon than salon. The Rua da Carioca is also one of Rio's oldest, where an annual costume festival takes place in the second week of August every year. The Bar Luís offers good solid German eats—veal Holstein, wurst and kraut, kassler—for between $4 and $9 a meal. Open from 11 a.m. until midnight, closed Sundays.

LUNCH COUNTERS AND PÉS SUJOS

There are innumerable galetos, *leitarias* (luncheonettes), and *pés sujos* scattered throughout the labyrinth of downtown streets. *Pés*

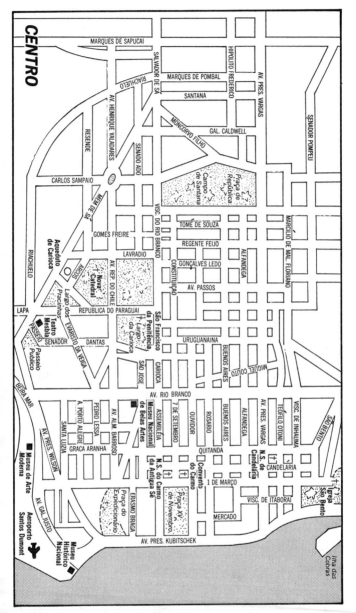

sujo is a slang name for those lovable greasy spoons that even the most discerning gourmets love to eat in from time to time, usually for the bar life as well as some little snack food that can be gotten nowhere else.

For Bahian-style food, try the **Oxaláa,** a lunch counter in the *Cinelândia* section, Rua Francisco Serrador 2 (tel. 220-3035). The counter is in Loja 1 (Store 1) inside a gallery of shops. All the Bahian specialties from moqueca seafood stews to vatapá and xim xim de galinha are served up in simple and large portions. Open during business hours, Monday through Saturday. The meals range between $4 and $8.

The following are among the most popular pés sujos (literal translation is "dirty feet") to be found downtown. **Arco do Telles,** Travessa do Comércio 2, open until 8 p.m. weekdays only. The specialty is calf's foot for $1. The **Ocidental,** on Rua Miguel Couto at the corner of Marechal Floriano, is open Monday through Saturday until 11:30 p.m., and the treat here is fried sardines, about 75¢ a dozen. The **Farão,** Rua do Lavrádio 192, open until 11 p.m. daily except Sunday, serves a mean *cabeca de galo* (rooster head) soup, made with kale, manioc flour, and two eggs per serving. The **Tangara,** Rua Álvaro Alvim 35, is the place for *batidas*—blended drinks made with cachaça and tropical fruits—for less than 50¢, including one made from *jilo,* an edible variety of deadly nightshade or belladonna.

7. A Santa Teresa Restaurant

One very special restaurant in the neighborhood called Santa Teresa, which sits in the hills overlooking downtown, is the **Bar do Arnaudo,** Rua Almirante Alexanrino 316 (tel. 252-7246). This delightful and slightly bohemian hangout, specializing in food from the northeast, is the ideal lunch or refreshment spot for anyone who's on a day excursion, visiting the sights of Santa Teresa. *Carne seca, carne de sol* (sun-dried jerky), and *sarapatel* (minced sweetbreads) are the typical dishes. No meal costs more than $4. But the way to try everything, for less than $10, including dessert and plenty of beer, is to order the large portion appetizers called *pratos diversos* on the menu. Open Wednesday through Sunday from noon until 10 p.m.

VI

THE SIGHTS OF RIO

1. THE BEST OF RIO'S SIGHTS
2. THE BEST OF THE REST

Rio's premier sights are two natural wonders which appeal to most visitors, whatever else their differences may be. Such is the fame of these two glories of nature that even 150 years ago in the 1830s, Charles Darwin, during the voyage of the *Beagle,* observed in his journal that "Everyone has heard of the beauty of the scenery near Botafogo." Darwin was referring in particular to the peaks of **Corcovado** and **Pão de Açúcar.** From these two heights— especially Corcovado—Rio can be seen for miles around. The views reveal the city's general layout, the contours of its 90-km (56-mile) shoreline, along with all its principal man-made and topographical features. Of the latter, Darwin humbly noted that "every form, every shade so completely surpasses in magnificence all that the European has beheld in his own country, that he knows not how to express his feelings."

1. The Best of Rio's Sights

The vistas and scenery praised by Darwin are still there for you to see today. No matter how much Rio develops, nothing seems to diminish or obscure the beauty of its natural setting. But the Rio of today is also a vastly different place from that sleepy South Atlantic town visited by the great naturalist in the 1830s, one that provides all the urban distractions that we would expect to find in one of the truly great cities of our own day. And, depending on one's particular interests, each of the places or groups of places described here— whether historic site or formal garden, inner-city forest or bayscape, art museum or jewelry exhibition—has its special recommendations.

CORCOVADO
A giant statue of Christ the Redeemer stands with outstretched arms on the summit of Corcovado, or Hunchback Mountain, 2,400 feet above sea level and dominates the skyline in Rio. During the

day, but especially at night when the statue is bathed in flood lights, the landmark can be seen clearly from many points in the city, stretching from Ipanema to the downtown and beyond. Photographs of the statue overlooking Rio have become almost synonymous with the city itself. But Corcovado was a beloved landmark in Rio, as Darwin's remarks demonstrate, long before the monumental statue was constructed.

Initial access to the peak was along a road that followed the ridgeline from the Alto da Boa Vista, an ascent that required more leisure time than most of Rio's citizens could afford. To democratize the experience of the renowned view, Dom Pedro II ordered the construction of a passenger train, completed in 1885, that could carry a group of sightseers to the summit and back in a short time. Initially a steam engine, and later Brazil's first electric train, the railroad has been modernized many times in the last century, and the climb today can be accomplished in only 20 minutes.

The imposing statue of *Cristo Redentor,* Christ the Redeemer, was conceived as a fitting monument to mark the centennial of Brazilian Independence in 1921. The project was underwritten by thousands of donations collected in churches throughout the country. Finally, in 1931, the statue was completed. Constructed of reinforced concrete and coated with soapstone, the massive figure with the welcoming arms rises 120 feet above a spacious observation platform, and weighs over 1,000 tons.

The view from this observation deck is truly unforgettable. Make sure you have a map along to help identify what you are seeing. Trace the shoreline from deep within the bay all the way to Leblon. In a single glance, embrace all of Lagoa and Jardim Botânico. Perhaps you will even see the mounts circling the field at the Jockey Club racetrack. Study Ipanema and Copacabana at a distance and then focus on the nearby back streets of neighborhoods like Botafogo, Laranjeiras, and Cosme Velho. Let your eyes hike over the bucolic highlands of Santa Teresa across the ancient aqueduct into the heart of downtown, where the buildings assume the disorienting scale of an architectural model. Watch the small planes circle close to that conical wonder at the mouth of Guanabara Bay, the Pão de Açúcar mountain, and then sweep across the harbor near Flamengo as they land at Santos Dumont airport. Then face away from the city and wonder at the enormity and the denseness of the surrounding forest that literally creeps to the very edges of Rio's most civilized corners. From the summit of Corcovado, all of Rio's disjointed parts fall into place, and the city suddenly becomes knowable in a way that could not be imagined before.

The best time to make the ascent is in the afternoon at around 4 or 5 p.m., when the sun is already low on the horizon and the light is evenly distributed above the landscape. Try to organize your visit to Corcovado on the clearest possible day as well. But even if you are forced to make your visit when the weather is overcast, don't fail to make the ascent on that account. The sensation of being above the clouds can be very powerful in and of itself, even if the panorama is somewhat obscured by the ocean mists.

Getting There

A number of options are available for reaching the top. But first you must decide if you want to go by yourself or with an organized tour. If by yourself, take a public bus or cab to the Cosme Velho train station. Bus 583 leaves from Copacabana, and a number of buses leave from the downtown Menezes Cortes bus terminal. The **train**—which climbs sometimes at a 30-degree angle and has a tractor system similar to that of a roller coaster—leaves every 20 to 30 minutes from 8:30 a.m. to 6:30 p.m. and costs approximately $2.25 round trip. The last train returns from the summit at 7 p.m. The train ride is a worthwhile excursion in its own right, as it crosses deep ravines with their own dramatic views and cuts intimately through the dense tropical vegetation on the surrounding slopes. There are a number of stops along the route to the top where residents who live on the hillside get on and off, so you get to see something of local life along the way as well.

You may also choose to ascend Corcovado by **cab or private car** along the paved road that zigzags up the slopes all the way to the base of the observation platform. From here, a series of stone stairways lead to the summit. Arriving by hired car is the most expensive option, but also the most convenient, especially if time is a factor. The arrangement you make with your driver usually includes his waiting for the return trip. Tour lines offer organized bus tours, some of which go directly to the top, while others take you to and from the Cosme Velho train station. (The names of various tour companies are given toward the end of this chapter.) These bus tours leave from your hotel and operate on fixed schedules, generally costing around $20. The buses are accompanied by tour guides who point out the sights, usually in four or five different languages, and answer your questions.

A Stop at Mirante Santa Marta

Many tours stop at the Mirante Santa Marta before climbing all the way to the summit. From this vantage point 1,200 feet above the ground, both Corcovado and Pão de Açúcar can be seen, and you will be treated to an even closer view of the surrounding neighborhoods. Some tours, especially the smaller groups traveling by van, will also make a quick detour near the train station to a nearby cobblestone courtyard called the **Largo do Boticário** to view the façades and setting of some lovely old town houses with wooden balconies and pan-tile fronts. While of no particular historic significance, the courtyard is a graceful residential cul-de-sac, entered through a metal archway, where gas lamps, a central fountain, shady trees, and its own bubbling brook add to the charm. At the entrance to the square is an art studio, occasionally open to the public when the semi-retired painter, Augusto Rodrigues, is receiving visitors. There is also an antique shop where English is spoken.

PÃO DE AÇÚCAR

Sugar Loaf Mountain is the eternal counterpoint to Corcovado. While Hunchback Mountain occupies an inland setting and is covered with lush vegetation, Pão de Açúcar stands virtually naked—a huge cone-shaped hunk of metamorphic rock composed primarily of granite, quartz, and feldspar that clings to the very shoreline of the great bay. Whether you are observing Pão de Açúcar from Corcovado or vice versa, the visual pleasures are equally stunning.

No roads lead to the summit of Sugar Loaf. Either you ride the cable cars or you climb. Most visitors choose the way of least resistance. The sleek gondolas, made from hardened aluminum and wrapped in acrylic windows, can carry over 1,000 passengers an hour on their two-stage ascent. The first ride takes you to the top of the *Morro da Urca* (Urca Hill), Pão de Açúcar's neighboring peak; a second car completes the journey to Sugar Loaf itself. During both legs of the climb, you are suspended in mid-air for approximately three minutes. It is reassuring to note that there has never been an accident.

The name, *pão de açúcar,* is of uncertain origin. Some say the mountain was named by the Portuguese who compared its shape with that of the ingots or "loaves" of raw sugar that were shipped to market from their many New World *engenhos* or refineries. A more esoteric—and probably romantic—theory holds that the name derives from the Tupi Indian phrase *pau-hn-acugua,* meaning a remote hill that is high and pointed. Yet it is undoubtedly true that the hill was made less remote when the first cable car system was installed in 1912, a simple affair of wooden carriages that remained in service until the more high-tech system in current use was inaugurated in 1972.

The first recorded ascent by a climber was that of an Englishwoman in 1817. Many more climbers followed, until all faces of the mountain were conquered. Today, climbing the Pão de Açúcar is a weekly event, as the safety lines of enthusiasts can be seen dangling from the rocks on any clear day. A more gentle ascent—but still a vigorous hike—can also be arranged, chaperoned by the organization that runs all the concessions on the mountain. As with Corcovado, however, the main reason for visiting Pão de Açúcar is for its unique view of bay and city. A sundown excursion is particularly exciting; there is no better vantage point in Rio from which to witness the transition from daylight to the natural and artificial illumination that envelops this stunning city after dark.

While Pão de Açúcar's altitude is only 1,300 feet (roughly the same height as New York's World Trade Center), the unique location of the huge rock gives it a virtually unobstructed view of much of the city. As is also the case when visiting Corcovado, it is extremely useful to have a map along to help you to distinguish one feature or area from another. Of special note is the close-up view of Botafogo harbor and the full visual sweep of the 15-km (9-mile) long bridge that connects Rio with its companion city, Niterói, on the opposite shore of the bay. Just south of Niterói begins another unbroken shoreline which includes the pristine beaches of Piratininga, Itaipú, Itacotiara, and Itaipuaçú. Both the mouth of the bay and the coast beyond Niterói can best be viewed from the garden walk on the far side of the hill.

In addition to its function as an overlook, the Pão de Açúcar complex is also home to various entertainment programs, several bars, and even a restaurant, most of which are actually located on the Morro da Urca. Every Monday night from about 10 p.m. until midnight, the samba school Beija Flor presents a cabaret version of Carnival with colorful costumes, music, and dance in a covered amphitheater. The show costs $10 a ticket. Live performances of top singers and musicians are also staged in the amphitheater, known as the *Concha Verde* (the Green Shell) on weekend nights, which in Brazil means Thursday through Saturday.

Getting There

Getting to Pão de Açúcar is considerably less involved than going up to Corcovado. Here, in fact, is one excursion where a bus ride may be entirely appropriate. Take bus 511 from Copacabana or bus 107 from downtown to the Praia Vermelha station, Avenida Pasteur. Or take a cab, which from Copacabana, for example, ought to cost no more than $3 to $4, and only slightly more from Ipanema/Leblon. Then just climb the stairs to the ticket office, pay the $2 round-trip fare, and ride to the top. The cable cars function from 8 a.m. until 10 p.m. on a continual basis if the demand is heavy, or at 30-minute intervals when traffic is light. Cars also function later to accommodate those attending special events. There is a gift shop in the boarding station for film or souvenirs, and a tourist information center, open during business hours only. For **information** about the shows, climbing excursions, or any number of other activities and special events, call either 541-3737 or 295-2397.

Urca

While in the area, be sure to walk or ride through the neighborhood of Urca, nestled at the foot of the hill of the same name. Urca is just a handful of streets seemingly unattached to the rest of the city, not particularly elegant, but with many private houses and a shady, small-town feeling. Residents there must feel themselves among the most privileged in all of Rio, being so close to the principal zones of the city, yet in so private and tranquil a setting overlooking both ocean and harbor.

THE BEACHES

Beaches in Rio are as basic an ingredient of daily life as food and shelter. And on the weekend, the beaches are life itself. Rio's coast is 80 miles long, and dozens of beaches dot the shoreline from one end of the city to the other. There are 23 beaches on Governor's Island alone, the island in the Zona Norte where the International Airport is located. There are no bad beaches in Rio, only beaches that keep getting better the farther you go from the center of town. There are bay beaches and ocean beaches, but, in the Zona Sul, at least, only the latter are good for swimming.

General Information

The ocean surf is often very powerful in Rio, and the **undertow** can be treacherous. Be careful not to overextend yourself, especially if you're not used to swimming in heavy seas. Experienced ocean bathers will find the bodysurfing rugged and exciting. Swimmers, on the other hand, must look for the most protected coves or await calm seas to practice their crawls. On those beaches where the waves are particularly high, you will usually find surfboarders. Surfers are fun to watch, and they usually keep to well-defined areas. Still, it's best to be alert in the water when flying surfboards are in the air.

During the week, especially in Copacabana and Ipanema, the beach attracts a fair crowd of fitness buffs from just after the sun comes up until it's time to go off to work. Then for the remainder of the day—at least during the **off-season** (April through June and August through October)—the beaches remain sparsely peopled. Even Copacabana and Ipanema are quiet during these months, except for a few nannies with preschoolers and the usual crowd of bon vivants. Tourists also come to Rio during the off-season, by choice or necessity. They may also be found weekdays on the major beaches, gathered in small pockets on the sand in front of their respective hotels. Thus you can always tell the Rio Palace crowd from that of the Othon, the Copacabana Palace, or the Meridien, but only during those months when the daytime crowd is light and the scene subdued. Vendors can always be found on Copacabana as long as there's someone to sell to, and many of the trailer cantinas on the beach side of Avenida Atlântica also remain open throughout the year.

The **high season** for tourism in Rio coincides with those months when Cariocas themselves are on vacation or holiday. The summer school holiday extends from Christmas through February (and into early March for Carnival when Ash Wednesday falls late on the calendar). July is the month-long winter school holiday. And while November, December, and March are not holiday months in Brazil (except for Carnival week), the tourist business remains strong in Rio at those times as well. Rio's beach life is at its richest and most intense on a daily basis during this high season.

On **weekends,** regardless of the season, as long as the sun is shining in Rio's obliging climate, capacity crowds will flock to the beaches from all over the city, providing a rare common ground for the mingling of Brazil's two vastly separate economic realities. On crowded days, no matter what beach you go to or where you sit, at least three minor sporting events will be taking place in the vicinity of your towel or umbrella (supplied by your hotel, or rented from a beach vendor). The game might involve a dozen men—of all ages —playing pick-up soccer. Or it may be a hard-fought game of volleyball, one of the best-loved sports in Brazil. Almost certainly you will see the fast-paced *fréscobol*, where two friends use large wooden paddles to smash a rubber ball back and forth in the air. Despite the apparent chaos and the blanket-to-blanket crowds, a convivial atmosphere reigns, and only rarely do the energies of one activity spill over into those of its neighbors. When the ball (or player) rolls onto your blanket, just throw it (or him) back.

Stepping gingerly among the reclining bodies are the scores of **vendors** who will offer you food and drink, souvenirs or beach mats, sun hats, and sun screen. The vendors seem like characters from a kind of *Threepenny Opera* by the seashore, colorful in person, and admirable in the dogged pursuit of their peddler's trade. Sometimes the vendors sing or use noisemakers, less to entertain than to penetrate the somnambulant state of sunbathers they hope to attract as clients. Cries of *sorvete* (ice cream), *água de côco* (coconut water), *amendoins* (peanuts), and *cerveja bem gelada* (well-chilled beer) can be heard from one end of the strand to the other as long as the sun is shining.

All of Rio's beaches are public, and none contain bathhouses or changing rooms, much less reliable rest rooms. (When a bathroom is required, cross the avenue to the nearest restaurant; the better the restaurant, the better the rest room.) Rio by day is strictly a come-as-you-are town. In the beach neighborhoods, people parade around everywhere in **bathing suits** all day. Women often use sarongs to cover their swimsuits, but you're just as likely—and strikingly—to see men and women traveling about in just their bikinis. The *fio dental* worn by many women translates as "dental floss," a graphic metaphor for how this swimsuit fits behind.

Only the principal beaches have **lifeguards,** and none too many at that. There is also a very discreet police presence on those beaches, like Copacabana, most frequented by tourists—usually a pair of patrolling young officers dressed in mufti (tank top, shorts, and baseball cap) who only stand out when you suddenly realize that the objects hanging from their waists are revolvers. The cops are there primarily to intimidate the urchins. Many of the street children are said to be homeless, and they likewise patrol the beaches for targets of opportunity in their hit-and-run banditry. If they don't see a camera or wallet, they'll run off with your sneakers. There are also poor children on the sidewalks, hanging out at the outdoor cafés, usually selling peanuts or chewing gum. The best way to deal with them when they surround your table is to smile and buy something from one of them, or just make a small donation to their cause —survival.

The Best of the Beaches

I'll begin with **Flamengo,** first beach of the Zona Sul and closest to downtown Rio. You might check it out if you're at the Hotel Glória or the Novo Mundo. As a bay beach, swimming is not advised, but it's fine for sunbathing. The surroundings are pleasant, and you have all of Flamengo Park behind you to explore. The kids might like the tractor-pulled train that tours the park, and the large playground.

Botafogo beach is next along the shore, a tanning spot primarily for local residents of this still charming neighborhood, Rio's most fashionable throughout much of the 19th century, and today undergoing a revival.

Near the Pão de Açúcar cable car station is the football-field-length **Praia Vermelha,** a somewhat protected ocean beach said to be popular with swimmers. A morning here could be tied in with a stroll around Urca, the nearby vest-pocket neighborhood, and maybe a day trip up to Sugar Loaf for lunch or a drink.

Leme and **Copacabana** are the first real pearls in Rio's chain of beaches. Wide, sandy ocean beaches at their best, they are remarkably clean—considering the use they get—and the South Atlantic here always seems to provide a moderately frothy sea.

Arpoador, Ipanema, and **Leblon** form the next stretch of shoreline going down the coast. Brimming over with its variety of scenes, from teenyboppers to tourists, neighborhood residents still predominate along this strand, with each family or group occupying its own piece of the turf. Ipanema, in particular, is always an exciting beach, an endless swirl of activity, of which the bold preening of young beauties in the scantiest of bikinis lends more than a thread of legitimacy to "The Girl From Ipanema" ideal.

São Conrado (or **Pepino,** the beach's traditional name) can teem with activity on the weekends, yet be virtually deserted Monday through Friday. Close to the deluxe Inter-Continental resort-hotel, the beach is the official landing strip for hang-gliders who sweep down from the surrounding mountains. The Gávea golf course runs along much of São Conrado beach. Interested golfers who wish to play the course may make arrangements through their hotel, but for weekdays only.

After São Conrado, the suburban and more remote beaches begin with a great sand reef some 15 km (9 miles) long, known as **Barra da Tijuca.** Barra is definitely a weekend beach, one of the most frequented in the city. If you're looking for a condo along a beach that is serene enough during the week and wildly active on the weekends, Barra is the place. The beginning of Barra—the "PP"—is Rio's current "in" beach.

Recreio dos Bandeirantes (or just Recreio, as locals refer to the beach) is a community of summer and weekend houses, one of the last that remains in Rio proper, right on the ocean. Some blocks in Recreio are fully developed with villas occupying every lot and boasting large grounds with gardens and swimming pools. Other blocks may contain only a single dwelling or two. The many empty house lots are the flattened remains of white sandy dunes, alive with beach vegetation. There are also large empty expanses of this sandy scrub land still undeveloped, especially the land nearest the hilly parts of the neighborhood. In an hour's walk through these sandy fields, you can reap two dozen varieties of wildflowers, thistles, and exotic seed pods, the delicate products of an ocean-bounded ecosystem. A good deal of the land in Recreio is still occupied by the poor, whose colorful shantytowns manage to seem so appealing from the outside and, at the same time, so forbidding. One does not enter the favela world easily in Brazil.

Beyond the high rock formations at the end of Recreio beach is the small strip of sand known as **Prainha**—Little Beach. You have to drive over those rocks to get to Prainha, a beachhead for the middle class against the tide of the masses they fear is about to sweep over them from the city's remote and crowded slums. The last beach, **Grumari,** approaches the city line and is the most undeveloped stretch of ocean beach that Rio still possesses. From here, you can move on to explore the southern shores of the state, along the lovely **Costa Verde** (the Green Coast), which is described in Chapter X.

PARQUE NACIONAL DA TIJUCA

The Tijuca National Park must be one of the largest—if not *the* largest—inner-city parks in the world. The park is an immense forest growing on the slopes of the **Serra da Carioca** (Sierra Carioca) a chain of mountains that cuts across the center of metropolitan Rio, dividing the Zona Norte from the Zona Sul. Stretching at one end from the Mirante Dona Marta, which overlooks the neighborhoods of Laranjeiras and Botafogo, to the Alto da Boa Vista and the Floresta da Tijuca at the other extreme, the park is a voluminous natural preserve of vegetation typical of the Atlantic forests which once lined the eastern coast of Brazil. Most (but not all) of the vegetation is second growth. The park lands were once occupied by the agrarian estates of early aristocrats and planters. These same slopes, over a hundred years ago, were mostly cleared and covered with plantation crops of coffee and sugar cane.

The park is etched with several major arteries, many smaller roads, and numerous paths and trails. A pleasant half-day, or even an all-day, excursion can be made in the park. A typical itinerary might be a long orientation drive, lunch at one of the two respected and well-isolated restaurants, and at least one stop to cool off in the cascades of water that fall from the rocky walls at various locales along the sides of the roads. Make sure you bring suitable dress and a towel so you can take the waters.

There are entrances to the park at the most extreme points throughout the city. So when you're traveling from one neighborhood to another, you can trade the urban backdrop for a tranquil green space by routing your drive through the park, if you don't mind taking the extra time. From downtown, for example, you would drive through Santa Teresa and then continue up the mountain chain into the park via Cosme Velho and Corcovado. From there, you could drive the whole length and breadth of the park and emerge through the gate in Jardim Botânico, on the far shore of the Lagoa district. On this drive you would pass two of the park's most famous overlooks. The first is the **Vista Chinesa,** with its Chinese Pavillion, a touching memorial to immigrants from China of the last century who were settled in the vicinity on what were at that time tea plantations. Up the road, the **Mesa do Imperador** (the Emperor's Table) was once a favored picnic spot for the family and court of Dom Pedro I. From both heights, you will have an unparalleled view of the city's southern sectors. The park is so vast that there are even entrances to it from as far away as São Conrado and Barra da Tijuca.

From Copacabana or Ipanema, the most direct route to the **Floresta da Tijuca** (Tijuca Forest), a separate entity within the National Park with many points of interest, is to enter the park in São Conrado and follow signs to the **Alto da Boa Vista,** where there is a formal common, the Praça Afonso Vizéu and an English tavern called the Robin Hood. The entrance gate to the Floresta is off this plaza. Heading straight on, you pass the **Cascatinha de Taunay,** a small waterfall named for the baron whose estate once occupied these lands. Farther on is the tiny **Capela Mayrink,** a delightful sample of an old rural chapel in pastel-pink and white with a reproduction of the original altar panels painted by Brazilian modernist, Cândido Portinari (the originals are now housed in the city's Modern Art Museum). The chapel is popular for society weddings, but has been closed to the public of late.

Past the chapel, the road parts and forms a series of loops through the remainder of the grounds. The two park restaurants are to be found beyond this point. If you fancy international food like curried shrimp or chicken Maryland, turn off to the left for **Os Esquilos** (the Squirrels; tel. 258-0237), open for lunch only, from 11 a.m. to 7 p.m. daily except Monday. To the right is a more rustic Brazilian restaurant called **A Floresta** (tel. 258-7802), where hummingbirds flit among the rafters, open from noon to 8 p.m. Both restaurants are favorite luncheon spots for locals when they want a respite from the swelter and motion of the city. Beyond the A Floresta restaurant, the road continues to **Bom Retiro,** where a trail leads to the **Pico da Tijuca** (Tijuca Peak), at an altitude of over 3,000 feet.

HISTORIC RIO

Rio has no "old town" per se. Yet there are numerous monuments to its past scattered throughout the downtown section and surrounding neighborhoods. Several of the city's most venerable architectural relics date, in whole or part, from the early 17th century. Of prime historical importance are several churches and monasteries, a few palaces and government buildings, the city's oldest parks and public squares, and one or two blocks of buildings where the architectural integrity of a particular era is more or less preserved intact. What follows are several itineraries for walking tours that can be accomplished in only a few short hours, yet provide you with a genuine opportunity to glimpse something of Rio's bygone eras, as well as fascinating aspects of the city today.

Since most sites of historical interest in Rio are located downtown, it would be wise to get some picture in your mind of how the center city is laid out. The two major boulevards are named **Avenida Rio Branco** (running north-south) and **Avenida Presidente Vargas** (which runs east-west). These two grand *avenidas* are products of 20th-century urban renewal. First came Avenida Rio Branco (originally Avenida Central), which was conceived and executed in order to embellish the city with a fin-de-siècle elegance typical of large European capitals of that day—and to avoid being outshined by the beautification of its major urban rival in South America, Buenos Aires. Before the city's southern and westward expansion into Copacabana and Ipanema, which at the time were outlying fishing communities, the Avenida Rio Branco functioned as the city's Champs-Élysées; along this wide, tree-lined boulevard were arrayed the city's most fashionable cafés and shops.

It was also along Rio Branco that the great samba schools first paraded at Carnival time. The second of the city's major internal thoroughfares, the Avenida Presidente Vargas, wasn't built until the 1940s, but it, too, was to transform the face of the city.

Many of the city's older buildings and narrow streets were demolished when these two space-devouring arteries were constructed. Whole neighborhoods were destroyed, among them the city's oldest slums, emptying downtown Rio of its former residential populations. The two wide avenues intersect dramatically at a point that at one time was the virtual epicenter of the original colonial settlement. It is therefore in the vicinity of this intersection that most of the buildings, streets, and plazas of historical interest can still be found—those narrow lanes and cobblestone squares that, through good fortune as much as good planning, were spared from the wheel of progress.

How to Get Downtown

Getting to the Centro from the Zona Sul is relatively easy. Take a cab by all means, if that is your preference. The frescão air-conditioned buses or the public buses heading for *Castelo* can take you directly to the Menezes Cortes terminal on Rua São José very close to where this tour begins. But remember, Rio also has a modern and safe subway system that runs from Botafogo with many downtown stops. You can reach the Botafogo subway station from the beach neighborhoods of the Zona Sul by either cab or bus. Regardless of your mode of transportation, the best place to begin your tour in earnest is probably Praça XV, a historic square near the oldest section of the waterfront.

A Prelude

For the purposes of this tour, however, I will assume you are riding the subway. Get off at the **Cinelândia** stop. Cinelândia means movieland, and there are several fine old movie palaces in this area. Foreign films, by the way, tend to not be dubbed, but play in their language of origin, with subtitles in Portuguese. This is also the neighborhood for downtown singles bars, both gay and straight.

When you alight from the train, follow the exit signs to the Rua Santa Luzia and head in the direction of the waterfront. At the end of this street at no. 490 is the **Igreja Santa Luzia** (tel. 220-4367). This gem of the baroque era, built in 1752, was freshly painted recently in striking stucco blue, and there is no better example of that golden age in the city than this delightful little church. Patrons of Saint Lucia celebrate her December 13th feast day by washing their eyes in the church's holy water, believed to possess miraculous properties.

A Landmark Restaurant

If you were thinking of lunch at the **Alba Mar,** the seafood restaurant occupying the old octagonal market depot on the wharf, you would cross the wide Avenida Presidente Antônio Carlos at this point and walk toward the water. On the way, you will pass the **Museu Histórico Nacional,** Praça Marechal Âncora (tel. 220-

2628), open Tuesday through Friday from 10 a.m. to 5:30 p.m. and on weekends and holidays from 2:30 p.m. to 5:30 p.m. This is the National History Museum, which is housed in a squat fortress-like building, sections of which date from 1603, although most of the imposing structure dates from the late 1700s. The museum's collection of paintings, furnishings, maps, and artifacts guides the history buff from Brazil's discovery in 1500 to the creation of its first republic. The building also contains the Military Museum.

The Tour

Continue on in a northerly direction from here, winding your way through the labyrinth of heavily trafficked streets until arriving at **Praça XV**—probably the best point of departure for this tour if you have arrived downtown by cab. The orientation from this distinguished landmark is relatively easy and, with the aid of a reasonable map, you can strike off in the direction of any of the sights mentioned in this description. Another good reason to begin at the Praça XV is that the square is a total environment from the past, with several colonial buildings that are open for inspection.

Praça XV is Rio's oldest square. From here the governing viceroys administered all of Brazil, and their official residence, constructed in 1743, was converted into the Royal Palace when Dom João and his family made Rio the seat of their empire in 1808. Originally called the Praça do Paço (Plaza of the Court), the name was changed following the Proclamation of the Republic, on November 15, 1889. Here also in the preceeding year, Princesa Isabel, eldest of Dom Pedro II's children, signed the document that abolished slavery in Brazil, the principal event leading to the downfall of the monarchy. The buildings today are used as exhibition and concert halls, and include a permanent photo display of both visual and historical interest.

Among the antiquities to be seen in the immediate vicinity of the Praça XV are two churches across the busy **Rua 1 de Marco.** The old cathedral **Nossa Senhora do Carmo da Antiga Sé** (1752), was used first by Carmelite monks, and its subsequently became the Royal chapel after the arrival of the Portuguese monarch, and finally the cathedral of the city. In this latter role, the church was recently replaced by the ultramodern Nova Catedral (New Cathedral), near the Largo da Carioca. The 1822 coronation of Dom Pedro I (Dom João's son) as Brazil's first emperor took place in the old cathedral, which contains a golden rose given to Princesa Isabel by Pope Leo XIII. Next door is the quaint **Convento do Carmo,** connected to its own chapel by Rio's only remaining public oratory under the tiled roof of an arch hewed from stone. The altar and much of the carving, including the portals, are the work of the important 18th-century Brazilian sculptor Mestre Valentim da Fonseca e Silva, the illegitimate son of a Portuguese nobleman and a slave from his household.

Recrossing the Rua 1 de Marco, opposite the north side of the square, enter the lane called the **Travessa do Comércio.** The arch above your head, the **Arco do Telles,** also dates from the 1700s. The narrow colonial street is all charm from the wavy cobblestone pavement to the flat-fronted houses with their wrought-iron balconies and large wooden doors. This route takes you right by the door of a popular *pé sujo* (greasy spoon), the Arco Telles, located at no. 2. Check out the chalkboard menu as you stroll by. This may be the restaurant surprise you've been looking for.

From here you can explore the surrounding cross streets, like the **Rua do Ouvidor,** which has a degree of lore associated with it. It is a street that has appeared often in Brazilian literature. *Ouvidores* were petty colonial officials, like magistrates, who worked for the crown and, as such, bedeviled the people of that era with their authority and their corruption. Today this old lane is Rio's major banking street. Going in the direction of the bay you will come to no. 35, the diminutive **Igreja Nossa Senhora da Lapa dos Mercadores** (The Merchants' Church of Our Lady of Lapa), built in 1750 and well worth a peek.

For blocks around on both sides of Avenida Rio Branco, which the Rua do Ouvidor crosses, there are shop-filled streets that are tempting whether you're in the mood to browse the merchandise or just want a distracting walk and some inner-city atmosphere. At some point, though, turn onto nearby Rua Quitanda and walk until you reach Avenida Presidente Vargas where you will see the **Igreja Nossa Senhora de Candelária,** a treasure that was earmarked for demolition in the avenue's initial construction plans. Fortunately a sober judgement saved the church, which remains on an island plaza of its own in the center of the avenue. Donations from sailors built this church, begun in 1775, to commemorate a terrible shipwreck, scenes from which are vividly depicted by panels on the church's dome. Outside, behind Candelária, the Avenida Vargas stretches beyond view in the direction of São Cristóvão and the Zona Norte. This was also the starting point for the Carnival parades that took place after the construction of the enormous avenue, until 1984, when an official parade grounds, the sambódromo, was inaugurated on the other side of town.

Two other sites of historic interest are located on this end of Avenida Rio Branco, the **Praça Mauá,** an old dockside square that has seen its share of history, and an early monastery, the **Mosteiro do São Bento.** Return to the intersection of Rio Branco with Presidente Vargas and, before turning toward the bay, look down the length of Avenida Rio Branco for a long view of the imposingly winged War Memorial in the distance. Then, walk to the Praça Mauá for a quick inspection of the still-active pier, and return along Rio Branco to Rua Dom Geraldo at the opposite end of which is the São Bento Monastery. The monastery complex is an unadulterated example of early-17th-century church and convent architecture, dating from the mid-1600s and built on the side of a *ladeira,* a steep incline overlooking the bay. To enter the monastery, take the elevator at no. 40—and you must be appropriately dressed (no shorts or halters). Enjoy a moment of quiet meditation on the lovely grounds and visit, above all, the rococo chapel with the gold-leaf interior. Look also for the 17th-century paintings of Friar Ricardo do Pilar, including *O Salvador (The Savior),* which hangs in the sacristy.

The Largo da Carioca

The next point of interest is Carioca Square, a crossroad for street life in the city, and about a 15 minute walk from Praça XV. There is a Metro stop right on the square called Carioca. The first thing you'll probably want to do when you get here is to check out the vendors and the entertainers who fill the square and line the neighboring blocks.

On a low rise overlooking the *largo* (square) is the **Convento do Santo Antônio** and its church, built between 1608 and 1615 and notable for the decorative use of *azulejos,* those Portuguese tiles that are hand-painted using only the color blue against a white ceramic background. Directly next door is the **Igreja São Francisco da Penitência,** on the corner of Rua Uruguaiana, a street noted for its bargain shopping. The church, built in 1773, is of the late baroque period, with an elaborately carved wooden altar and ceiling murals by José de Oliveira that are worth pondering.

Heading east toward the Avenida Rio Branco, only a block away from the Largo da Carioca, you will immediately see the **Teatro Municipal,** a small-scale replica of the Paris Opera, set back slightly on a square called the Praça Floriano. This is Rio's temple of high culture, which has hosted the Brazilian arts as well as many international performers since opening in 1909. The season begins in February and runs through December, after which the Theater remains closed for repairs during January. Programs include ballet, symphonic concerts, and opera, as well as other major theatrical productions, including a yearly performance of *The Nutcracker* during the Christmas holidays. Check the box office while you're here to see if there's something going on that you'd like to see. And also check out the **Café do Teatro** (described more fully in Chapter V), if only to ogle the movie-epic décor.

Practically across from the Teatro, at Avenida Rio Branco 199 is the **Museu Nacional de Belas Artes,** the Museum of Fine Arts (tel. 240-0160), Rio's most important art museum. The collection of Brazilian paintings in the second-floor gallery provides a comprehensive visual account of the country's artistic development, and of its social and cultural history as well. Of special interest is the painting *Café* by the Brazilian modernist, Cândido Portinari. The museum is open Tuesday and Thursday from 10 a.m. to 6:30 p.m., on Monday and Wednesday from noon to 6:30 p.m., and on Saturday, Sunday, and holidays from 3 to 6 p.m. There is a nominal admission charge.

Around the corner from the Fine Arts Museum at 80 Rua Araujo Porto Alegre is the headquarters building of Brazil's National Art Foundation, FUNARTE, with a small concert hall called the **Sala Sidney Miller,** where performances of Brazilian regional music are staged regularly immediately following the end of the workday. Tickets for these recitals cost approximately $1, and you may check the entertainment section of the daily newspaper for an up-to-date listing of musical programs and performance schedules.

On to Lapa

Continue down Avenida Rio Branco—you're going toward the War Memorial now—until coming to Rua do Passeio. Turn to the right here toward the neighborhood of Lapa. On your left you will pass the **Passeio Público,** Rio's oldest park, which once bordered the water's edge before landfill pushed back the bay. The park is a bit of a no-man's-land these days, in need of repairs and some regular tending, but its basic appearance is still quite captivating since the original layout and landscaping dates from 1775 when public gardens reflected a very different view of nature than they do today.

When you reach the **Largo da Lapa,** look for the **Sala Cecilia Meirelles,** a concert hall, at no. 47. This is a favorite venue in Rio for classical orchestral and chamber concerts and for modern popular music as well. A little farther along, on Avenida Mem de Sa 15, is the **Asa Branca** gafieira, a musical hall of a different type which is described more fully in Chapter VII. The Asa Branca building is one of many in the neighborhood dating from the middle of the last century that have had their exteriors lovingly restored. Lapa was once a bohemian quarter and the hub of Rio's cabaret life. Something of that era seems to linger in the air, making Lapa a delightful place for an unstructured stroll.

If your consumer curiosity is piqued, drop in at the Mesbla department store—Brazil's largest chain—and look around. Make sure you check out the store's rooftop restaurant.

From the Largo da Lapa, walk up the Avenida República do Paraguai and cross under the aqueduct, officially the **Aqueducto da Carioca,** but known simply as **os arcos** (the arches). To remedy the shortage of fresh water within the city proper, the aqueduct was begun in 1724, linking the springs of hilly Santa Teresa with a public fountain in what is now the Largo da Carioca. Since 1896, when the first tracks were laid, the Lapa arches have shouldered a **trolley-car line,** the only one that still functions in Rio. Today passengers follow the ancient route of the water from the terminal on the Avenida República do Chile, near the Largo da Carioca, up through the winding streets of Santa Teresa.

The large conical dome that dominates the horizon beyond the arches is not a nuclear power plant, though use of this design in an urban setting seems grimly in pace with the times. What is strange, however, is that the city's **Nova Catedral** (New Cathedral) on Avenida Chile just above the Largo da Carioca should have assumed such a shape. The building is massive, its exterior segmented by four enormous stained-glass windows in solid primary colors. Inside, there is standing room for 20,000 persons. Personally, I would feel as if I were delivering my prayers through the funnel of a jet turbine to the great engineer in the sky. (We all have our biases, and when it comes to churches, mine is for the baroque of stone, timber, and plaster over the high tech.)

The Nova Catedral stands on flattened terrain that was once a hill, the Morro do Santo Antônio. In Rio, urban renewal and slum clearance has on several occasions taken the form of removing the entire hill occupied by a favela, or poor neighborhood, and using the earth for landfill somewhere else, usually a nice upper-class neighborhood. Thus did the hill of Santo Antônio become the *aterro* (landfill) of Flamengo Park, which was completed in 1960.

From the Largo da Carioca you can take the subway in either direction, depending on the next historical environment you wish to explore. Nowhere else in Rio, however, will you get as concentrated a sampling of historical sights and exhibitions as is available in the vicinity of the Largo da Carioca and the Praça XV. Many of the remaining museums and miscellaneous sights can best be visited individually or, in the case of the next itinerary, the Zona Norte, possibly linked to other excursions of interest. There is the **Feira Nordestinho** (an open-air market) every Sunday morning from 6 a.m. until 1 p.m. in São Cristovão, an old neighborhood of the Zona Norte close to downtown. Other attractions that could bring you to the area are a visit to an **escola de samba** (samba school) rehearsal, or a soccer game at **Maracanã** stadium.

The Zona Norte

There are several points of interest in and around São Cristovão. Take the subway to the São Cristovão stop, where you will be visiting the nearby **Quinta da Boa Vista,** a royal residence for all of Brazil's monarchs. The pink-and-white mansion was built in 1803 by a wealthy Portuguese colonial named Lopes and bestowed on Dom João VI and the royal family when they arrived in 1808. Dom João was the architect of Brazil's major cultural institutions, including the **Museu Nacional,** which is today housed in the former palace. The entrance hall contains the Bêndego meteorite, which was discovered in the state of Bahia in 1888, perhaps the world's largest at almost 12,000 pounds. Displayed throughout are all the elements of a natural history museum as they pertain to the Brazilian experience: birds, mammals, reptiles, insects, plants, minerals, prehistoric relics, and artifacts of the country's various indigenous cultures. There is a separate **Museu de Fauna,** a museum of Brazilian fauna, at the Quinta da Boa Vista as well. The National Museum (tel. 264-8262) is open Tuesday through Sunday from 10 a.m. to 4:45 p.m.

The grounds of the Quinta da Boa Vista (which means, incidentally, the country house with a nice view) are what you would expect from what was once a private royal park, including an elegantly geometric garden filled with sophisticated marble statuary. But the paths of the old estate are used for jogging these days, and swimmers crowd the lake, especially on weekends when the park is most in use.

The **Jardim Zoológico** (the Zoo) is also located on the grounds. Brazil has many bird and animal species that are not found in North America or even elsewhere on its own continent. Those who plan a trip from Rio to the Amazon region will have ample opportunity to view these creatures. If not, Rio's zoo is a very good place for an introduction to the country's unique birds and animals. There are capybaras and boas, jaguars and monkeys, tapirs and toucans, and much, much more. The zoo is open from 8 a.m. until 4:30 p.m. every day except Monday.

Although the **Igreja Nossa Senhora da Penha,** in Penha, is distant from downtown, true lovers of church architecture, as well as adventurous train buffs, might find the trip worthwhile. Our Lady of Penha sits high on a hill, where 365 steps cut from the rock ascend to the church door. Some penitents make the climb on their knees in a gesture of atonement or thanksgiving (a funicular transports those who cannot or do not wish to negotiate the steps). Inside the church are hung crutches and plastic facsimiles of body parts, the votive offerings of those who have been delivered by the intercession of Our Lady from their suffering. This particular form of devotion seems peculiar to the Roman Catholic church in the Portuguese-and Spanish-speaking countries.

If you don't go to Penha by cab or car, you could try the suburban train, the Leopoldina line. Pick up the train at the Barão de Mauá Station in São Cristovão, or take it all the way to the Penha neighborhood.

Between Downtown and the Zona Sul

If you head back toward the Zona Sul from your downtown tour, you can make a stop at the Glória subway station and visit the octagonal church called **Nossa Senhora da Glória do Outeiro** (Our Lady of Glória on the Knoll). This famous society church, built in 1714, is located behind the Hotel Glória on the Praça da Glória 135 (tel. 225-2869), and is open to the public Monday through Friday from 8 a.m. to noon and from 1 p.m. to 5 p.m. Emperor Pedro II was married in Our Lady of Glória, and his daughter, the crown princess Isabel, was baptized there. The Glória's interior also contains carvings by Rio's baroque artist Mestre Valentim, most notably the main altar. Access to the church's collection of sacred art can be arranged by contacting one of the priests. On August 15th, the church is ablaze with decorative lights in honor of the Feast of the Assumption, providing a striking sight against the darkened background of the surrounding mountains.

If you want to get a closer look at the War Memorial, the **Monumento dos Mortos da II Guerra,** this would be a good opportunity. Walk from the church to the Praça Paris, a park that was indeed laid out in Parisian style with formal hedges, fountain, and reflecting pools. Do not attempt to cross the Avenida Beira Mar—instead locate the nearest underpass or overpass. Please keep in mind that pedestrians are always in season from the point of view of any Carioca who is behind the wheel of a—usually speeding—automobile. There is a small museum next to the War Memorial that documents Brazil's role in the Italian campaign during World War II.

On the downtown side of the War Memorial, but still within Flamengo Park, is the **Museu de Arte Moderna** (the Modern Art Museum; tel. 210-2188), or MAM as it is known locally. The building and the grounds are of more interest than the collection, much of which was destroyed by a fire in 1978. The MAM is in the process of reacquisition of works, and is used primarily as a site for visiting exhibitions. It's open Tuesday through Sunday from noon to 6 p.m. Films are shown daily, and there is also a reliable restaurant on the premises.

Opposite the Catete subway stop at Rua do Catete 153 (entrance on Rua Silveira Martins) is the **Museu da República.** The Museum of the Republic is quartered within the Catete Palace, formerly the official residence of Brazil's presidents until the transfer of the country's capital to Brasília in 1960. Getúlio Vargas committed suicide here in 1954 while still in office, and the bedroom where his body was found has been preserved. The collection here begins where the National History Museum leaves off, with the founding of the Republic. There are exhibits of presidential memorabilia and furnishings. The grounds of the palace, planted with towering royal palms, and the impeccable garden are also open to the public—or will be when the restoration work that has been going on since 1984 is completed. Until then, there are two guided tours each month. To reserve a place, or to find out if full operations have been resumed, call either 225-4302 or 265-9747.

THE MUSEUMS OF FLAMENGO AND BOTAFOGO

On Avenida Rui Barbosa, across from no. 560 at the southern end of Flamengo Park, is the **Carmen Miranda Museum** (tel. 551-2597). The Portuguese-born chanteuse and one-time Las Vegas headliner helped put Brazil on the map for many Americans in the '30s and '40s with her Latin rhythms and outrageous hats of dangling fruit and full-skirted *baiana* costumes, many of which are on display in this small tidy collection. This is a definite nostalgia trip for those who once swayed to the verses of Carmen's trademark song "Tico, Tico No Fubar." Open Tuesday through Friday, 11 a.m. to 5 p.m., and on weekends and holidays from 1 p.m. to 5 p.m. The Flamengo station is the closest subway stop to this section of the park.

There are a number of smaller museums in Botafogo that are worth a visit for those inclined toward a deeper understanding of Brazilian culture and history. Near the Botafogo subway stop is the Rua São Clemente, where at no. 134 you will find the **Museu Casa de Rui Barbosa** (tel. 286-1297, extension 45) the house of the remarkable statesman and jurist that has been opened to the public since 1930. Author of Brazil's first constitution after the founding of the Republic, Rui Barbosa was also a lifelong abolitionist. In his zeal to obliterate the memory of that cruel institution, Barbosa ordered all official records and documents relating to slavery destroyed following emancipation. This act of narrow nationalism was strangely out of place for a man who read widely in seven languages and devoted his life to scholarship and the principles of international law. Barbosa's library of over 30,000 volumes, complete with marginalia penned in the language of the text, is open to the public, as are the many rooms of this rambling pink mansion. Open Tuesday through Friday from 10 a.m. to 4:30 p.m., and on weekends and holidays from 2 p.m. to 5 p.m.

The **Museu do Índio** (Indian Museum) is located off Rua São

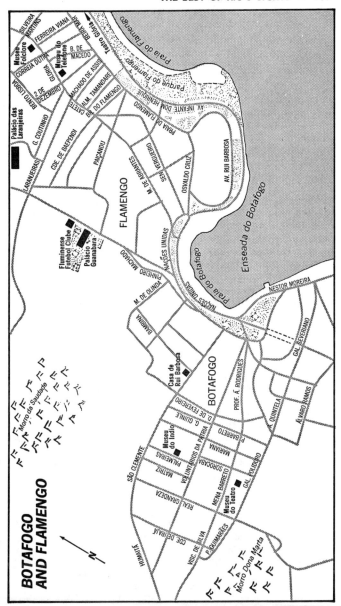

BOTAFOGO AND FLAMENGO

Clemente, some blocks farther into Botafogo, at Rua das Palmeiras 56 (tel. 286-2096). This exhibition of Indian artifacts is small but intelligently displayed. After an hour's study of the photographs and cultural objects, you will have a fairly good idea of the diversity of Brazil's tribes and the manner in which they once lived. Particularly beautiful are the items of dress and adornment that were expertly crafted from the raw material of nature—feathers, bones, shells, vines, and noble hardwoods—into headdresses, jewelry, and various practical utensils for eating or storing food. Tapes of native language and music are also available, and there is an inventory of films which document the contemporary lives and struggles of Brazil's remaining Indians. Open weekdays from 10 a.m. to 5 p.m.; closed weekends.

SANTA TERESA

If you want to get a representative taste of old Rio and you only have a limited amount of time available after visiting the obligatory sights of Corcovado and Pão de Açúcar, go to Santa Teresa. The hilly neighborhood, close to the center of town, was settled early in Rio's history, primarily by the well-to-do who sought the elevation as a refuge from the heat and noise below. The architectural integrity of the neighborhood is remarkable. Private homes—some extremely lavish—and small commercial buildings preserve a pre-20th-century scale throughout the district, and picturesque narrow streets wind dramatically among the rising slopes.

The main attractions in Santa Teresa, beyond the quarter itself —which merits a long drive, or better yet, a good old-fashioned constitutional—are a restaurant called the Bar do Arnaudo, and a museum, the Chácara do Céu, the former private residence of a wealthy industrialist that houses the art treasures of his rich and selective collection.

In the past, when one wanted to introduce a friend to the charms of Santa Teresa, there was no question that the way to get there was via the old **bonde,** the streetcar trolley that leaves from near the Largo da Carioca and rides above Lapa along the old aqueduct. But the bonde, especially where tourists are concerned, has been the object of considerable controversy in recent years. Gangs of young marauders have apparently found the trolley an easy target for their muggings, and the incidents are said to have occurred with alarming frequency in recent years. Because the trains were open on all sides, to allow for the constant boarding and disembarking while the train remained in motion, they were particularly vulnerable to these lightning assaults. Today, police ride shotgun to discourage the bold assailants, who have always operated in broad daylight. The trains, moreover, are always packed, and the citizens of Rio, in growing outrage at the street crime epidemic, have been increasingly coming to the aid of assault victims—a case where the remedy is at times uglier than the offense.

It is difficult to make a judgement as to whether a tourist ought or ought not ride the bonde, though I'm tempted to answer in the affirmative, if for no other reason than the train's bad reputation has made the authorities and passengers more alert, a condition that is not favorable to thievery. Nevertheless, tourists often stand out and, in the minds of the muggers, are likely to represent fairly risk-free targets. In conclusion, I personally believe that you can ride the bonde these days without great risk if you keep a low profile, leave your valuables in the hotel, and follow the lead of the thousands of passengers who ride the train daily without incident.

If you opt for the experience of the trolley ride, ask the driver to leave you off in the vicinity of the **Chácara do Céu Museum,** Rua Murtinho Nobre 93 (tel. 224-8981). The walk is somewhat circuitous and will lead you down one of the many stairways cut into the hillside, but the museum sits on a rise at the end of this dead-end street, and there are signs that indicate the way. By bus, take the no. 206 or 214 from the downtown bus terminal, Menezes Cortes to Rua Dias de Barras and follow the signs. The word *chácara* in Portuguese conveys the image of a gentleman farmer's country home, and *céu* means sky or heaven. This former home of the industrialist Raymundo de Casto Maia, however, has more of the Bauhaus about it than the barnyard. The home is very modern, and the grounds are landscaped and beautiful, but urban in their inspiration, not rural.

The modernist influence pervades the mansion in its design, its furnishings, and in its art, one of the best small collections of impressionist and modern paintings in the country. While of a later vintage, the collection here has a force similar to that of the Frick in New York City, but on a much reduced scale of grandeur. The studies of Don Quixote in colored pencil by Cândido Portinari occupy an entire room. The work of other greats, Brazilian and foreign, are distributed throughout the mansion. They include canvases by Di Cavilcanti, Monet, Degas, Matisse, Miró, Modigliani, and Picasso. The library is the warmest room in the house, which almost seems to have been conceived as a gallery rather than as part of a dwelling. A large ground-floor space is given over to some very whimsical exhibitions, as in 1987 when bathroom interiors of the past—complete with all the fixtures—were juxtaposed with those of the present. Prints, catalogs, and postcard reproductions of the collection are sold in the lobby. The museum is open Tuesday through Saturday from 2 p.m. to 5 p.m., and on Sunday from noon until 4:30 p.m. If you arrive by cab, make sure you have your driver wait, since it will be difficult to hail a cab in this vicinity for the return trip.

The **Bar do Arnaudo,** Rua Almirante Alexandrino 316 (tel. 252-7246), is the perfect place for refreshments or lunch before wandering over to the Chácara do Céu. The bar is located near the **Largo de Guimaraēs,** Santa Teresa's main square, also easily accessible by trolley or bus. Arnaudo's is a traditional rendezvous for artists whose works are often displayed on the walls. This is nonetheless a family-run restaurant, featuring the country-style food of the northeast where the owners grew up. The food is so good that it's hard to choose a single platter from the menu. Instead, ask Dona Georgina to serve you a little bit of everything in the large-portion appetizers. Open from noon until 10 p.m. daily except Monday and Tuesday.

JARDIM BOTÂNICO

A visit to the Botanical Garden must certainly rank high on the list of activities for nature lovers and birdwatchers. The gardens were the pet project of Dom João VI, who ordered the initial plantings soon after arriving from Portugal in 1808. This was the age that inspired the greatest naturalists who ever lived, including Baron

Von Humboldt and, subsequently, Darwin. Dom João was clearly caught up in the naturalist vision of his day, which combined mercantile practicality with a dreamy romanticism. The garden was created as both nursery for the adaptation of commercially desirable plants and as a great temple to nature, suitable for private walks and meditations. One has only to study the famous painting that depicts Humboldt and his native guides deep in the Amazon forest of the late 18th century to grasp the power of that melancholy vision. It was in this age that man discovered nature as the spiritual counterweight to the rise of materialism and the advances of science that everywhere accompanied the political and industrial revolutions raging in the midst of the old order. The naturalist, after all, was merely cataloging the very nature that mankind was now embarked on destroying, while the creator of parks and gardens went about the task of both enshrining nature in discreet patches and of cultivating the merchandizable plants that were culled from the naturalist's store.

The conscious motivation for Dom João VI no doubt had more to do with the challenges of growing spices and fruits introduced from the East Indies—nutmeg and cinnamon, breadfruit and avocado. From the West Indies came many species of palm trees that were not indigenous to Brazil. No one driving by the great wall of the Jardim Botânico in Rio can fail to be moved and impressed by the 100-foot-high royal palms that stand at the periphery of the garden like sentinels and line the elegant avenue leading in from the main entrance. Along with these, the garden is filled with thousands of equally archetypal trees and plants, its 340 acres divided between "natural" stands and more cultivated groves. The native plants are particularly fascinating, like the Régia Victória, a water lily native to the Amazon with a giant pad up to 20 feet in diameter, and the orchids, with their intoxicating aromas that saturate the air. As for birds, there have been some 140 sightings, including occasional flocks of toucans, a creature whose luminous cobalt-blue eyes must be the most beautiful of any species on the planet.

Getting to the garden by bus is relatively easy. It borders the Avenida Jardim Botânico, a principal thoroughfare from Gávea to Botafogo, where it becomes the Avenida São Clemente. Many bus lines travel this route, like those marked "via Jocqui" or "Jardim Botânico." The garden is open daily from 8 a.m. until 6 p.m., and there is a small admission charge.

GUANABARA BAY

For those who wish to be not just *in* the water, but also *on* it, there are several boat excursions available.

Paquetá has been a popular weekend and tourist destination for many years. No motor vehicles are allowed on the island, but you may hire a horse and carriage for about $5 an hour, or for $1 an hour there are bicycles for rent. Since Paquetá is quite small, these modes of transportation are completely adequate for getting around. The island has several beaches and hotels and is crowded on the weekends, but quiet during the week. Once a pristine fishing village, Paquetá has lost some of its allure since its heyday as a summer colony 30 years in the past. But it is an island in a beautiful bay, and accessible by inexpensive ferry service. The ferry leaves from a pier near the Praça XV downtown and costs 50¢ each way for the 1½-hour trip. Regularly scheduled ferries leave about every two to three hours Monday through Saturday between 5:30 a.m. and 11 p.m., and from 7 a.m. until 11 p.m. on Sunday. There is also a hydrofoil service that leaves every hour on the hour from 8 a.m. until 5 p.m. from the same dock, making the trip in a third of the time, and for only $1 each way during the week, $3 on weekends.

Boat Rental: A variety of crafts, from windsurfers to cabin cruisers may be rented through private agencies and owners. For more information, either visit or call the **Marina da Glória** (tel. 285-3749).

MARACANÃ

Maracanã is the name of Rio's legendary soccer stadium, built to hold as many as 200,000 spectators. Sports fans are the only ones likely to spend their time in Rio at a soccer match. But since soccer is Brazil's middle name, the true sports fanatic is very likely to be tempted by the opportunity to see the game played at its very best, in that free-wheeling, individual style that has made Brazilian players both feared and admired by their opponents throughout the world. The soccer season runs from March through July (though there are elimination rounds and international contests throughout the year) and the game of the week takes place on Sunday at 5 p.m.

The subway stops near Maracanã, and you can go there on your own for most games and be assured of getting a ticket. But given the size of both the stadium and the crowds, it is strongly suggested that you book a tour for this particular activity. The cost will be somewhat higher than if you did it on your own, but you'll be guaranteed the best and most comfortable seats in the covered section called *cadeira especial*, transportation to and from your hotel, and most important, a reliable escort who will help you negotiate the large crowds and the unfamiliar turf. Most tour companies provide game packages to Maracanã, which can usually be booked through your hotel.

Maracanã Stadium is also used to host super-concerts and other special events. Frank Sinatra has performed there, and the Pope once said Mass in Maracanã before a crowd of 180,000. In addition to its soccer field, Maracanã also has a total sports complex, with facilities for Brazil's other professional or Olympic sports, including swimming, volleyball, and basketball. The gymnasium, called the Maracanazinho (Little Maracanã), holds 20,000 people and also serves as a concert hall for top names in music from home and abroad.

GEMSTONE AND JEWELRY WORKSHOP TOUR

One of the great visual attractions in Brazil—beyond her natural grandeur and historic architectural patrimony—are the dozens of varieties of gemstones that are scooped from the country's mineral-rich earth. You don't have to fancy finished jewelry to appreciate the mystical attraction of the brilliant colored crystals, known as semiprecious stones for decades, but now—given their value and scarcity—referred to more appropriately as gemstones. In recognition of their general appeal, the H. Stern company has organized a tour of their lapidary workshops that allows you to witness craftspeople as they cut and polish the stones, design and construct their settings in gold and silver, and assemble the finished jewelry into rings, necklaces, and bracelets. The tour takes about 15 minutes and is conducted in one of seven different languages with the use of headphones. Don't forget to visit the small museum in the small building on completion of the tour to see some of the world's largest uncut gemstones and the fascinating displays of polished gems as well, particularly the dozens of tourmalines in their many varieties of shapes and colors.

The free tour takes place during business hours in the H. Stern Building, located in Ipanema at Rua Visconde de Pirajá 490. H. Stern will even provide you with round-trip transportation—by private car or taxi—between the workshop and your hotel. Just contact a representative at one of the company's many outlet stores in hotels throughout Copacabana or elsewhere in the city, and arrangements for the tour will be made in a prompt and obliging manner. Clearly the tour is a form of sophisticated promotion, and the company would naturally like to attract your business. After completing the tour, you will be invited to a jewelry showroom or to a large and well-stocked souvenir shop, but there is absolutely no pressure to buy. Anyone with the slightest curiosity about gemstones—where they come from, how they are mined, and how they are milled into priceless stones—will definitely find the H. Stern tour of great value.

---

2. The Best of the Rest

For those with even more time to get acquainted with Rio, the following museums and activities have much to offer.

OTHER MUSEUMS

Museu do Palácio do Itamarati (Itamarati Diplomatic Museum), Avenida Marechal Floriano 196, Centro (tel. 291-4411). Itamarati is the name still used when Brazilians refer to their Foreign Service, once housed in this palace when Rio was still the country's capital. Initially a private residence, the palace was built in 1854 and later served as official home for Brazil's presidents from 1889 to 1897. The museum's collection consists of tapestries, old furnishings, and other historical artifacts, some of which relate to the life of Brazil's most distinguished Foreign Minister, the Barão do Rio Branco, who was a major force in South American diplomacy during the 19th century. Open Tuesday through Friday from 11:30 a.m. until 4:30 p.m.

The **Museu da Cidade** (City Museum), Estrada de Santa Marinha, Parque da Cidade, Gávea (tel. 322-1328). Located on the grounds of what was formerly a private estate and is now a well-tended public park, the City Museum documents both the development of Rio and the central role the city has played in the history of Brazil. The displays are laid out chronologically by century, and there is a special room devoted to the evolution of Brazil's pharmaceutical industry, which relied heavily on herbal remedies that were known to the country's native peoples. The grounds themselves are nestled among the Gávea foothills and are popular for picnicking and hiking. The museum is open Tuesday through Sunday and holidays from noon to 4:30 p.m.

On the Morro da Urca, the halfway stop en route to the top of Pão de Açúcar, there is a special collection of wood carvings called the **Museu Antônio de Oliveira** (tel. 541-5241), open daily from 9 a.m. to 6 p.m. The hundreds of carvings form a diorama, automated in part, that depicts small-town life in Brazil and rural Carnival scenes.

The **Museu de Foclore Edson Carneiro** (Museum of Folklore), Rua do Catete 181, Catete (tel. 285-0891), is a separate collection of craft goods, musical instruments, and items from everyday life located at the Museum of the Republic. Open Tuesday to Friday from 11 a.m. to 6 p.m., and on weekends and holidays from 3 to 5 p.m. One of this museum's main attractions is the periodic concerts featuring Brazilian folk and regional music.

For an introduction to Brazilian classical, folk, and popular music, visit the **Museu da Imagem e do Som** (Sound and Image Museum), Praça Rui Barbosa 1 (tel. 262-0309, extension 181). The museum also houses a noncommercial movie theater, and numerous photographs and modern paintings. Open Monday through Friday from 2 to 6 p.m.

Near the Gávea Golf Club in São Conrado is the **Vila Riso,** Estrada da Gávea 728 (tel. 322-1444 or 322-0899), a restoration of a colonial era *fazenda* or farm. Staff don colonial garb and will take you on a 3½-hour tour, including lunch, for $20. The tour takes you through the old-fashioned gardens and presents a medley of Brazilian theatrical music dating from the 1860s to the World War I. Lunch is buffet style, and includes feijoada and churrasco. You must make a reservation to take this tour, which is offered on Tuesday only from 12:30 until 4 p.m., though there is talk of adding additional days during the high season if the demand warrants. Arrangements will also be made for pick-up and return to your hotel.

ACTION AND AMUSEMENTS

Rio has a small, but animated amusement park, the **Tívoli,** along the shores of the Lagoa, open on Thursday and Friday from 2 to 8 p.m., on Saturdays from 3 to 11 p.m., and on Sundays from 10 a.m. to 10 p.m.

Next door is the city's only open-air **drive-in theater,** and across the street is the **racetrack** called the Jockey Club. Fans of the ponies will enjoy the grandstand restaurant (tel. 297-6655 for reservations) along with the races, which take place every Monday and Thursday night and on Saturday and Sunday afternoon. Handicappers should check the sports pages of the *Jornal do Brasil.* The track only costs about 25¢ to enter, $1 for the enclosed grandstands (where no one dressed in shorts is admitted). Bets are taken for win (*vencedor*) and place (*place*) only.

Rio also has a **Planetarium,** Rua Padre Leonel Franca (tel. 274-0096), located in Gávea, for those who are interested in a formal presentation of the Rio starscape.

TAKING THE TOURS

Rio has many companies that package tours, small and grand, which may in general be booked directly through your hotel. Some typical tour packages are:

Corcovado and the Tijuca Forest, taking in all the major overlooks, including Corcovado, the principal attractions of the forest and the beaches of Barra, Leblon, and Ipanema.

Pão de Açúcar and City Tour, including the beaches of the Zona Sul, Sugar Loaf, and downtown sights like the Lapa aqueduct, the sambadrome, and Maracanã Stadium.

Rio by Night might include a big production show and a tour of several nightclubs and discos.

If you're looking for this type of guided tour, the first place to inquire is at the **porter's desk of your own hotel.** Many hotels actually provide their own buses and itineraries.

Tour Operators

Among local tour operators, **Blumar Turismo,** Rua Santa Clara 50, sala 1209, Copacabana, (tel. 255-6692), is a dynamic young company serving as ground contact for various U.S. travel agencies and wholesalers, and specializing in adventure packages, Brazilian musical and cultural circuits, resort destination services, sports-oriented tours (such as the Rio Marathon, for which they are the exclusive agents), and in the corporate sphere, technical and incentive group visits.

Other companies that are reliable and experienced are **South American Turismo,** Ltda., Avenida Nossa Senhora de Copacabana 788, sixth and seventh floors (tel. 255-2345); **Kontik-Franstur,** Avenida Atlântica 2316 A (tel. 255-2422); and **Gray Line,** Avenida Niemeyer 121, Suite 208 (tel. 274-7146).

For a more custom-tailored tour, contact **Expeditur,** Rua Visconde de Pirajá 414 (tel. 287-9697). Expeditur specializes in tours to the Amazon and Pantanal, but they also have a fleet of vans and tour guides in Rio who can give you a more personalized view of the city. "Projeto Roteiros Culturais" (Cultural Tour Project) offers high-brow tours of museums, colonial and imperial Rio, and the Botanical Garden, and can be contacted via their round-the-clock number (tel. 322-4872) or at their offices in Copacabana, Rua Santa Clara 110, Suite 904. Daytime tours are generally in the $20 range, and tours by night run twice that amount or more, since they tend to include a show with drinks, and sometimes dinner. **Brazil-Trek,** Rua Frei Pinto 59 (tel. 281-9646), escorts hikers on park trails and on more vigorous climbs up Rio's various well-known peaks, like the Pedra da Gávea and Pedra Bonita.

Cultural Rio

Since 1983, Professor Carlos Roquette has been conducting all-day walking tours, covering Rio's historical and cultural attractions. Professor Roquette, who speaks English and French in addition to his native Portuguese, helps bring interested visitors into contact with the details of Rio's architectural and artistic heritage. Tour bookings may be made by calling Professor Roquette's 24-hour telephone line: 322-4872. The cost of the tour is $20 per person, with a minimum of five participants.

Rio Like A Native

In all my travels throughout Brazil over the years, I never chose to participate in an organized group tour until I learned of **Brazil Nuts** (79 Sanford Street, Fairfield, CT 06430; tel. 800/553-9959, or 203/259-7900), whose staff personally escorts behind-the-scenes visits to Rio, that particularly cater to aficionados of contemporary Brazilian music.

THREE GOOD BOOKS

There is an excellent book of photographs of "Old Rio" available in most good book stores. The title is **O Rio Antigo do Fotógrafo Marc Ferrez** ($15) and contains over 200 photos of Rio taken between 1865 and 1918. **Rio,** with text by Vinícius de Morais and Ferreira Gular and photos by Bernard Hermann is available from Les Editions du Pacifique, in both English and French editions. Another book, significantly more esoteric, but wonderful for its illustrations, city plans, and photographs is **Evolucão Urbana do Rio de Janeiro** ($7) by Maurício de A. Abreu, about Rio's urban growth from colonial times to the present, available in Portuguese only.

VII

RIO'S NIGHTLIFE

1. LIVE MUSIC AND DANCING
2. BARS AND STAGE SHOWS

Do Cariocas ever sleep? This is a question you may find yourself asking after spending any time at all in Rio de Janeiro. Practically any night of the week, no matter where you are in the city, the restaurants are filled and the clubs and bars are jumping! *Movimento* the Brazilians call it—motion. Movimento plays as important a role in the daily life cycle of Cariocas as the *Praia* (the Beach). During the week, of course, there is not as much movimento as there is on the weekends, when favorite nightspots are filled to the rafters and pulsating with the *papo* (table talk) and steamy rhythms of whatever music happens to be occupying the same air space as the animated conversation.

And music is as inevitable an ingredient of Rio's nightlife as are sand and surf to the makeup of a beach. If there is no band around to make the music for them, Brazilians will make their own. Key chains, match boxes, the edge of a table—whatever. These are the instruments that Cariocas will employ for the spontaneous *batucadas* (rhythm jams) that break out from table to table wherever Cariocas gather to let down their hair.

And song. Brazilians love to sing—especially the great *samba* tunes of yesterday and today. They love to "join in," whether at clubs or concerts, the lack of inhibition being practically universal in this country of Carnival, where people of all backgrounds and states of life are bred from childhood to feel free about singing and dancing in public.

Things don't really begin to happen at night in Rio until after midnight. After work, people go home to *tomar banho e descansar* ("to take a shower and rest up") for the long night's festivities ahead. By around 10 p.m., the restaurants and clubs begin to slowly fill, and most of them then remain open until the last customer toasts the dawn for the final time. Sunday and Monday nights are the slowest, depending on the time of the year. Tuesday and Wednesday are so-so. By Thursday night, the clubs are jumping all over town. Friday and Saturday nights are outa-sight.

1. Live Music and Dancing

As if to tune you up for the night ahead, most deluxe and first-class hotels have small samba groups circulating in their restaurants and at poolside during lunch. During the cocktail hour in many hotel bars, there is usually a piano player who plays Brazilian and international standards, and takes requests.

Restaurants that also double as clubs feature cabaret-style shows with music and dance. And most nightclubs offer supper along with their full-blown stage productions.

Samba and jazz clubs take up the slack during the wee hours, and the main discos and dance halls also feature live bands, so you are always sure to find a place suitable to your particular brand of foot stomping.

Traditionally, many nightclubs in Rio admit couples only, though this is no longer a hard and fast rule. You should check at the porter's desk of your hotel as to whether a particular club allows singles to enter or not. All clubs with live music charge an "artistic cover," generally between $3 and $8, and sometimes a minimum as well. Nightclubs are more expensive, starting at $10 and climbing to $50 for organized tours, which include dinner and a drink or two.

The Lambada Craze

Not since the heyday of *bossa nova* in the mid '60s has a dance sensation been as hot in Brazil as the *lambada,* which is sweeping across not only that country but such world capitals as Paris and New York. The word *lambada* might best translate into English as "whiplash;" indeed this word provides a suitable indication of the *lambada's* signature motion. Performed at its best, the *lambada* is wild and sensual, requiring well-conditioned and well-practiced dancers. Most people can manage the *lambada's* basic sway and the syncopated side step, which could frequently be seen in dance halls of an earlier time, when Havana was the playground of the Caribbean. Since then the *lambada* has been simmering in the bistros of Brazil, influenced by scores of *merengue* and *bolero* records that became inexpensive when all things Cuban, including music, fell into official disfavor here after the rise of Fidel Castro. And while *lambada* is most popular throughout the Brazilian northeast, where many clubs are devoted exclusively to the dance, it is also popular in most of Rio's traditional dance halls, called *gafieiras.*

Samba

When Antônio Carlos Jobim and João Gilberto wrote the tune "So Danco Samba" ("I Just Dance Samba") they were expressing the almost-universal preference of their countryfolk for a music and dance form that is truly Brazilian. But the samba also owes much to the drum rhythms brought from Africa by the country's original slaves. This early drum music had a religious significance, used in the spiritist rituals that are known today as *candomblé, macumba,* and *unganda.* In these ceremonies, drum music drives the frenetic supplications pressed upon the gods to descend and take possession of the faithful whose worship takes the form of wild, trance-like dancing. As each devotee is "mounted" by his or her god, he or she whirls and swoons until falling to the ground in a state of blissful exhaustion. The samba is the secular and popular form of music and dance that has evolved from the chanting and gyrations of these religious practices.

Samba is also the centerpiece of Carnival. If you go to Rio during Carnival, you will experience samba in its most magnificent manifestations. If, however, your trip to Rio occurs during some other time of the year, you can still sample the samba culture in a more or less authentic form, depending on time, degree of interest, and individual taste.

The **Escolas de Samba** (samba school's) rehearsals are a nontouristy way to check out the samba scene. To date, only **Beija Flor** (tel. 791-1571) has scheduled rehearsals in the Zona Sul on Saturday at 9:30 p.m. in Lagoa, near the drive-in theater. The location of Beija Flor's outdoor rehearsals seems to shift from time to time, however, and it would be wise to verify the venue and schedule listed here with personnel at your hotel. But to get the real flavor of the samba schools, you must see them rehearse in their own spaces, all of which are located at various points in the Zona Norte. The most convenient from the Zona Sul are **Unidos de Vila Isabel,** Rua Maxwell 174, Vila Isabel (tel. 268-7052), every Saturday after 10 p.m.; **Mangueria,** in the Palácio do Samba, Rua Visconde de Niterói 1072, near Maracanã Stadium (tel. 234-4129), Friday through Sunday at 10 p.m.; and **Salguerio,** Silva Teles 104 in Tijuca (tel. 238-5564), on Saturday at 10 p.m. The rehearsal spots are relatively close to downtown.

Jazz

Jazz is alive and well, and living in Rio. Whether your preference is for bebop, modern, or Latin, you are likely to find a group playing somewhere in the city that suits your tastes, especially if you're willing to make the rounds of the various clubs. Check the entertainment section of the local newspapers under *Música para Ouvir* (listening music) for name-groups—Brazilian and international—that are making the scene.

Jazzmania, Rua Rainha Elizabeth 769, in Ipanema (tel. 287-0085), is considered the best pure jazz club in Rio. Located over the Barril 1800, a large beachfront café, Jazzmania always features some top talent from the Brazilian or international jazz milieu. Sacred to the memory of Jazzmania are the great artists who have played the club over the years, enshrined in the form of glossy black and white publicity photos that line the walls. Patrons frequent Jazzmania for the music and not the scene. You pay a small cover charge to get in, then saturate yourself with some of the most sophisticated modern jazz being played in the world today.

At **Chiko's Bar,** Avenida Epitácio Pessoa 1560, in Lagoa (tel. 287-3514), every night of the week there's a combo playing. Chiko's is one of the most popular bars in town for both couples and singles. You may not know the musicians' names, but the music is hot and professional. If you stick around until the early morning hours, you may witness a real old-fashioned jam session, as jazz musicians drift in from their gigs all over town and play at their best for their friends and themselves. You can also eat a full dinner at Chiko's or dine in the attached Castelo da Lagoa restaurant.

Canecão, Avenida Venceslau Braz 214, Botafogo (tel. 295-3044), opposite Rio Sul Shopping Mall, is really a concert hall that plays host to both pop entertainers and well-known jazz ensembles. Typical of the club's extravaganzas was a recent Tom Jobim concert, where superstar Milton Nacimento was coaxed from the audience and joined the dean of Bossa Nova in some impromptu duets. Canecão can seat over 2,000 people, and is also a supper club. Tables are arranged horseshoe fashion within this enormous amphitheater, with some cheaper theater-style seats in the upper reaches for those who don't wish to snack during the concert. The supper concession is run by the well-known cookbook author and restaurateur Maria Teresa Weiss, and it features Brazilian specialties including salgadinhos, the little pies that are the traditional fast food of Brazil. In addition to the featured act, a house band provides continuous music during breaks. Tickets vary in price, depending on the popularity of the headliners, and gallery seats without tables can usually be had for $5.

People Bar, Avenida Bartolomeu Mitre 370, in Leblon (tel. 294-0547), has a glitzy, new wave interior of black and gold wallpaper and mirrored table tops. People's clientele are chic and young, dressed to the nines, as if so many gorgeous mannequins from the nearby boutiques of Ipanema had suddenly come to life in a fantasy world of beautiful people. In stark contrast to a club like Jazzmania, the scene here is more significant than the music, which can be quite good, but tends to be drowned out in a sea of chatty narcissism. People's is "in" and not particularly large, so if you want to be assured of a table, you must arrive here at an hour that is uncharacteristically early for a Rio nightspot—10 p.m. at the latest—otherwise you will spend the evening on your feet, even when you are not dancing.

A slightly older crowd frequents another popular singles bar, **Biblo's,** Avenida Epitácio Pessoa 1484 (tel. 521-2645), one of several nightspots that overlook the Ipanema side of the Lagoa. Downstairs, a combo plays disco and Brazilian pop standards, and there is a small space for patrons who wish to dance. The upstairs at Biblo's is used more for intimate dining, to the accompaniment of a pianist or guitar player.

The bars at the Rio Palace, Meridien, and Sheraton hotels also feature live jazz on a regular basis.

Fado

The only club in Rio to showcase the traditional Portuguese fado is **A Desgarrada,** Rua Barão da Torre 667 (tel. 239-5746), in Ipanema. The menu here also features Portuguese cooking. Open Monday through Saturday from 8 p.m. on, with nightly shows beginning after 10:30 p.m.

Cheek-to-Cheek

As a dance hall, the **Asa Branca,** Rua Mem de Sá 15, in Lapa (tel. 252-4428), is a throwback to the Big Band era of the '30s and '40s. The club is housed in a lovely old commercial building in this once bohemian nightlife quarter where Rio's socialites mingled with the demimonde in the night. Inside the cavernous hall, long cloth-covered tables are set up bingo-style, facing the stage and contoured around a sizable dance floor. Beginning around 9 p.m., a house band begins to warm patrons into the right mood for the big show, usually some major Brazilian talent. The dancing is spirited and intense, as a Nat King Cole look-alike croons sweet ballads, or peppy jazz tunes. The Asa Branca offers an extensive supper menu, and ticket prices vary depending on the popularity of the main attraction.

Attached to the Sol e Mar restaurant is the **Bâteau Mouche Bar,** Avenida Repórter Néstor Moreira 111, in Botafogo (tel. 295-1997). This is a supper club for those who prefer the foxtrot over flash dancing. One advantage of this environment is the bayside location and the surrounding scenery of Botafago, custom-made for romance under the stars.

Two other popular traditional dance spots are worth a visit. The **Carinhoso,** Rua Visconde de Pirajá 22 (tel. 287-3579), on the Copacabana end of Ipanema, features a restaurant and two bands nightly. **Un, Deux, Trois,** Avenida Bartolomeu Mitre 123, in Leblon (tel. 239-0198), is divided into a downstairs restaurant and a supper club with orchestra upstairs. Separate reservations are required on the weekends if you want to dine and dance in the separate environments.

Discos

The downtown **Café Nice,** Avenida Rio Branco 277 (tel. 240-0490), by day an executive lunch room, becomes a swinging supper club and disco by night. It's not an "in" place on the tourist agenda, which is why Adam Carter of Brazil Nuts in Brooklyn, NY—who accompanies tours to Rio—likes to take his groups there. Café Nice is a very popular singles' spot for Brazilian men and women. The music is first rate, and the food and beverages are good and inexpensive.

Calígola, Praça General Osório, in Ipanema (tel. 287-7146), was Rio's No. 1 disco in 1987. Located on the bottom floor of the same building that houses the Le Streghe Italian restaurant, the dance floor at Calígola is designed like a pit in the Colosseum, and surrounded by columns and other period details to recall Imperial Rome. The Calígola is, as the Brazilians say, *superlotado* (filled to overflowing) on the weekends. You must have a confirmed reservation to get in. Ask someone at the porter's desk at your hotel to call ahead and provide you with a written verification of the reservation, a standard practice in Rio under such circumstances.

Help, Avenida Atlântica 3432, in Copacabana (tel. 521-1296), has the reputation of being a wild spot, for a mostly younger crowd and hungry single males who feast on the B-girls who hang out there. But the crowd is by no means homogeneous. Inside, giant screens project the reigning MTV rock videos of the day, and flashing lights bathe dancers on the large circular floor in semidarkness. The great advantage of Help for those staying at beachside hotels in Copacabana is the convenient location. The modest $4 entrance fee, which includes your first drink, is also not hard to take. Upstairs at the same location is another smaller disco called **Sobre as Ondas,** featuring the latest samba and Brazilian pop music.

Zoom, Praça São Conrado 20, in São Conrado (tel. 322-4179), is the newest disco popular with the younger set. Informal, but not quite as raunchy as Help, Zoom occupies the same building in São Conrado as the Pescador Restaurant.

Similar in spirit and clientele is a disco called **Circus,** Rua General Urquiza 102, in Leblon (tel. 274-7895), located above the Bella Blu Pizzaria.

The newest "in" spot is **Babilônia,** Avenida Afrânio de Melo Franco 296, Leblon (tel. 239-4448). Open Wednesday through Sunday from 10:30 p.m. till dawn. Dancing for the under-18 crowd on Sunday from 4 till 8 p.m..

While not actually a discothèque, another great place to hear live rock in Rio is a Copacabana bar called **Let It Be,** Rua Siqueira Campos 206. Decorated with posters of rock's greatest heroes and heroines, Let It Be is unabashedly on a '60s nostalgia trip. Local rock bands blast out the old standards, and taped originals pick up the slack during the breaks. A mere $1 cover fee gets you through the door.

Private Clubs

There are several discos, generally quite popular, which restrict entrance to members or to those who acquire temporary membership through their four- or five-star hotels.

Of all the private discos, the **Hippopótamus,** Rua Barão da Torre 354, in Ipanema, remains the hottest, catering primarily to Rio's high society and the international jet set. You can watch the rich at play for a price. Nonmembers pay $50 per couple to gain admittance to the Hippopótamus, assuming they can wrangle the necessary invite. Less exclusive are the **Palace Club,** in the Rio Palace hotel and **Rio Jazz Club** in the Hotel Meridien, both of which are open to their respective guests and in general to foreign tourists who seek admittance.

Gafieiras

Gafieiras are old-fashioned dance halls. The best are those that retain their links to the popular culture and attract a cross section of social and economic classes. Bands with plenty of brass play all the old standards, Brazilians and otherwise, and you wouldn't expect to see any of the musicians playing at society weddings.

Among the best are **Estudantina,** Praça Tiradentes 79, Centro (tel. 232-1149), open Thursday through Saturday; **Forró Forrado,** Rua do Catete 235, in Catete (tel. 245-0524), open Thursday through Sunday; **Elite Club,** Rua Frei Canaca 4, Centro (tel. 232-

3217), open Friday through Sunday nights. Gafieiras open generally around 10 p.m. and cost about $1 at the door.

---

2. Bars and Stage Shows

PIANO BARS

Almost all the major hotels, including the Inter-Continental, Caesar Park, Miramar, and Othon Palace have piano bars, where you can enjoy your drinks in an environment where music is confined— at least during the week—to the background.

VIDEO BARS

If drinking in a bar and screening tapes from MTV is your kick, you won't find a more agreeable environment than the brand-new American bar, **Neal's**, Avenida Barra da Tijuca 6250 (tel. 399-6577). Neal's is very popular on weekends, especially when temperatures are high and the humidity is sticky. The bar is airy, open to the elements along the walls, and just far enough out of town to induce a welcome sense of escape from the urban crowds. Neal's old location offers the same American fare, with videos, at Rua Sorocaba 695 in Botafogo (tel. 266-6577).

TOURIST SHOWS

It's hard to tell whether the following shows are actually popular with tourists or not. They are passed off as authentic portraits, in song and dance, of everything folkloric in Brazil, from Carnival to candomblé. And though these shows are created for and aggressively marketed to foreign tourists, the impresarios then turn around and claim: "This is what the tourists want." Needless to say, you will find few locals at these shows, other than those, of course, who are performing in them. Sadly, these shows are as close as most tourists get to Brazilian culture. They're not to my taste, but if you like big productions à la Vegas and Atlantic City, here they are—though, to be frank, they're not even that good.

At the **Scala I & II**, Avenida Afrânio de Mello Franco 292, in Leblon (tel. 239-4448), the show is like something left over from the heyday of Batista's Cuba: gaudy, tawdry, and slightly amateurish, but with none of the raunchy eroticism those pre-Castro spectacles were renowned for. There is a fair amount of topless nudity, usually confined to the *mulatas,* a Brazilian euphemism for black women. For $50 you get the show plus dinner and transportation. If you go at all, it is advisable to skip the meal and the tour and just go on your own to catch the show. The Scala II, on the other hand, is a showcase on occasion for top Brazilian and international talent.

The **Beija Flor** Carnival show at Pão de Açúcar every Monday night has already been described in the section on Rio's sights. Compared with Carnival or a genuine samba school rehearsal, however, the performance here has all the drama and authenticity of a TV game show.

The other big production shows are **Oba-Oba,** Rua Humanitá 110, in Botafogo (tel. 286-9848), and **Plataforma 1,** Rua Adalberto Ferreira 32, in Leblon (tel. 274-4022).

KARAOKÉ

This is a craze which spread throughout Brazil during the '80s and is now on the wane. The house provides taped instrumental background music from a repertoire of some 250 songs, and you provide the singing. If you don't know all the words, these will also be provided on printed forms. Karaoké clubs can be found in most of the country's major cities. In Rio, the clubs to try are **Canja,** Avenida Ataufo de Paiva 375, in Leblon (tel. 511-0484), **Limelight,** Rua Ministro Viveiros de Castro 93, in Copacabana (tel. 542-3596), and **Manga Rosa,** Rua 19 de Fevereiro 94, in Botafogo (tel. 266-4996).

CONCERTS, OPERA, AND BALLET

The **Teatro Municipal,** Praça do Floriano, Centro (tel. 210-2463), stages all three during its year-round season. Check newspapers for current programs.

Other venues for classical music are the **Sala Cecília Meirelles,** Largo da Lapa 47, Centro (tel. 232-9714), and the **Sala Nicolau Copérnico,** Rua Padre Leonel Franca 240, in Gávea (tel. 274-0096), in the Planetarium.

For dance, classical and modern, there is the **Teatro Vila Lobos,** Avenida Princesa Isabel 440, in Leme (tel. 275-6695).

GAY NIGHTLIFE

Much of gay male nightlife centers on the **Galeria Alaska,** Avenida Nossa Senhora de Copacabana 1241, where there are several bars and a drag (transvestite) theater. A section of the beach in Copacabana that is popular with gays fronts the Copacabana Palace Hotel, while in Ipanema the stretch of beach between Rua Farme de Amoedo and Rua Vinícius de Moraes is often frequented by gays. There are additional gay bars in the vicinity of Cinelândia, the downtown movie theater district.

RED LIGHT & EROTICA

Rio's most respectable red-light district is located in Copacabana off Avenida Atlântica, between Avenida Princesa Isabel and the Praça Lido. These blocks contain numerous pick-up bars, some of which, like the **Erótika,** Avenida Prado Júnior 63 (tel. 237-9370) and the **Don Juan Boite Show,** Rua Duvivier 37, have erotic stage shows. Single men sitting at night in cafés along this section of Avenida Atlântica will almost certainly be approached by streetwalkers, who may double as pickpockets—so beware.

VIII

CARNIVAL AND SPECIAL EVENTS

1. STREET CARNIVAL, BALLS, AND PARADES
2. RIO'S OTHER SPECIAL EVENTS

No other country in the world has a national holiday as elaborate or as all-consuming as Carnival in Brazil. Nor as long! For over a week, all normal activity grinds to a halt throughout the country, as Brazilians everywhere, from the tiniest backwater hamlets to the most sophisticated urban centers, fill the streets to reenact a pre-Lenten ritual that has been celebrated with a special zeal in Brazil for over a hundred years. And nowhere is the spectacle staged with more panache or grandeur than in Rio de Janeiro—so much so, that for many non-Brazilians, the city and the event are fused into a single, inseparable reality.

The official time span reserved for the revelry of Carnival is only four days, beginning on a Friday evening and running until noon of Ash Wednesday, which generally falls in mid to late February, and, rarely, in early March. In actuality, the organized festivities are spaced over at least a two-week period. And for those whose participation takes the form of a public performance—members of the neighborhood associations called **Escolas de Samba** (Samba Schools)—Carnival is virtually a year-long preoccupation. By August each *escola* has already settled on the theme it will enact through song and dance during the Carnival parades. By November, intense rehearsals are in full swing, and the associations' seamstresses are working overtime to create costumes, consistent with the chosen theme, for as many as 4,000 members. The theme songs also have to be written, and recordings are aired by Christmas so that the public already has the latest crop of sambas committed to memory by the time Carnival rolls around.

The parades are the yearly celebration's most formal element. And they are indeed spectaculars that even Hollywood might envy for sheer scale of conception and volume of participation. Each year the samba schools attract thousands of visitors to Rio, and their performances are beamed over TV to every corner of Brazil with all the hype and pomp Americans might associate with the annual Super Bowl.

But Carnival is not merely a commercial creation for the consumption of tourists and TV audiences. Carnival is a state of mind that infects the entire Brazilian culture. Or better, it is a state of collective mindlessness, because it's anything but cerebral. All Cariocas —excepting those killjoys who yearly flee the city to escape the madness—take to the streets by day and attend the mass parties by night. These affairs may be the ritzy, glitzy balls of the elite or the frenzied popular dances of the poor, held in tin-covered pavilions in the most wretched of favelas. No matter! The spirit of total release from the psychological prisons of daily existence—whatever the social class and status of a particular participant—is what unites all the citizenry in a momentary utopia of mass euphoria and abandon. For many, the letdown is swift and inevitable. As the song *"Manhã de Carnival"* (Carnival Morning) from *Black Orpheus* puts it, *"Tudo se acabar na secunda feira"* ("On Monday [following Ash Wednesday], everything comes to an end") and it's back to business as usual for another year. But then again, if one assumes the cyclical view, it really isn't the end, but the beginning. There's always next year's Carnival to look forward to in this endless human quest for release and redemption.

1. Street Carnival, Balls, and Parades

A strong argument can be made that the best part of Carnival is also its simplest, most accessible element—dancing through the streets in the company of perfect strangers. Life affords few opportunities to be linked with fellow humans who are not of one's acquaintance in such moments of uncensored good will. After this experience, the mundane evasions of daily life (the avoidance of eye contact in elevators, for example) will seem just that much more incomprehensible and absurd.

The streets of Copacabana, Leme, Ipanema, and Leblon—to name only those neighborhoods where most foreign visitors are likely to be lodged during Carnival—are a perpetual swirl of activity from early in the afternoon until dawn. Mornings, in contrast, are silent and calm, not only in these barrios, but throughout the rest of the city as well. Even during Carnival, people have to sleep sometime. After lunch, which may have to be in your hotel since many of your favorite restaurants will be closed, the pockets of revelers begin to form. On designated blocks, **bandas** (the traditional neighborhood bands) take up their positions as the evening draws near. Then the bands begin to play and march through the streets, attracting hundreds of revelers in their wake. Some people are dressed in *fantasias* (as costumes are called), others not. There are no dress codes. Many men are in drag; others play the fool. Women wear next to nothing and vamp as if their lives depended on the most erotic displays of seduction imaginable. Many people dress in beach wear or shorts—which are reasonable choices given the high temperatures and humidity of the Brazilian summer.

The basic dance step of the samba is not difficult. Essentially you jump up and down with your hands above your head to the driving rhythm of the percussion bands. As for the more complex steps, just watch and imitate. Who knows, you might be a natural. The one thing you can't do is stand around and watch shyly from the sidelines. The only human behavior—other than violence, of course—that is frowned upon during Carnival is timidity. And remember, you don't need a ticket to be a part of Carnival in the streets; this is one worthwhile experience in life that's completely free.

The most well-known bandas and their jumping-off points are as follows: The **Banda do Leme** on Rua Gustavo Sampaio behind the Meridien Hotel; the **Banda da Vergonha do Posto 6** (the Shameful Band from Post 6), near the Rio Palace Hotel; and the **Banda de Ipanema,** Praça General Osório, site of the weekly Hippie Fair. Practically every block in these neighborhoods has its own band, however, and there's nothing to prevent you from hopping from one to another for as long as your energy holds out.

THE BALLS

The traditional Carnival balls are to the upper and middle classes what street Carnival is to the *povo* (the people). The other distinctions are that the balls require tickets—from as little as $15 to as much as $100 per person—and their general atmosphere is even more lavish and erotic than anything taking place on the streets. Some participants at the balls wear costumes of extraordinary complexity and beauty, costumes whose costs can range into the thousands. Most participants, however, wear as little as possible. Nudity or near nudity is the order of the night. Ballrooms are swollen to capacity with revelers dancing back-to-back and belly-to-belly, and the music never stops until morning. These events are not for the prudish; you will get no fair hearing if your bottom is pinched. The major balls are as follows:

The **Hawaiian Ball** is the event that kicks off Carnival each year. The ball takes place on Friday night a week before Carnival at the *Iate Clube do Rio de Janeiro,* Rio's Yacht Club on Avenida Pasteur on Botafogo, where tickets may be purchased directly. The celebrants spend much of the evening outdoors dancing under the sky on the club's beautifully landscaped ground.

On Thursday night—a day before official Carnival begins—one of the city's most traditional balls, the **Vermelho e Preto** (the Red and Black) is hosted by Flamengo, Rio's most popular soccer club. While relatively cheap at about $30 a couple, the ball has a reputation for being among the raunchiest of them all.

The **Pão de Açúcar Ball,** perhaps Carnival's most fashionable, takes place on Friday night high above the city on Urca Hill. Tickets may be purchased for approximately $75 per person at the office of the event's organizers at Rua Vicconde de Pirajá 414, Room 909, in Ipanema (tel. 287-7749).

Other traditional balls, like the **Champagne Ball** and the **Gala**

Gay (one of several homosexually oriented events), are scheduled in Rio's major showcase houses, like the Scala in Leblon or the Help discothèque in Copacabana. Travel agencies specializing in booking the Carnival trade are the best sources for learning where these events will be scheduled in a given year. Most of the major hotels produce their own spectaculars for those who want to celebrate close to home, for instance, the Copacabana Palace's **Golden Room Ball** on Monday night.

THE PARADES

The **Passarela do Samba** is Carnival's main event. On Sunday and Monday nights, the year's 16 most prominent **Escolas de Samba**—the voluntary samba clubs that tend to be integrated into the very fabric of all Rio's blue-collar and favela neighborhoods— compete for first prize in the spectacular parades staged downtown in the **Sabódromo.** Tickets are required to view the parades in this special stadium that was inaugurated in 1984. And several grandstands are reserved exclusively for tourists, whose tickets are usually included in the packages they purchase at home before arriving in Rio. Otherwise tickets are sold at offices of the Bank of Rio de Janeiro **(BANERJ)** in locations throughout the city; the main branch is downtown at Avenida Nilo Pecanha 175 (tel. 224-0202). The best source of information on all Carnival activities is the event's major sponsor, **Riotour** (tel. 232-4320). As a last resort, tickets may be purchased from scalpers who buy them by the lots when they first go on sale, and later do a land-office business with the tourists. Needless to say, a scalper's ticket will cost you more than face value. But remember, you shouldn't accept their first offer; a good round of bargaining can be as satisfactory to a scalper as a high markup.

The parades are scheduled to begin on each of the two designated evenings at 7 p.m., but they rarely get off before 9 p.m. and can run until noon of the following day. The logistics involved in coordinating the productions are awe-inspiring. The schools can each involve the participation of 3,000 to 4,000 members organized into as many as 100 separate components.

Each school's performance conforms to an *enredo*—a theme which is generally political or patriotic—and tells a story as the dancers and musicians strut their stuff in the 45 minutes allotted per *escola*.

Each parade begins with the **abre-ala,** a float that is the sampler or title page of the whole ensemble, followed up by the **comissão de frente,** traditionally the school's directors and honchos who, rather than dance, execute a series of formal salutations to the audience. Many schools have departed from the traditional use of the commissão component in recent years, using it to showcase celebrities or even for laughs—as when one school put burros in its front line. Next comes the body of the school, with everyone in lavish fantasia, the costume that reflects its theme.

From here the school is divided into its various elements, the group's dancers who whirl and twirl in unison, including the **ala das baianas,** the women in the traditional costumes of Bahia; the flag bearer and dance master, a couple who execute a formal choreography; individual dancers and musicians whose steps will knock your socks off if anything does; and the **bateria,** the percussion band with the force of a locomotive, numbering as many as 300 musicians, that drives the whole machine. Each element in the parade is judged and given a score. The winner then appears for a curtain call at the victory parade scheduled for the Saturday after Ash Wednesday. This is Carnival's finale.

The Passarela do Samba is only one of the several official competitions. The less professional schools, called *blocos,* parade along Avenida Rio Branco practically all week long. Some blocos can number as many as 10,000 participants in a single, joyous spectacle of mass celebration. Other groups, like the *frevo* and *rancho* schools, reenact regional or historical versions of Carnival. These events are free and very crowded, so leave your valuables in the hotel.

The best way to reach downtown during Carnival—when traffic crawls, at best, at a snail's pace—is to take the Metro, which runs 24 hours a day during this period only. It's perfectly safe, and cheap, but don't forget to purchase round-trip tickets so you don't have to stand on line for the return.

2. Rio's Other Special Events

A number of other special events or activities take place in Rio throughout the year. Some of the more interesting from a visitor's point of view are these:

FESTA DE IEMANJÁ

The Feast of Iemanjá turns New Year's Eve into a genuine pagan celebration, a homage to the goddess of the sea whose worship was introduced to New World culture by its African inhabitants. The celebration takes place on virtually all of Rio's beaches, most notably in Copacabana and Ipanema. The white-garbed celebrants begin to arrive on the beaches during the day to mount their endless circles of candles and the altars of offerings—from flowers to cosmetics—that will be cast upon the waves at midnight in the hope that they will be acceptable in the sight of Iemanja, the mother of all. Whether as a participant or an observer, this unique celebration is a memorable experience.

FESTAS JUNINAS

June is the month that Catholic Brazil celebrates the feast days of its favorite saints, Anthony (June 13), John (June 24), and Peter (June 29). Parties are held primarily in private clubs and at home. The predominant theme is a recognition of Brazil's peasant culture and the rural experience in general. Children dress up in their versions of country costumes, and barbecues and bonfires are also typical elements of these celebrations. If you're in town during these times, you can try to have your hotel arrange an invitation for you at a private club. The low-keyed parties are typical of Brazilian home comfort and hospitality, and are a very pleasant way to get closer to the culture for anyone who cares to.

MACUMBA

Macumba is the name of the spiritist religion as it is practiced in Rio and its environs. In Bahia, you will hear the term candomblé. While in São Paulo, the term unganda is used. All of these practices are similar, if not entirely the same in all their rituals.

Many tour agencies in Rio include a macumba rite in their list of sightseeing activities. The tourist should be aware, however, that these events are not genuine. Anyone who has a genuine interest in witnessing or learning more about macumba should try to strike up an acquaintance with a true practitioner—and these are not lacking in the city—and try to tag along informally. Only in this way are you likely to get a look at the real thing, which is not only impressive as a religious ceremony, but allows you to hear some of the most inspired drum music you will ever hear in your life.

IX

A RIO SHOPPING SPREE

1. FAIRS AND MARKETS
2. THE FASHION SCENE
3. SOUVENIRS
4. THE SHOPPING CENTERS
5. GEMSTONES

Rio is a shopper's paradise. The very woes that contribute to Brazil's eternal battle for economic stability—runaway inflation not the least among them—have ensured a favorable shopping climate for tourists who arrive here with one of the world's hard currencies in their pockets. Even the much besieged American dollar still ranks in this privileged company when weighed against the more enfeebled currencies of the so-called developing countries. Simply stated, this means that no matter how weak the dollar is, the venerable greenback remains far stronger than the Brazilian cruzado and promises to retain this favored position for the foreseeable future.

One implication of this imbalance is that Brazilian goods, especially when purchased in Brazil, tend to be 30% to 50% less expensive than items of comparable quality procured in the U.S., Canada, or Europe. Since Rio is one of Brazil's great marketplaces —filled with shops and shopping malls, souvenir stores and street fairs—visitors to the Cidade Maravilhosa are presented with innumerable opportunities to exercise their consumer power. Rio, for example, is a major center (along with São Paulo) of the Brazilian garment industry. Most tourists may come to Rio for the sunshine and the lifestyle, but those visitors who are also serious shoppers are mindful of the great deals to be found in clothing, leather goods, and jewelry—the very goods that are perpetually desirable and most easily transported home.

Shopping in Rio need not be limited to a search for bargains in baubles, sportswear, and handbags at fashionable boutiques within a stone's throw of your hotel. Shopping expeditions can become urban adventures, carrying you widely through the city for a far more intimate view of day-to-day economic life among your Carioca hosts. And nowhere does the popular commercial pulse beat more dramatically than at the open-air markets and fairs that are regularly scheduled in a variety of neighborhoods throughout the city. But whether you approach shopping in Rio as an end in itself or as a means to explore the city somewhat off the beaten track, you are likely to find many more items that please your eye and tempt your purse than you can carry home when your vacation is over.

A NOTE ON U.S. CUSTOMS

Because of Brazil's status as a developing nation, many items that U.S. residents purchase there, including gemstones and jewelry, may be duty free. This policy is referred to by the abbreviation GSP, which stands for General System of Preferences. In a nutshell, personal items that you bring home from Brazil are exempt from duties, even if you exceed the normal $400 limit, if at least 35% of the labor and materials that went into their production originated in Brazil. Exempt items must still be listed on your formal declaration, but they will not be taxed. Major jewelers provide their clients with affidavits in the case of items that satisfy these criteria. Other qualifying purchases can be substantiated by receipts from the seller that indicate the product was *fabricado no Brasil* (made in Brazil). A free booklet entitled *GSP and the Traveler* can be obtained by writing the U.S. Customs Service, Washington, DC 20229.

DISCOUNTED CRUZIEROS

The best guarantee of making purchases in Rio at a substantial savings is the ready availability of "cheap money." The distinction between the "official" and "parallel" exchange rates is explained in Chapter II under "Currency." Given the importance of this issue, however, a word or two of repetition is in order.

Change all your money in Brazil on the "parallel" market whenever possible. Refer to Chapter II for how this is done. The difference between the semilegal black-market rate and the official rate is usually at least 50%, and can soar to 100% or more depending on the vagaries of the economy. Avoid changing money through hotels and banks, which are obliged to trade at the official rate only. Pay for all your purchases in cruzieros—"cheap cruzieros," that is—or in dollars (or traveler's checks) if you are offered a good rate of exchange. Traveler's checks will generally be worth slightly less than cash in the parallel money market. Credit cards will be computed at the new tourist rate of exchange which is slightly below the parallel rate. And if you have not already pre-paid your accommodations before arrival, you will find it particularly advantageous to use cash obtained on the parallel market when closing out your hotel account. The trick, however, is to change money only as needed.

Remember, the parallel market is perfectly legitimate; you will not be engaging in a shady act by trading in it. If you are contemplating a really big purchase—an investment in gemstones, for example—and don't care to burden yourself with large amounts of cash when traveling, many of the better shops will accept your personal check at a favorable rate of exchange.

SHOPPING HOURS

Shops in Brazil tend to be open Monday through Friday from 9 a.m. until 6 or 7 p.m., and on Saturday until 1 p.m. Shopping malls generally remain open until 10 p.m. Most, but not all, stores re closed on Sunday, which is a day for street fairs at several locations in the city.

---

1. Fairs and Markets

ARTS AND CRAFTS

The **Hippie Fair,** or Feirarte as it is also known, occupies every inch of the spacious Praça General Osório in Ipanema on Sunday all year round. At about 9 a.m. the artists and artisans begin to mount their booths and displays, which remain there throughout the day until sunset. Paintings and wood carvings occupy most of the plaza and, as is generally the case with open-air art markets, you have to search carefully for anything original among all the dross. There are many stalls of artisans selling costume jewelry, predominantly silver pieces, but also works in bone, hematite beads, and of course, gemstones, both loose and in settings. Leather goods are also much in evidence, primarily belts and handbags, as well as wallets, sandals, and portmanteaux. Check the stitching before making any leather purchases. Other items of interest are handmade toys and utensils, hammocks, and musical instruments, like the squeaky *cuícas* used in Carnival bands, though in this case more ornamental than practical. Most of the vendors know enough English to be able to bargain. Never accept the first price, unless you just can't imagine getting the object in question any cheaper. The great advantage of the Hippie Fair is its location near the beach in Ipanema, convenient for a walk-through when you need a break from the sun. The great disadvantage is that the event is unabashedly staged for tourists. Caveat emptor.

The **Feira do Nordeste** (Northeast Fair) is the other Sunday street market of major interest. Much less artsy than its counterpart in Ipanema, the Northeast Fair caters more to the everyday needs of working people and is also somewhat of a weekly popular festival. There are many stands offering prepared dishes typical of the diet consumed in Brazil's northeastern states. But be careful when you poke your nose among the produce and meat stalls. The sights are splendid and fascinating, but the odors can be overpowering. The sounds you will hear are also delightful and not just the normal cacophony of the marketplace, but the more measured twangs of the many groups and individuals playing regional music. While the Hippie Fair may be a more suitable place to buy souvenirs for friends and family, you should think of the Northeast Fair as a cultural event, and a very entertaining one at that. And you will no doubt find something to purchase in the hundreds and hundreds of booths that spread out in all directions.

The fair's one drawback is its location in the Campo de São

Cristóvão on the Zona Norte side of downtown, near the National Museum at the Quinta de Boa Vista. The most direct route is by cab through the Rebouças Tunnel, the same centrally located tunnel you will take to get to Corcovado. You can also get to the fair by subway, taking the Metro from Botafogo to the São Cristóvão stop. The Northeast Fair is open from 6 a.m. until 1 p.m., on Sunday only.

ANTIQUES MARKETS

A weekly antique market, **Feira de Antiguidades,** is set up outdoors on Saturdays from 9 a.m. to 5 p.m. downtown, near the Praça XV and the Alba Mar restaurant. Most items at this event are more typical of flea markets than antique fairs. Still, the word is that there are finds to be made for those who are patient and know what to look for. Among the more transportable items are stamps, coins, and antique weapons. Also downtown, the Passeio Publico **stamp and coin markets** take place on Sunday mornings. At the opposite end of the city, in Barra da Tijuca, a smaller antique fair and flea market has taken root in recent years every Sunday on the grounds of the Casa Shopping Mall from 10 a.m. to 6 p.m. The well-regarded **Rodeio Churrascaria** is also located within the Casa Shopping complex.

More serious antique buffs might want to take in an auction. There are several convenient **auction houses** in Ipanema and Copacabana, like the Investirarte located in the Cassino Atlântica mall, attached to the Rio Palace Hotel. Check the Saturday and Sunday editions of the local newspapers *O Globo* or *Journal do Brasil* under *"Leilão,"* the Portuguese word for auction.

STREET MARKETS

Open-air fruit and vegetable markets take place throughout Rio's neighborhoods on a rotating basis. They usually begin at dawn and are over around midday. For color, smell, and general kaleidoscopic crowd activity, nothing in the day-to-day world of the Cariocas surpasses these markets as public spectacles. Every minute you spend at one of these markets is an education, whether to study and taste the produce or to watch the hearty *favelados* as they dismantle the stalls and load them on the festively painted flat-bed trucks. The whole event has the energy of a circus coming to town. And when the tents have moved on, all that's left is the strong odor of spoiled produce embedded in the pavement that awaits the arrival of the sanitation trucks.

In **Copacabana,** there are open-air markets on Wednesday on Rua Domingos Ferreira, on Thursday between Rua Belford Roxo and Rua Ronald de Carvalho (close to Avenida Princesa Isabel), and on Sunday on Rua Décio Vilares (near the Praça Edmundo Bittencourt). **Leme** has its market on Monday on the Rua Gustavo Sampaio. The **Ipanema** street markets are on Monday on Henrique Dumont, on Tuesday at Praça General Osório, and on Friday at Praça da Paz. And the **Leblon** market is on Thursday on Rua General Urquiza.

FLOWER MARKET

The center of the flower market is downtown on the Praça Olavo Bilac, off Rua Gonçalves Dias, near the Uruguaia Metro stop. You may not wish to purchase cut flowers necessarily, but they're always beautiful to smell and look at. Most of the varieties are familiar, but there are always a few surprises. For fancy floral arrangements or corsages, there is a flower shop at the Copacabana Palace Hotel on Copacabana beach.

Generally, it is forbidden to enter the U.S. with botanical or agricultural products from abroad. But there is at least one plant that U.S. Customs allows, the **pau d'água**. At some point during your stay in Brazil you are bound to see someone at a flower stall or on the street selling what looks like the segmented and leafless limb of a tree. These are *pau d'águas,* or water sticks. You take it home, stick it in water, and it sprouts into the most amazing tropical plant —the waxy, palm-like fronds grow right out of the stalk in great profusion.

---

2. The Fashion Scene

Many travelers to Rio, particularly women, find the city's clothing fashions much to their tastes and very pleasantly affordable when compared with prices at home. The principal street for fashions is Ipanema's **Rua Visconde de Pirajá,** which is lined with boutiques from one end to the other. Many fine shops are also located on the side streets of both Ipanema and Leblon. The main items of interest are formal and sports apparel, shoes and sandals, and swimwear. The favorite fabrics for dresses and outfits— generally in the $30 to $100 range—are cotton, linen, jersey, and silk. Acrylic knit dresses, ideal for traveling, are also quite popular. Tops, skirts, and pants made of smooth and often multitoned leather, are more expensive. Well-made sandals and pumps of many styles cost between $10 and $20, while highly styled dress shoes in soft, sculptured leather are between $50 and $75.

For Italian-style knits and women's clothing, try **Mariazinha,** Rua Visconde de Pirajá 365A, next to the **Forum,** a gallery of several shops, including **La Bagagerie, Elle et Lui** for both sexes, and **Soft Shoes** for footwear. **Tokyo Rose,** in the same complex, specializes in the briefest of bikinis.

Polo Ralph Lauren, Rua Visconde de Pirajá 401A (tel. 267-2741), specializes in sportswear for men and women. Shirts and shorts for men are priced in the $35 to $40 range, and women's skirts and blouses begin at $45 and $63, respectively. Open Monday through Friday from 9:30 a.m. till 8 p.m.; Saturdays until 2 pm. Directly across the street, a large building complex called the **Quartier Ipanema,** Rua Visconde de Pirajá 414, houses dozens of shops and boutiques catering to every need and price range. At midscale in men's shoe prices, there is **Mr. Cat** (tel. 267-5645). The store's most expensive item, wing tips with leather soles and heels, is priced at $60; a variety of other less expensive styles, including the

Brazilian version of the "topsider," are also available. All shoes are packaged in an attractive flannel sack. Mr. Cat's six branches in Rio mostly are located in the shopping centers. Open 9 a.m. till 8 p.m. Monday through Friday, until 3 p.m. on Saturdays.

Workout, at no. 414, has decorator sweat suits, and **Red Green,** at no. 422, offers a wide selection of reasonably priced women's sports apparel. **Bee,** at no. 483, specializes in informal children's wear and T-shirts for the whole f a.m.ily.

Muni's, Rua Visconde de Pirajá 430A (tel. 287-8299), is a popular footwear chain with 13 branches throughout the city and a good place for inexpensive sandals and beach shoes.

The **Galeria 444** (between Rua Maria Quitéria and Rua Garcia D'Ávila) is an arcade of shops and galleries including **Bum Bum** for bikinis and beachwear, and **Benneton** with men's and women's apparel. The Brazilian airline VASP has a ticket office in 444.

Also at 444 is a novelty shop called **XYZ** (tel. 521-4097) featuring T-shirts, accessories, and Brazilian handcrafts. XYZ also has a branch in Copacabana at Rua Barata Ribeiro 611, (tel. 236-7334). Open Monday through Friday 9 a.m. to 8 p.m. and till 2 p.m. on Saturdays. **Van Gogh** (tel. 521-5244), at street level in the 444 gallery, carries white linen, silk, and Pan a.m.a suits ($200–$250), trousers ($135), and shirts ($50). Open daily 9 a.m. to 7 p.m., Saturdays till 2 p.m.. The store has an affiliate, **Petite Homme** (tel. 541-3793), that stocks the exact same line for boys aged 2 to 16. Open Monday through Saturday from 10 a.m. till 10 p.m.

A great concentration of the neighborhood's toniest boutiques line the Rua Garcia D'Ávila where, incidentally, at the street's intersection with Rua Visconde de Pirajá, you'll find the headquarters building that houses jeweler H. Stern's main showroom. At **Les Griffes,** Rua Garcia D'Ávila 108, you will see many items sporting the n a.m.es of the big designers displayed in separate showrooms in this two-story chrome and glass environment, all made in Brazil under the necessary licensing arrangement. For designer jeans, there is **Quorum,** at no. 134, and don't forget **Twiggy's,** at no. 160, for evening wear and other *haute couture a La Brasiliene.*

Farther up the block in the direction of Leblon is **Eduardo Guinle,** Rua Visconde de Pirajá 514A (tel. 259-6346), specializing in cotton (from $15) and linen (from $37) men's shirts. Open daily from 9 a.m. to 7 p.m., Saturdays till 4 p.m.. Across the street is **Mr. Wonderful,** Rua Visconde de Pirajá 503A (tel. 274-6898), where designer Luis Freitas began to showcase his fashions in the late '60s. Today, Mr. Freitas exploits the "nerd" look, his mannequins sporting Pan a.m.a hats, pastel bermudas, and loud '50s-style polo shirts, an ensemble that suggests . . . well, a young Truman Capote dressed for a summer barbecue. The shop's large, uncluttered space, with blue neon lighting and loud rock music is also worth seeing. Open Monday through Friday from 9 a.m. till 8 p.m., Saturday till 3 p.m.

Another chain store, this one for the younger set, is **Toulon,** Rua Visconde de Pirajá 540 (tel. 239-2195), with some branch outlets throughout the city. It carries skateboards, stickers, denim sportswear, and much more. Open Monday through Saturday from 9 a.m. to 8 p.m.

Shopping Leblon

For years shops in residential Leblon, situated originally on the neighborhood's main thoroughfares, were limited to high-priced showrooms for the latest materials and furnishings in interior design. In recent years, chic boutiques have begun to spring up along the shaded side streets of Leblon like delicate dandelions after a spring rain. The best of Leblon includes **Asparagus** on Rua Carlos Gois 234, with knits for all seasons; **Cenário & Figurino,** Rua Alm. Pereira Guimaraẽs 65B, for original beaded evening gowns; and **Sônia & Romero,** Avenida Ataulfo de Paiva 528A, also featuring dressy (and pricey) evening wear. For children's clothing try **Smuggler,** Avenida Ataulfo de Paiva 566, and **Cantão,** at the same address, for bathing suits. Outrageous, oversized costume jewelry is the thing at **Bijou Box,** Rua Alm. Pereira Guimaraẽs 72B, where state-of-the-art baubles in plastic and ceramic are served up from bins.

AN ARTIST'S STUDIO

While you are in Leblon, you might make arrangements to see some interesting oil primitives and wood carvings, and possibly meet a charming, married pair of international artists. The studio of wood sculptor and painter **Batista and Mady** is on the Jardim Botânico side of Leblon, Rua Pacheco Leão 1270. For an appointment, call 227-8702 or 294-6715.

---

3. Souvenirs

Brazil, like any country, has what would have to be considered its traditional souvenirs. Typical of these *tchotchkes* are butterfly trays, wood and clay figurines, agate ashtrays, stuffed snakes, and, of course, T-shirts.

The most typical of all Brazilian souvenirs is the **figa,** a good luck charm in the shape of a fist with the thumb protruding between the second and third fingers, available in a variety of materials from carved wood and stone to silver. According to tradition, however, the charm is only potent if you have received the figa as a present. This item is therefore a nice, simple gift for the folks back home.

Most of the souvenir trade is centered on Copacabana, between Rua Paula Freitas and the Praça do Lido, primarily along the Avenida Nossa Senhora de Copacabana. Look for **Evelyn,** Avenida Nossa Senhora de Copacabana 471, and also the shops **Macumba Souvenir** and **Liane** in the same vicinity. Other popular souvenir shops are **Foclore,** Avenida Atlântica 1782, for Indian artifacts, and **Copacabana Couros e Artesanatos,** Rua Fernando Mendes 45A, for leather goods, especially in crocodile.

Worthy of note is the fact that the very long **Avenida Nossa Senhora de Copacabana,** which runs parallel to the ocean one block in, is the major shopping street in the Copacabana neighborhood. Copacabana, with its 300,000 residents, has been called a ghetto for the rich, and in Rio it is billed as the most densely populated neighborhood in the world. No wonder then that this principal thoroughfare provides an endless pageant of animated street life from early in the morning until late at night, and contains shops of every type, including its own share of fancy and fanciful boutiques. To be experienced and enjoyed in full, the avenue should be strolled from one end to the other.

Notable outlets along the way include the **Pronto Entrega 30,** on the side street Rua Siqueira Campos 30, a 12-story mart functioning in a semiwholesale, semiretail capacity. The selection of ready-to-wears here is enormous, but a minimum purchase of six pieces is normally required. Those who are nostalgic for the old Woolworth's atmosphere should be sure to stop at **Lojas Americanas,** in the 500 block of Avenida Nossa Senhora de Copacabana. Viva the lunch counter! After your grilled ham and cheese sandwich (sandwiche mixto), drop in across the street at the **Centro Commercial Copacabana,** a warren of 200 shops selling just about anything you can imagine, at discount prices.

Downtown Shopping

Those who opt to stroll the historic lanes and streets of downtown Rio will certainly want to poke their heads into any number of stores that strike their fancy along the way. For the opposite of Ipanema chic, wander over to **Rua Uruguaia** (which is closed to vehicular traffic) and its surrounding streets. You'll see many clothing stores and perhaps score a real bargain. At Rua do Rosário 155 is **Kosmos,** a shop specializing in old engravings and prints of the city, like those of Jean Baptist Debret, the French artist who has left an amazing pictorial record of early-19th-century Rio.

---

4. The Shopping Centers

Over the past ten years, the shopping mall phenomenon has exploded throughout Rio. This occurrence doesn't seem to have reduced the consumer movement in neighborhood shops, but rather to have added a new dimension to the city's shopping habits. The malls, for example, tend to stay open later than most neighborhood shops. They also provide free and ample parking, which is always a challenge in heavily populated areas like Ipanema and Copacabana.

Barra Shopping, Avenida das Américas 4666, Barra da Tijuca, is said to be the largest shopping center in South America. Under its vast skylit roof, Barra Shopping houses 322 shops, according to the last official count. In addition to large department stores like Sears and Mesbla, there are dozens of restaurants, lunch counters, and even an amusement center with rides and video games for the children. Barra can also boast Rio's only ice-skating rink. Shuttle buses run between 40 of the major hotels and the shopping center on a fixed schedule. The first bus leaves from Leme at about 10:15 a.m. and the final bus of the day returns at 9 p.m. For details on scheduling, check at the porter's desk of your hotel. Barra is about a 30-minute cab or car ride from Copacabana, and stores are open from 10 a.m. until 10 p.m. Monday through Saturday. Entertainment and recreational areas are open seven days a week from 10 a.m. until midnight.

Carrefour, Avenida das Américas 5150, right next door to Barra Shopping, is a gigantic supermarket and home center. Anyone with a passion for large supermarkets and sufficient time in Rio to warrant the visit, ought to browse the aisles of Carrefour just for the experience. Row after row of edible commodities, fresh, packaged, and canned, will dazzle your eyes and set your mouth watering. Students of labels and packaging techniques will thrill to the overwhelming selection of goods to admire. On a practical note, pick up a few large bottles of mineral water or beverage of your choice to stock the fridge in your hotel room rather than paying those outrageous mini-bar prices. Open from 8 a.m. to 10 p.m. Monday through Saturday. While you're there, especially if you're feeling a tinge of homesickness, check out the nearby branch of the "golden arches."

Casa Shopping, Rua Alvorado 2150, in Barra da Tijuca, is the newest shopping center in Rio. Tiles, tubs, wallpaper, and furnishings—everything you need for home design is here in many shops that all have first-floor entrances on the street. There are also numerous restaurants, including the famous Rodeio, and several cinemas. The open-air antique fair also takes place here on Sunday. Store hours are the same as at Barra Shopping.

Shopping da Gávea, Rua Marquês de São Vicente 52, Gávea. Gávea is an inland neighborhood bordered by Leblon and the Jockey Club racetrack. Because of the Catholic University there, it is somewhat of a college neighborhood. The Rua Marquês de Sao Vicente is a main drag, a westward extension of the Avenida Jardim Botânico. Shopping dá Gávea is a very tony mall, with high-fashion shops, art galleries, and showrooms of designer furnishings. Of special interest is the branch of **John Somer,** Brazilian manufacturers of fine pewter, the word for which in Portuguese is *estanho* (literally, "tin," the principal metal used to make the product).

Rio Design Center, Avenida Ataufo de Paiva 270, Leblon. Here's where Cariocas go when they want the latest in home decorations and designer furnishings. If you know what you're looking for and can comparison shop based on prices back home, you may find an object or two here that will make the fuss and worry over shipping worth the effort. Think of the Design Center as a kind of toyland for homeowners, a place to browse for ideas and inspiration. Then go down to the basement level café and sculpture garden to spin your nesting fantasies over a cool beverage.

Rio Sul, Avenida Lauro Muller 116, in Botafogo, is the closest full-sized shopping center to Copacabana, located on the other side of the Tunel Novo at the end of Avenida Princesa Isabel. While only a decade old, Rio Sul is the grandparent of shopping malls in Rio and, with over 400 stores, remains both trendy and well stocked. In addition to the many boutiques, there's a toy store, kids' clothing stores, and full-blown department stores like Mesbla and Lojas Americanas. Rio Sul also operates a free bus service to and from many major hotels, and is open Monday through Saturday from 10 a.m. until 10 p.m.

The **São Conrado Fashion Mall,** across from the Inter-Continental Hotel, is a medium-size, but extremely chic mall with branches of many top shops. It's particularly convenient for those staying in nearby resort hotels, but also a bit less of a jaunt from Copacabana and Ipanema than Barra da Tijuca. Open Monday through Friday from 10 a.m. to 10 p.m., and on Saturday from 10 a.m. to 8 p.m.

---

5. Gemstones

Brazil is said to produce 90% of the world's colored gem-stones. Furthermore, the low cost of labor in Brazil means that stones and finished jewels purchased in the country are 20% to 40% cheaper than comparable products elsewhere. For this reason, and because of the stone's intrinsic beauty, visitors to Brazil are often excited by the prospect of finding attractive gemstones, set in traditional jewlery or loose, to carry home, not only for use as adornments and remembrances of their terrific Rio vacation, but also as wise investments. The visitor in Rio—the country's gem-stone capital—can be forgiven for thinking that practically all Brazilians deal in gemstones, so aggressively are the precious rocks marketed to arriving tourists. This misconception can make the task of a reliable gemstone purchase that much more difficult. Assuming you are not a gemological expert, how do you know you are getting a stone that is worth what you are paying for it? In fact, how do you even know if you're getting the stone you think you're paying for?

These potential dilemmas can best be remedied by purchasing your stones and jewelry from one of Rio's major gem dealers, who stand behind their products and provide buyers with certificates of appraisals and other safeguards like credit, exchange, or repurchase guarantees. The two largest and best-known jewelers in Brazil are the H. Stern Company and Amsterdam Sauer, the Hertz and Avis of Brazilian gemstones. Both enterprises are vertically integrated companies. That means that they handle all phases of the gemstone operation from mining through retailing. You won't have any trouble finding retail outlets for either company. Their stores are located at the airports, in all the major hotels, and at many other points throughout the city.

Brazilian jewelers offer all the world's precious stones at reduced prices, including rubies and sapphires. But the best deals to be had are on those gems that come from Brazil's own mines. These are amethyst, aquamarine, citrine, emerald, opal, topaz, and tourmaline. Diamond production in Brazil remains high, though not in the quantities of the boom days two centuries ago. Indeed Brazilian diamonds are rarely mined these days, but are small specimens of the alluvial type, sifted from the flowing waters of many river systems. The price per carat of a given stone depends on numerous factors, not the least of which is its visual beauty—a quality that is difficult to gauge. In general, the fixed criteria of a gem's worth are based on a stone's color (both its shade and degree of transparency) and on its clarity and absence of flaws. Although in some cases, as with cat's-eye tourmalines or star sapphires, the flaw is considered intrinsic to the stone's beauty and value. The major characteristics for each of the Brazilian stones—including what some believe are their healing and mythical properties—are listed below:

Amethyst is the most highly prized quartz variety of gemstone. Colors range from pale lilac to rich purple, with stones of the deepest and most constant shades having the most value. The current price for amethysts in Rio ranges from $1 to $30 per carat, but beware the many pale stones or even glass imitations that flood the market. Believed to protect against blood disease and drunkenness, the amethyst signifies purity and is the birthstone for February.

Aquamarine, next to emerald, is the most highly prized of the beryls. The stone ranges from pale to deep blue, the price often depending on the depths of its shading. While the price of this blue beauty can span anywhere from $5 to $1000 per carat, expect to pay a minimum of $100 a carat for any aquamarine of even middling quality today. Frequently free of flaws, the aquamarine is said to calm the nerves and to revive a lagging marriage. Sailors have long worn the stone as protective amulets. Aquamarine is the birthstone for March.

Citrine is quartz, essentially an amethyst that grades from smoky brown to deep yellow in color, also priced in the $1 to $30 range per carat. The citrine looks like precious topaz, but costs far less, so you must be particularly careful when purchasing the latter stone. Still, the citrine is beautiful in its own right, and it is believed to have powers to aid failing eyesight. Citrine is the alternate birthstone for November.

Emerald is the most valuable of the beryls, and has been in fashion for millennia. A fine stone of good color—deep green with no tint of blue or yellow, and flaw-free can cost $50,000 a carat, though lesser stones can be purchased for $50 a carat or less. Since their relatively recent discovery, Brazilian emeralds have been accepted in the world gem market as on a par with any of their cousins mined in traditional emerald-rich countries like Colombia. Emeralds are believed to strengthen the memory and to protect against temptation and seduction. The Emerald is the birthstone for May.

Opal, composed of silicone oxide, is called the queen of gems. The most popular are white with fireflies of red, gold, blue, purple, and green. The rarest and costliest are black, harlequin patterned. The opal is considered bad luck, unless it is your birthstone. Lucky for those born in October.

Topaz is brilliant and sparkling. The most important color range is from yellow to brown, with rich sherry-brown the most expensive—up to $1,000 a carat. The gem also comes in pale pink (the rare imperial topaz) and in blue, which is becoming increasingly popular as aquamarines get more and more expensive. Blue topaz is relatively inexpensive, from $2 to $25 per carat, while imperial topaz can fetch between $20 and $2000 a carat. Said to heal insomnia, the topaz is also to be worn as a ring against untimely death. The topaz is the birthstone for November.

Tourmalines come in virtually any color you can imagine, but the most popular is emerald green. Some crystals have two or three color bands. These are called watermelon tourmalines because they are almost always green on the outside and pink in the center. Red tourmalines are called rubilites. The price of tourmalines ranges from $5 to $600 a carat. Tourmalines are believed to attract good will and friendship and are the alternate birthstone for October.

In all, there are about 90 different types of gemstones, though only 20 are of particular interest to jewelers. The names of some of these other stones you may see offered for sale are garnet, agate, hematite, peridot, and amazonite.

The headquarters for **H. Stern and Company** is the modern 18-story building in Ipanema at Rua Visconde de Pirajá 490 (tel. 259-7442). The company, founded by Hans Stern, a refugee from Nazi Germany and a brilliant success story, now has 170 stores and retail centers throughout Brazil and in 13 countries worldwide—including New York City at 645 Fifth Avenue (tel. 212/688-0300), which exists primarily to service North American clients who have made their purchases in Brazil. Stern makes the following warranty for his products: "If we say something is perfect, it is perfect. If we say it is genuine, it is genuine." Mr. Stern also offers the following tips for prospective gemstone buyers. First, choose the color you really like. Then experiment with a variety of stones, holding them next to your skin, preferably in natural lighting. If you have any doubts about a stone for whatever reason, ask the staff gemologist at the store where you are making the purchase to verify its authenticity. For your second and third purchases, buy a similarly colored stone as the first, beginning, say, with a ring, and them moving on to a bracelet or earrings. Always get a certificate of appraisal for any gemstone purchase in excess of $500. See Chapter VI for details on the company's free tour of its workshops.

Amsterdam Sauer, Rua México 41 (tel. 220-8332), is H. Stern's closest competitor. The company also has many outlets throughout Rio, including those at the Rio Palace, Meridien, and Caesar Park hotels. The New York office at 580 Fifth Avenue (tel. 212/869-5558) does no retail business, but services North American clients and handles the company's export business. Founder Jules Roger Sauer's background is remarkably similar to that of Hans Stern. He also just managed to flee Europe on the eve of World War II. Sauer is the author of the excellent illustrated book, *Brazil: Paradise of Gemstones,* which is printed in seven languages including English (available in bookstores throughout Rio for about $10).

Other reliable gemstone dealers and jewelers in Rio include

Rodtiti, Rua Visconde de Pirajá 482; **Moreno,** Rua Visconde de Pirajá 500, and with an outlet in Cassino Atlantico in the Rio Palace Hotel; and **Balulac,** Rua Visconde de Pirajá 487. All of these retail outlets are within a (you'll excuse the pun) stone's throw of Stern and Sauer in Ipanema.

X

RIO'S DAY TRIPS AND WEEKEND SPAS

1. DAY TRIPS
2. COSTA DO SOL
3. COSTA VERDE
4. COASTAL SÃO PAULO

Cariocas themselves, at least those who have the means, seldom spend the weekends or holidays in Rio. The beaches of Copacabana and Ipanema tend to fill up rapidly on Saturday and Sunday, a scene which can be quite pleasing and exciting to the tourist, but less appealing to the full-time resident. Anyone else spending more than a week in or around Rio, having satiated their appetite for the urban beach scene, might easily include one of the following side trips in their itinerary. To escape the crowds, people generally head in one of three directions. The two nearby beach resort areas are the Costa do Sol and the Costa Verde (the Sun Coast and the Green Coast). Those seeking relief from the hottest days of summer in January and February might prefer a more cooling environment in the mountain regions, rather than the shore, where the heat and the action during the high season can be quite intense.

From a visitor's point of view, however, all of the locales described in this chapter may certainly be visited at any time of the year, as their attraction is merely modified, not determined, by the seasons. Naturally, cost of lodgings and food tends to parallel the transition from high to low season. The relative isolation and calm of the low season (most of the year) will cost you less than during those times of the year when the spas fill up with vacationers: summer, winter school vacation during the month of July, and major holidays (see "Fast Facts Brazil" in Chapter I). The choice, then, is between the people-scene of the high season, when the clubs are jumping, or the privacy-scene of the low season, when you can have the towns and beaches much more to yourself. So as not to give a totally misleading impression, however, (or perhaps to confuse you even further), there is always *something* going on in most of these destinations, especially on the weekends, throughout the year.

1. Day Trips

NITERÓI

A short ferry ride away, Niterói, the former capital of the State of Rio de Janeiro, is Rio's companion city across the bay. Ferries and hydrofoils depart regularly from the dock near Praça XV in downtown Rio. Bus service across the bay bridge is also frequent, leaving from the Rodoviária Novo Rio bus station in Sao Cristóvão.

Once you've arrived in Niterói by ferry, bus 33 departing from the terminal will take you to the beaches of **Icaraí, São Francisco,** and **Jurujuba.** The ride is picturesque, but the beaches (like those on the other side of the bay) are less than pristine. The view of the Rio shoreline, however, is dramatically beautiful, particularly so as you travel in the vicinity of the twin beaches dubbed **Adam and Eve** (Adão and Eva). Beyond Jurujuba is the 16th-century fort of **Santa Cruz,** one of Brazil's oldest fortifications, open daily from 8 a.m. until 4 p.m.

Bus 38 from the ferry terminal carries passengers to the spectacular ocean beaches of **Piratininga, Itaipú,** and **Itacoatiara,** about a 45-minute ride from Niterói. In Itaipú, there is an archeology museum in the ruins of the 18th-century convent of Santa Teresa. To the east of Niterói and its own metropolitan beaches stretches the long, seductive Costa do Sol, which is described later in this chapter.

PETRÓPOLIS

When Cariocas want to exchange the seaside landscape for that of the mountains, Petrópolis is one of the closest and most popular destinations. The tradition was started by Pedro I, who bought a farm there in the 1830s and was continued by his son Pedro II, who so loved the more temperate climate in Petrópolis, that he moved the country's capital to the fledgling city during the summer months, or during those times when Rio was rife with disease and epidemics. Much of the court followed the emperor's example, so there remain numerous mansions with large gardens left from the empire period in a town that is today a mixture of modern textile plants and narrow cobblestone streets. Petrópolis is only 66 km (41 miles) from Rio, reached by a dramatic climb along a steep mountain road with many stunning views of the surrounding mountains and valleys.

The first sight of general interest, just before entering Petrópolis, is **Quitandinha,** once Brazil's most fashionable casino, before gambling was abolished in 1946. Today, Quitandinha is a middling resort, slated to become an apart-hotel sometime in the near future. But the grounds and the buildings in the grand Norman style, are worthy of a look for the old Hollywood-esque glamour they still reflect.

In the town itself, there is the Emperor's former palace, now the **Museu Imperial** (Imperial Museum), which houses the crown jewels and other royal possessions, including an early telephone given to Pedro by Alexander Graham Bell. In appearance, the palace remains much as it was during the occupancy of the imperial family. The Imperial Museum is open Tuesday through Sunday from noon to 5:30 p.m.

The **Palácio Cristal** (Crystal Palace), Praça de Confluência, was built by Dom Pedro II's son-in-law, the Conde D'Eu, a Frenchman who imported the structure from his native country to house the great flower exhibition of 1884. Petrópolis is still known for its nurseries today. Flower lovers should visit **Florilia** on Estrada do Alcobaça, just outside town, to see the permanent exhibition of orchids. Florília is open from 9 a.m. to 5 p.m. daily, and cuttings (called *mudas* in Portuguese) may be purchased.

The house of Brazilian aviation pioneer **Santos Dumont,** Rua do Encanto 124, is open Tuesday through Friday from 9 a.m. to 5 p.m., and from 11 a.m. to 5 p.m. on weekends. An architectural oddity, the house was built by Dumont at a time in his life when mystical obsessions had outdistanced his earlier scientific curiosity. He believed, for example, that he should always walk up stairs leading with his left foot. The staircases in his houses were built deliberately narrow to accommodate this eccentricity. Nevertheless, Dumont was a man of indubitable genius, and many displays of his inventions in the house attest to this fact.

Cotton knitwear is the principal product of industrial Petrópolis, and reasonable bargains can be had on *malhas (mahl-yaz)*, as the garments are called, along the Rua Teresa.

Buses for Petrópolis leave frequently from Rio's downtown Menezes Cortes Bus Terminal, and the round-trip fare is approximately $5.

Where to Eat

Full tea is served from 8 a.m. until 10 p.m. at the **Florilia** restaurant, on Rua Maetro Otávio Maul, which includes tea, toast, honey, jam, and cakes for $2.

A good dish of trout smothered in a peanut sauce can be had for $10 at **La Belle Meunière,** Estrada União Industrial 2189 (tel. 21-1573), 10 km (6 miles) from the center of Petrópolis.

Within the town, the best restaurants are to be found on Rua João Pessoa and Rua do Imperador.

TERESÓPOLIS

Centered on the mountain town of Teresópolis is the **Parque Nacional da Serra dos Orgãos** (Sierra of the Organs National Park), so named because the surrounding peaks have the appearance of a pipe organ. The huge park boasts numerous trails to hike and peaks to scale.

Teresópolis is located beyond Petrópolis, 95 km (58 miles) from Rio. On the way, be sure to stop at the **Mirante do Soberbo,** an overlook with a panoramic view of the Guanabara Bay and the verdant, craggy mountaints that stretch from the backyards of Rio far into the interior. Nature's feats of erosion are obvious along the zigzag of rocky forms outlined against the horizon, especially in the case of a prominent and solitary projection called the **Dedo de Deus** (God's Finger), which rises to an elevation of several thousand feet. There are many ponds and waterfalls in the park for bathing, and stable horses may be rented within the grounds in an area designated the Pracinha do Alto.

The night and street life in Teresópolis itself is centered on the area known as **A Várzea.**

As is the case for Petrópolis, the Teresópolis buses leave regularly from Rio's downtown bus station. Many tour companies offer day-trip excursions that take in both towns and their environs.

Where to Eat

The **Taberna Alpina,** Rua Duque de Caxias 131 (tel. 742-0123), offers a good Spanish-style codfish plate for $8. For inexpensive "international" food, try **Ângelo,** on the Praça Higino da Silveira (tel. 742-0007).

NOVA FRIBURGO

Higher still among these mountains, approximately 150 km (93 miles) from Rio, is Nova Friburgo, a town originally settled by Swiss immigrants, and today a favorite summer retreat for Cariocas wishing to escape the summer swelter of their city. Many chalets in the **Conegô** suburb still attest to the influence of the European colonization, as does the elegant layout of the city's principal squares.

An energetic and steep climb up to the **Pico da Caledônia** offers a magnificent view of the valley, the city to one side and a lake district to the other. A different perspective can be viewed from the **Morrô da Cruz,** reached by cable car from the Praça dos Suspiros.

Near Friburgo are two small towns that were only electrified in 1984 and retain in their ambience familiar elements of rural Brazil. First is **Lumiar,** 36 km (22 miles) away, reached from the Rio-Friburgo highway by exiting at Mury. A further 6 km (3½ miles) along on a hard-packed dirt road is **São Pedro.** Both towns are hospitable to visitors. You will be welcome to take a refreshing dip in the local swimming hole, the *poço feio* (the ugly well).

Nova Friburgo is a three-hour bus ride from Rio.

Where to Eat

There are more than 30 quality hotels and inns in the region. Most offer full board for guests, and their restaurants are also open to the public.

TRÊ RIOS

A number of agencies are now offering white-water rafting expeditions along the Rio Paraibuna, about 1½ hour's travel beyond Petrópolis. The rafting takes you along the rapid current, shooting over numerous small falls—some with drops of up to 15 feet—and takes about 4½ hours to descend the river. The excursion, which costs about $58 per person, including transportation and lunch, can be booked in Rio through **Klemperer Turismo** (tel. 252-8170) or through their main offices in Petrópolis, Avenida Afranio de Mello Franco 333 (tel. 0242/43-4052).

Klemperer also manages a camping resort in the Serra dos

Orgãos Park, called **Cabanas Açu.** Ten double-occupancy suites occupy five rustic, but comfortable, cabins on a gently sloping hillside with the scenic mountains near at hand. Guests spend their time hiking, searching for secluded mountain pools, canoeing on the streams and lakes, or in organized sports on the grounds of the resort.

ITATIAIA NATIONAL PARK

The other great park within the state of Rio de Janeiro is Itatiaia, about 161 km (100 miles) inland from Rio in a southwesterly direction, not far from the steel mining town of Volta Redonda and accessible along the Via Dutra, the principal highway to São Paulo. The park has excellent facilities for camping, hiking, and climbing. To book a campsite, contact the park administration at least two weeks in advance by writing Administraçao do Parque Nacional de Itatiaia, Itatiaia 27540 RJ. Further information on the park can be obtained in Rio from the **Clube Excursionista Brasileira,** Avenida Alm. Barroso 2, eighth floor (tel. 220-3695).

ITACURUÇÁ

This beach resort town is in fact our first stop along the Costa Verde. Only 82 km (51 miles) from Rio's Barra da Tijuca, a trip to Itacuruçá can also be considered a legitimate one-day excursion. The favorite activity of visitors is to cruise the clear blue waters of the Sepitiba Bay in a coastal sloop (called a *saveiro*) and visit some of the many offshore islands. The transparent waters are excellent for snorkeling to see the many colorful varieties of tropical fish which made the bay their home. Sepetiba Turismo in Rio on Avenida Nossa Senhora de Copacabana 605 (tel. 235-2893), offers a cruise of the bay from 10 a.m. until 4:30 p.m. which embarks from a pier in Itacuruçá on Saturday, Sunday, and Monday. The cost is about $15, which includes a snack of fruit on board and lunch on the Ilha de Jaguanum, while bar items and other beverages are paid for separately. Transportation by bus to and from your hotel can also be arranged by the tour agency.

Where to Eat

On the way to Itacuruçá you will pass **Pedra de Guaratiba,** where two of Rio's most popular out-of-town restaurants, **Cândido's** and **476,** are located. (For details, see Chapter V).

---

2. Costa Do Sol

East and to the north of Rio, along the Atlantic coastline, are located the numerous towns and harbors that have come to be known collectively as Rio's Costa do Sol. The Sun Coast begins at the beaches in the vicinity of Niterói, passes through Búzios, the best-known of its resort towns, and goes on to its most distant point, Macaé, 187 km (116 miles) from Rio.

BÚZIOS

Once a rustic and obscure fishing village, **Armação dos Búzios** (the official name in full) is now most often referred to as the St. Tropez of Brazil. Ironically, it was the French actress Brigitte Bardot who really put Búzios on the map. Bardot, one of the most popular international stars of the '50s, sought in Búzios a refuge from publicity during frequent vacations to Brazil. In her wake, many others among the rich and famous began to flock to Búzios, transforming the simple coastal hamlet into one of the chicest of all Brazilian summer colonies and side-trip destinations. Búzios occupies a small peninsula, approximately 170 km (105 miles) from Rio de Janeiro, about a three-hour trip by car, cab, or bus. It's most easily accessible by air taxi which makes the one-way journey in 40 minutes.

Getting to Búzios

If you were going to rent a car at all in Brazil, this might be the time to do it. Not only will you be able to explore the whole length of the Costa do Sol on your way to and from Búzios, but once you've settled into the resort, you'll find it very convenient to have your own wheels for getting around from beach to beach or restaurant to restaurant. If you choose to drive your own car, cross the Rio/Niterói bridge and follow the main road BR-116 in the direction of Araruama, making the turnoff for Búzios after driving for approximately 75 miles (at the km 124 marker). Your hotel in Rio can also provide transportation to Búzios in the form of a **private car and driver,** or you can hire a **radio taxi** to take you there as well. Needless to say, the cab will not wait, but you will be required to underwrite the cost of its return to Rio, nonetheless—in all a very expensive proposition. Finding a vehicle to take you back could be a problem, but not an insurmountable one.

A number of **tour agencies** make the run between Rio and Búzios on a regular basis. **Blumar,** Rua Santa Clara 50, Room 1209, Copacabana (tel. 255-6692), for one, provides a full range of tours and services for tourists who wish to explore Búzios and its beaches. In Búzios itself, try **Ekoda,** Rua José Bento Ribeiro Dantes 22 (tel. 0246/23-1493).

Still another option is to take a **bus** for about $2 from Rio to nearby Cabo Frio, which is only a 30-minute cab ride from Búzios. A public bus also runs between the Cabo Frio and Búzios, and when combined with the bus from Rio this is by far the cheapest way to get to the spa. If you have reservations at one of the better inns, they will sometimes arrange to meet you in Cabo Frio, especially if more than one person is involved.

The fastest way to get to Búzios is by **air taxi. Costair** makes the trip in about 40 minutes, leaving from Rio's downtown Santos Dumont Airport and landing in Búzios on a dirt strip in the middle of a great marsh. The $82 round-trip flight is worth it alone for the close-up view of Pão de Açúcar as the plane negotiates the curve of Guanabara Bay on takeoff and landing. The view on the way down the coast isn't half bad either.

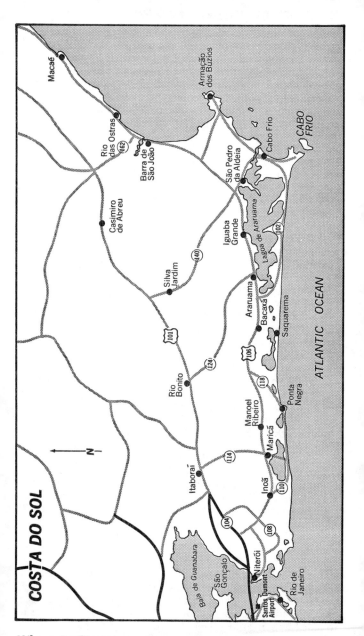

Where to Stay

At the entrance to the Búzios peninsula, on the bank of a narrow river, is the reception center for the island resort of **Nas Rocas** (tel. 0246/23-1303, or 251-0001 in Rio for reservations). A seven-minute ride by trawler takes you across an inlet to the private island created a tamer version of the Club Med–style resort. Nas Rocas occupies the entire island, which can be circled by footpath at a comfortable pace in no more than 45 minutes. Nas Rocas is totally self-contained, providing lodging, all meals, aquatic sports from windsurfing to snorkeling, tennis, and a variety of organized activities from pool games to exercise classes, and even a schooner for island-hopping and tours of Búzios' famous coves and beaches.

At Nas Rocas, there are 80 two-room suites in 40 separate and attractive bungalows, which overlook either the inlet or the open sea. Each suite has a large veranda, bath with shower, mini-bar, color TV, and air conditioning. The daily rate per person, including two meals, is $90. Food is served buffet style, with a minimum of two main dishes—usually fish and meat—and all the trimmings.

The grounds on the island are resplendent with flowers. Every season has its blossoms. The decorative plants are all imported to the island from the mainland, and are lovingly tended by Sr. Hélio, the principal gardener, who receives ample assistance from many of the resort staff of 240 workers. The primitive, native growth on the nonlandscaped sections of the island is equally attractive. Botanists, professional or amateur, are welcome to tag along with Sr. Hélio, who will be happy to share (in Portuguese) his knowledge of Brazilian flora as he makes his daily rounds.

The hotel provides taxi and bus transportation to take guests into Búzios, which is actually 10 km (6 miles) farther down the peninsula. Or you can rent a dune buggy, a very popular mode of transportation in these parts. To get to Búzios proper from Nas Rocas, you must cross over a single-lane bridge with an extremely acute arch in the shape of a camel's hump. Then you will pass through the village of **Manguinhos,** a ramshackle affair not without its charm—really a strip of houses, cafés, stores, and markets. The 27 beaches of the area (or 36, depending on whether or not you count several coves that won't accommodate more than a handful of bathers) begin in this municipality, where off the road and up a winding hill is the **Barracuda** (tel. 23-1314), one of the best *pousadas* (inns) in the region. The popular Barracuda has only 21 rooms in gorgeous vine-covered bungalows, very comfortably furnished with all the amenities. Each bungalow has an attached terrace with hammock overlooking the water. The daily rate per double, including breakfast, is $80. The inn has a particularly attractive pool and patio area, and the much-praised Tartaruga (Turtle) beach, is over the hill about 200 meters (650 feet) away.

Another ten minutes down the road brings you to the very center of the old fishing village of Búzios, still somewhat intact, but surrounded by some of the fanciest boutiques, restaurants, and inns this side of Ipanema. One local lady, a British expatriate, attributed to Búzios the character of St. Tropez of 20 to 30 years past. "Totally disorganized," she claimed, by which she meant informal and not overly self-conscious as yet of being the great watering hole of the society set.

Society is here, to be sure. Many of the well-heeled from Rio have summer homes in Búzios. Sr. Modiano, of Nas Rocas, for example, has a beautiful rambling house on the beach, the crown jewel of his 2,500-acre estate where he is planning to build, over the next five years, Búzios' first real hotel, a full-scale boat marina, and a new airport that will accommodate medium-sized passenger jets.

The principal center of Búzios, from the standpoint of its greatest concentration of fashionable shops, fine restaurants, and first-class pousadas, is the **Armação,** a term which loosely designates an area of several blocks, but primarily the establishments found on and around the *Rua das Pedras*. The street's official name is *Rua Bento Ribeiro Dantas,* but it is known traditionally as the Street of Stones because of its unusual paving surface. Most of the streets in Búzios that are not simply dirt roads are paved with cobblestones. But on the Rua das Pedras, you will still see the colonial-era paving method of using large, thick flagstones, which stick up at every imaginable angle, forcing all vehicles to amble slowly down this long block at the speed of a walking horse.

On this colorful, if perilous street, is the **Estalagem,** an inn, restaurant, and music bar, the property of an American rock and jazz bassist, Bruce Leitman. In season, there is live music at the Estalagem every night, and in the off-season, only over the major holiday weekends. The inn has only eight rooms off an open courtyard, painted brightly in white with blue. Rates are about $35 a night per person.

Other top-rated inns—some 50 in all—can be found scattered among the surrounding hills and beaches, which are for the most part a 15-minute to half-hour walk from the heart of the Armação. Two special inns in particular are worth noting. The **Pousada Casas Brancas** (tel. 23-1458), perched over the Praia da Armação, offers guests first-class elegance in a dozen suites overlooking the water for $85 a night. On the *Praia dos Ossos* (the Beach of Bones), the plain but appealing **La Chimere** (tel. 23-1043 or in Rio 220-2129) has rooms for $40 a night, single or double occupancy. Another hilltop hideaway is **Byblos,** Morro do Humanita 8 (tel. 23-1162), with 17 suites, and rates beginning at $44 a night for a single or double.

Beyond the Armação area, the undeveloped lands of the Búzios peninsula represent some of the most scenic and unspoiled natural beach environments you will find in this part of Brazil. Unlike Cape Cod, say, or other U.S. Atlantic Ocean–beach communities for that matter, which are essentially flat and bordered by networks of elevated dunes, Búzios is hilly with lush vegetation. The vistas in the hills beyond the town are breathtaking in spots, and uniformly beautiful. Try to arrange for a car with a very good suspension system when touring these backroads and undeveloped areas of Búzios —or at least prepare yourself for a jolting ride.

Where to Eat

Búzios is considered Brazil's third most distinguished culinary capital following only São Paulo and Rio, though on a much smaller scale to be sure. The original **Le Streghe** is located in Búzios on the Rua das Pedras, and you can get the same fine Italian food there as at the companion restaurant in Ipanema. Veal and pasta, the latter made daily in the restaurant's own *cucina,* form the bedrock of the mostly Italian menu at Le Streghe. And prices, as at the restaurant's Ipanema branch, are surprisingly reasonable, with most dishes falling within the $5 to $10 range. The **Au Cheval Blanc,** an excellent French restaurant, is located several doors down on the same block. Platters here are classically French, so that whatever you are eating —meat, fowl, or fish—the sauce is the thing. Meals may be taken in the interior dining room or on the outdoor deck which looks out over the busy Búzios harbor and the comings and goings of the town's colorful trawler fleet. The bar at Au Cheval Blanc is a comfortable gathering place in its own right, decorated more like a small salon than a typical restaurant cocktail corner. Prices at the Au Cheval Blanc are also unexpectedly moderate, with few entrees surpassing the $10 mark. Another pleasant choice for French cooking is the inn **La Chimere** on the Ossos beach, where the dining room is open to the public. Opposite the same beach is **Satíricon,** for seafood specialties à la Romana. Whether you select an elegant filet from the catch of the day or the platter of pasta smothered with several of the sea's most delightful edibles, your palate will have fond memories of the fare at Satíricon, where dishes are priced between $4.50 and $12.

Búzios also possesses many less fancy eating establishments, as is befitting a beach town, including the usual array of cabañas on the beaches serving fresh seafood at reasonable prices.

As for the nightlife, most of the clubs and bars are concentrated within several blocks of each other in the center of town. You won't have any trouble finding the latest "in" spot once you are there. Reservations at better restaurants, like those described above, are generally required on weekends and during the high season. Since none of Búzios' restaurants have phones, however, you must drop by the restaurant you've selected for dinner during the day to sign up for the evening meal.

OTHER COSTA DO SOL DESTINATIONS

One could devote many weeks in Brazil just getting to know the stretch of coastline and string of beaches between Niterói and Macaé. The main route to follow is RJ 106, which is picked up on the outskirts of Niterói. The road runs north of the lagos fluminenses, great lagoons high in saline content from which the region's principal product, salt, is harvested.

At Bacaxa there is a turnoff that leads to **Saquarema,** a resort town surrounded by beautiful beaches, wide and sandy white, where Brazil's surfing championships are held annually. There are many inns in the area, and the **Pousada do Holandês,** Avenida Vila

Mar 374 on the Praia de Itauna, comes highly recommended, as does the **Panorama,** Avenida Saquarema 1680.

The next major port of call along RJ 106 is **Araruama,** which fronts the immense lagoon of the same name. Here, in contrast to Saquarema, the waters are calm and the sands said to possess medicinal properties. The colonial city, **São Pedro de Aldeia,** on the eastern end of the lake, is a local center where lodgings are available in a town that retains charming traces of the Old World atmosphere.

Cabo Frio, one of Rio's most traditional weekend spots, is worth a detour, if for no other reason than to experience a truly Brazilian resort with few international trappings. By far the region's largest town, Cabo Frio is filled with restaurants, hotels, and many campsites on or near neighboring beaches. Most foreign tourists these days skip this somewhat fading spa in favor of the elegance and isolation of Búzios, located another 30 minutes down the peninsula by cab or bus. After Cabo Frio—which means Cape Cold, a historical reference to the cool climate that has attracted Cariocas for generations—RJ 106 turns abruptly north toward the small port town of **Barra de São João,** where there is a church dating from 1630, the Capela de São João Batista, and the birthplace of poet Casimiro de Abeu, whose house is now a museum and library.

Farther on is the tranquil village of **Rio das Ostras,** renowned for its shellfish, and finally **Macaé,** a municipality that stretches from the ocean to the nearby mountains, embracing in between a historical district of colonial-era plantations.

---

3. Costa Verde

The Costa Verde (Green Coast) is below Rio to the south and west, and stretches along the Rio-Santos Highway (BR 101) to the town of Parati near the border with the state of São Paulo, some 300 km (180 miles) away. Green is far too pedestrian a word to describe the spectrum of colors that envelop the traveler along this route, now curving and winding over mountainous terrain clad in every shade of luscious jungle vegetation, now hugging the shores of the island-cluttered bays whose waters glisten with such subtle tones that only a brilliant colorist would dare to give them names. Call them green if you must, even emerald in a burst of promotional zeal. But in the end, the eye will register a thousand variations that the mind is ill-equipped to classify, and for which the mouth has no sound.

Sit where you will in car or bus on this journey. You will not miss the show. There are no obstructed views, so total is the spectacular scenery in which you are immersed. On one side, are the hills and rock outcroppings that in places extend their extremities, dripping with verdure, to the very edges of the water. Elsewhere this same swollen topography has been cleared into rolling pastures and cultivated fields. Frozen on their surfaces, in the form of ancient corrals and fazenda houses, is the vision of an agricultural past. In some places, only the scent of the sea is present, so you breathe the more deeply just to savor the pleasing, salty freshness of the air. But water is rarely out of sight for long, as you speed by the succession of graceful coves with their impeccable strands, and the horizon of the sea everywhere interrupted with a numberless multiplication of islands in every size and shape. And you think, "I must stop here on the way back, no there . . . oh, but definitely there."

The true miracle of this landscape is that it continues even beyond Parati, virtually to the gates of the belching, industrial zone that surrounds São Paulo. The whole journey to São Paulo along the Rio-Santos road takes about seven hours, assuming you break for only the most necessary pit stops. A week by stagecoach would be a more reasonable pace. Here we will take the trip in Rio de Janeiro State as far as the preserved colonial town of Parati, and then beyond to the beach resort of Ubatuba and the mountain hideaway of Campos do Jordão, both of which are actually within the borders of São Paulo State. Rio's Costa Verde segment of this excursion is divided into three distinct environments, and three major towns. First is the Baia de Sepitiba, with the town of Mangaratiba. Next comes Angra dos Reis, which embraces the Baia de Ilha Grande. And finally, there is Parati itself.

MANGARATIBA

What distinguishes Mangaratiba is not the town so much as its surrounding beaches. The great scenery of the Costa Verde really begins from this point onward. The fact that Mangaratiba is not a resort town may make it all the more attractive to those who value peace and quiet on uncrowded beaches more than the people-scenes and organized fun of resort areas. Or, if you want, have your cake and eat it too. Stay at the nearby **Frade Portogalo**—about 20 km (12 miles) farther south and use Mangaratiba as the base for your unstructured explorations. There is a daily ferry from Mangaratiba to **Ilha Grande,** the largest of the offshore islands, which in the mornings continues on to Angra does Reis (see below). Also nearby is the village of **Itacuruçá,** from where saveiro cruises may be booked for exploration of the other 36 islands of Sepitiba Bay. (See "Day Trips" above.)

Where to Stay

The Mangaratiba region now also boasts a brand new **Club Med** called the **Village Rio das Pedras,** Rodovia Rio Dantos-BR 101-kilometer 55, (tel. 021/789-1568). Two readers who stayed there offer the following description: "It was everything you'd typically expect from a Club Med—sun, sports, fabulous food, music, and entertainment. But to our surprise, it was more than a generic beach resort. We met friendly travelers from all over Europe and South America, and enjoyed traditional Brazilian food and samba music. In fact the Club Med samba night was one of the best parties we'd ever been to." (Lisa Renaud and John Rosenthal, New York City).

On the Rio-Santos road at the marker km. 71 is the **Hotel Frade Portogalo** (tel. 0243/65-1022 or 267-7375 in Rio for reservations), high on a hill overlooking the bay. A novel chair lift carries guests from the pool area down to a little village of attached condos, where there is a French restaurant, a boat marina, and a beach. There are 80 first-class accommodations at the Portugalo, priced at $60 per double occupancy.

The luxury **Hotel Pierre** (tel. 788-1560) on the Island of Itacuruçá, is reached by a five-minute boat ride, and includes breakfast and dinner in its rate of $90 per double.

Another island hotel is the **Hotel Jaguanum** on the Ilha de Jaguanum, a 30-minute boat ride from Itacuruçá. The island affords beautiful surroundings for walks and bathing, and the hotel charges $55 per double, including all meals.

ANGRA DOS REIS

While Sepitiba Bay offers more than 30 islands to explore, the Baia da Ilha Grande, which washes the shores of Angra, contains an archipelago of over 300 islands, including the fascinating Ilha Grande from which the bay takes its name. Angra is one of Brazil's oldest towns, in continuous settlement since the early 1500's. Numerous relics from the colonial past are scattered throughout this sprawling hillside town which has declined considerably since its heyday as a great port and agricultural center. The main attraction here—other than the coastline of unspoiled beaches and picturesque palm-lined coves—is the **Ilha Grande.** The large island was once a pirate colony, but is today occupied by several fishing hamlets and a Brazilian penal colony. The island's interior is virtually uninhabited, covered by a tropical forest which rises and falls over somewhat hilly terrain. This island is the ideal place for trekking overland from one hamlet to another, and for camping in seclusion on the beach of a suitable cove.

Where to Stay

The **Pousada Mar da Tranquilidade** (tel. 0243/288-4162) is located in Abraão, the principal hamlet on Ilha Grande, and the point of debarkation for the ferryboat. The inn, charging $35 for double occupancy, is attractive and clean, the best option on the island for those not wishing to camp or find simpler accommodations in one of the fishing hamlets, where residents will provide a suitable pallet or hammock for a pittance. Reservations at the inn are necessary to be assured of accommodations. Angra is a wonderful place to visit for island-hopping or camping on the beaches, but it is not the place to lodge yourself in a hotel when Parati is only an hour or so down the road.

Embarking from the port of Angra at noon on Monday and Friday, however, is the **Frade Mar,** a floating four-star hotel aboard a large schooner. The sailing ship, with 12 first-class cabins and semi-private baths, cruises the bay, making several ports of call—including Ilha Grande—and offers a wide range of aquatic sports from fishing to wind surfing. The price for the cruise is around $270 per double. Reservations are made at the central number for the Frade Hotel chain in Rio, 267-7375.

PARATI

The only blemish along the road from Angra to Parati is Brazil's first nuclear power plant, near Cunhambebe, the very existence of which sends shudders up the spines of Brazilian ecologists who worry about the potential for radioactive pollution of the nearby waters. Other than that, the scenery is the same delicious ensemble of sea and mountains that characterized the earlier stage of the journey, a visual backdrop that is never tiresome.

You'll enter Parati by way of an access road off the main highway, and the scene along it is typical of rural Brazil everywhere. There are the inevitable groups of shirtless men lounging in front of the many open-fronted commercial shops, while other players in this mundane pageant are driving by in a variety of conveyances, from rickety trucks to horsecarts to bicycles. The side streets are all unpaved, and bare-bottomed toddlers play in the mud while their mothers with babes in arms sit cow-eyed in the open doorways. These are the folk that Brazil's history has always left in its wake, even in a town like Parati, which was always relatively prosperous, indeed a veritable power during colonial days, and a thriving tourist attraction today.

The Story of Parati

Parati's harbor was deep enough and just the right scale for ships of the colonial days, which called there often to load their holds with precious stones and gold from nearby Minas, and later with the coffee and sugarcane that was cultivated so successfully on the surrounding hills. The cane cultivation led to the creation of an ancillary industry, the production of *aguadente de cana,* the archaic name for what is today generally known as pinga or cachaça. Actually, cachaça was originally distilled from honey, while only cana or pinga came from sugarcane alcohol. Parati, in any case, became the pinga capital of Brazil, and is still considered to produce the highest quality sugarcane brandy in the country.

The heart of Parati, today, is a seven-square-block area, set on a jutting neck of land between harbor and river, that might easily have been plucked from the mid-1700s and placed in the present, so authentic is the preservation of its buildings and streets. Development ceased in Parati when a new road was laid in 1723 from the mine fields and plantations of Minas to Rio, bypassing the once active port. And so Parati slept for almost two and a half centuries in virtual isolation from the rest of the country. But the miniature city never decayed, sustaining itself on local agriculture, fishing, and, as always, on the production of pinga. A new road connecting the town to Angra in the 1950s opened Parati anew, first to artists and bohemians, who were captivated by the tranquility and ambience of the place, and lately to the casual tourist.

The Sights and Festivals

The historic core of Parati has now been declared a national monument by Brazil, and a world treasure by UNESCO. Motor vehicle traffic has been banned from its narrow, stone-paved streets.

Many of the historical buildings are private homes, but a fair number also house shops and inns, though the air of commercialization remains extremely faint despite the obvious gentrification. Parati is so genuine in its every detail that even the most effete bohemian would still feel at ease here, and the artist no less inspired.

It hardly bears mentioning that one must visit Parati in the daytime, although I highly recommend an overnight in one of the superb inns. It doesn't take more than a couple of hours to see the entire town, including the delightful slave's church, the **Igreja do Rosário** (1725), on the Rua do Comércio across from the post office. Note the black face of the statue of St. Benedict.

The harbor is very quiet, and at the dock are moored the colorful fishing craft that today carry tourists on excursions around the bay.

There are several interesting festivals held in Parati every year. The most important is the **Festa do Divino,** a religious festival of great significance in Portuguese culture dating from the 13th century, and preserved in Parati from the legacy of its own colonial past. The festival culminates on Pentecost Sunday, after ten days of diverse activities, sacred and profane, including medieval pageantry with songs and processions, craft fairs and sporting competitions. The **Festival da Pinga,** a kind of Brazilian Oktoberfest, takes place in August from the 22nd to the 24th. Holy Week and Carnival are two other important periods of celebration in Parati.

The Bay and Environs

Numerous saveiros also cruise the waters off Parati to take in a panorama of sights that can best be viewed from the sea. Parati was protected by several strong fortifications, which remain as a historical testament to the days when a million tons of gold were shipped from its wharves. It is also claimed that there are, in all, 65 islands and 300 beaches that may be visited in the vicinity of the town.

Also visible from the water, opposite a point called Boa Vista, is the steam-driven mill of the Quero Essa pinga factory.

The schooner **Soberano da Costa** makes a daily cruise of the bay, which includes stopovers for swimming, leaving at noon and returning at 4:30 pm. Two pinga factories, the **Engenho Murycana** and the **Engenho Quero Essa,** both located on colonial fazendas, may be visited by land.

Staying the Night in Parati

Parati offers lodgings, within its historic district, in some of the most attractive inns to be found anywhere in all of Brazil. The **Estalagem Mercado de Pouso,** Rua Dona Geralda 43 (tel. 0243/71-1114), occupies an extreme corner of the town, with its back to the wharf and the splendid Santa Rita Church to its front. The inn has 19 rooms and 5 suites, all under thick-beamed ceilings with views of interior gardens, or in ateliers that look over the tiled rooftops of neighboring buildings—in all, an extraordinarily beautiful interior environment. The rate per double occupancy is $40 for a room and $55 for a suite.

The Frade's **Pousada Dom João** is located at the other extreme end of the town on the Rua do Comércio 01 (tel. 0243/71-1205), near the river and behind the Igreja Nossa Senhora dos Remédios. With 40 rooms, the inn also has a swimming pool and a gorgeous outdoor patio and garden. Reservations are made in Rio (tel. 267-7375), and transportation is offered by the Frade company, which provides regular bus shuttle service from Rio to all of its hotels along the Costa Verde. The cost per night is $50 for a double room.

Two other choices in the same price range and with similar luxurious accommodations and amenities, are the **Pousada Padieiro,** at the opposite end of the Rua do Comércio at no. 74 (tel. 0243/71-1370); and the **Pousada do Ouro,** Rua da Praia 145 (tel. 0243/71-1311).

Budget Choice

The **Hotel Solar dos Gerânios,** Praça da Matriz (tel. 0243/71-1550), is a Swiss-run inn occupying a building with much of the original interior intact, including a massive stone central stairway that leads to a second-floor corridor with a number of very simple rooms without baths. The inn is also filled with antique furnishings collected by the owners and left in their unfinished state, a condition that strangely enhances their aesthetic appeal. Double accommodations are $15 per night.

For camping, there is the nearby Praia do Jabaquara.

Eating in Parati

All the better inns in Parati, including those listed above, have their own excellent restaurants. For a good homecooked Brazilian meal of steak or chicken breast with all the usual side dishes, try the **Restaurante Santa Rita,** across from the Igreja Santa Rita at the corner of Rua da Matriz. For $4 or $5 per person, including beverage, you can eat simply but extremely well there.

A fancier choice is the **Restaurante Ancoradouro,** Rua Dona Geralda 345 (tel. 71-1394), around the corner from the Pousada Mercado do Pouso. The menu is international, and entrees fall in the $5 to $10 range.

The **Do Lixo Ao Luxo,** on Rua Do Comércio (tel. 71-1124), is a combination bar, restaurant, and antique shop. The name means "From the Garbage to the Rich," and the colonial-era goods, including cast-iron cooking stoves, are certainly expensive and very beautiful.

Tourist Information

The old jail house, next to the Igreja Santa Rita, has a desk where you can get a program of the latest happenings in town. There also is a tiny gift shop on the premises with some attractive and well-made craft items. Open daily from 9 a.m. until 4 p.m. (tel. 71-1256).

4. Coastal São Paulo

Roughly 48 km (30 miles) down the coast from Parati, having crossed into São Paulo State while continuing along the Rio-Santos shoreline highway, you will come upon a flat coastal strip where a string of 73 beaches are all incorporated into the municipal sphere of a resort town with the melodious name of **Ubatuba.**

The myriad beaches stretch over a distance of almost 72 km (45 miles) in both directions from Ubatuba, an old and fair-sized seaside community with a year-round population of 35,000. The word *ubatuba,* incidentally, is indigenous and literally means "place where the shafts grow," referring to the poles used by the earlier inhabitants to fashion their fishing spears. During Carnival—which always falls during the week before the Catholic penetential season of Lent—Ubatuba's population swells to some 400,000 souls. Most visitors during this particular time of the year, the majority of whom hail from Rio and São Paulo, come for the same singular reason: to escape Carnival. Clearly, Brazilians are not universally fond of their national festival.

By the same token, the Carnival period is not the time for foreign visitors to visit Ubatuba, a locale that is best viewed as an off-season resort, when the vacation crowds have diminished and the resort's hotel rates plummet to half of what is charged during the high season—December through February, and during the July school holiday.

WHAT TO SEE AND DO IN UBATUBA

You could spend your entire time in Ubatuba trying to figure out which of the 73 beaches is the most perfect according to your own criteria. If, however, the sun should fail you on a given day, or if your peripatetic rhythms prevent you from staying prone in the tanning position for more than a few hours at a time, there are a number of touring and activity options which might be of appeal.

Of historical interest is the previously mentioned colonial-era town of Parati (assuming you have approached Ubatuba from São Paulo and not Rio). There are also a number of **ruins** in the area: an old coffee plantation's slave quarters, Brazil's first glass factory, and a fort built at the turn of the century on nearby Anchieta Island, now a wildlife sanctuary, a ten-minute boat ride from the mainland.

A full range of **aquatic sports** from skindiving to sailing is also available. The tourist agency **Ubatur,** Rua Flamenguinho 17 on the Saco da Ribeira beach (tel. 0124/42-0388), offers tours, schooner excursions, diving equipment, and boat- and car-rental services.

WHERE TO STAY AND EAT

As with many Brazilian resort areas, you have the option of staying close to the center of activity or in relative seclusion, according to the dictates of your mood and constitution. The in-town hotel of choice has to be the **Ubatuba Palace Hotel,** Rua Coronel Domiciano 500 (tel. 0124/32-1500, or 011/280-8496 in São Paulo for reservations). This venerable 59-room hotel is a block from the Avenida das Praias, the town's principal oceanfront thoroughfare, where the evening promenade takes place and where nightlife is centered on the avenue's many cafés, restaurants, and beer gardens.

The rooms at the Ubatuba Palace all have deep-green louvered doors, and front on common balconies which offer a view of the town. Furnishings are comfortable and attractive in a *fazenda* (ranchhouse) style, right down to the pious placement of crucifixes over the queen-sized beds. The hotel's several two-room suites are huge, with private balconies. Regular-season single-room rates are quite reasonable at $90 for two, including half pension, and the off-season price is a steal at $25 per person, including breakfast and your choice of either lunch or dinner.

It will require no hardship to eat in the Ubatuba Palace dining room where the food, ranging in price from $6 to $15 à la carte, is of genuine gourmet quality. The shrimp crêpe, with its creamy sauce, will melt in your mouth. The hotel also offers a very attractive pool and lounging area, and a steamroom.

Surrounding this hotel is a warren of small streets filled with craft shops and stores of every variety, laid out among the obligatory church-dominated plazas and small parks. The overall effect of municipal Ubatuba, however, is of an informal beach town where people in bathing costumes are in a constant parade either toward or away from the beachfront.

One choice for a more remote, resort-style hotel is the **Torremolinos,** Rua Domingos Della Mónica Barbosa 37, at Enseada Beach (tel. 0124/42-625). There are 37 rooms in this modern, three-story beachfront hotel, which has the look of a Frank Lloyd Wright original. Most of the brightly decorated rooms face the ocean and open onto small balconies. Two pools—one for adults, the other for children—and a large tiled patio area with chaise lounges and umbrellas, separate the hotel from the sandy beach. The hotel has a restaurant and a poolside snack bar, and it's about a 15-minute car ride from Ubatuba. The daily rates at the Torremolinos are comparable to those of the Ubatuba Palace, both during the *temporada* (high season) and the *baixa* (low season).

The nearby **Mediterrâneo,** also on the Enseada beach (tel. 0214/42-0386), is true to its name, architecturally speaking. The grand white façade with the awninged windows, is certainly imbued with a look of the European Riviera. Set against verdant rising hills and surrounded by tropical vegetation and lawns, the hotel looks out over the breaking sea. Steps from a large one-story-high terrace with pool lead down to the beach, where tables, chairs, and umbrellas have been placed for the convenience of the guests. The 30 rooms, depending on the season, range from $65 to $75 a night for two, breakfast included.

For between $23 and $26 a night, for double occupancy and breakfast, you can stay off-season at the **Hotel Village Tropical,** also located at the edge of Enseada beach (tel. 0124/42-0055). The 24-room, two-story building has interior courtyards and open-air corridors filled with plants, like a Brazilian ranchhouse. There is also a beautifully planted *quintal* (yard) between the hotel and the beach, but no pool. High-season rates climb to between $50 and $55 per night.

CAMPOS DO JORDÃO

A logical place to visit after a stay in Ubatuba, especially for those touring independently by car or bus, is the mountain resort town of **Campos do Jordão.** The drive up the winding sierra from the shore at this point—via São Luís do Paraitinga and Taubaté—can be an unforgettable journey. The road curves around the hills in an ever-ascending spiral and becomes as narrow as a logging trail in places. A perpetual mist hangs in these mountains, slowing your pace to that of a caravan. After some three hours of this often breathtaking climb, you arrive in the mountain retreat of Campos do Jordão.

When *Paulistanos* (as the residents of São Paulo city are called) want fresh air and cooler temperatures, this is where they come. July is the coldest month in Campos do Jordão, when the mercury frequently hovers at the frost line overnight, but warms up to a comfortable afternoon temperature of 50°F to 60°F on many days. The natural setting of this resort town is not so unlike its counterparts in New England, although architecturally its style is alpine, reflecting the European origins of many of its inhabitants. Narrow, winding roads climb the surrounding peaks, revealing around every curve the drive of a fine hotel or, at roadside, a chalet-style inn, all set among the towering evergreens of a dense conifer forest. By late March, the few hardwood trees—mostly maples seemingly so out of place in this country of predominantly tropical vegetation—already display autumnal coloring and cover small patches of ground everywhere with their fallen leaves.

Campos do Jordão is entered through a formal portal which opens into the town's commercial center. Beyond this neighborhood, called Abernéssia, are the more swank residential and touristic sections of Juaguaribe and Capivari, where most of the shops, boutiques, and restaurants are located. Local crafts include products of the *malha* cottage industry—handmade pullovers and cardigans, a reminder of the town's frequent sweater-weather climate. But the greatest resource of the town is its pure mountain air, kept crisp and healthy at its protected mile-high altitude.

For further information, or to book reservations for Campos do Jordão directly in São Paulo, call **Campostur,** Rua 7 de Abril 404, sixth floor (tel. 255-1156).

WHAT TO SEE AND DO

The **Festival de Inverno** (Winter Carnival) occupies the entire month of July each year, with special events and festivities scheduled for every day. Classical musicians flock to Campos do Jordão in July, and daily chamber music concerts are a big part of the scene.

For year-round enjoyment, there is the **Parque Florestal,** located in a remote corner of the town, along a mountain dirt road where cows graze freely under the boughs of the evergreens on the forested hillsides. The park has a trout hatchery, and many of these speckled beauties can be seen swimming in the local streams. There is also a working water-powered saw mill and wood-working shop, and many separate picnic environments. You can rent horses at a stable near the park's entrance, the gently sloping terrain and open woods seemingly ideal for riding. Hiking and backpacking are also popular pastimes in the surrounding countryside.

The town also has a **mountain train** that makes hour-long excursions to a nearby village lower down the slopes, São José dos Campos.

A ski lift off the town's main square carries interested sightseers to a local mountaintop, the **Morro do Elefante,** for a panoramic view of the town and the surrounding Paraiba valley.

WHERE TO STAY AND EAT

There are over 50 hotels of differing categories in the region. Most hotels include full board with their rates, so guests tend to eat "at home" while in Campos do Jordão.

The **Hotel e Restaurante Vila Regina,** Avenida Emílio Lang Júnior 443 (tel. 0122-63-1036), is typical of the mid-range inns in Campos do Jordão, with 22 modern and comfortable rooms. The daily rate for two is $105, which includes all three meals. The restaurant is decorated hunting-lodge style, and specializes in baked trout along with a host of other international and Italian dishes. As an apéritif, try a *negroni*—a cocktail made from sweet vermouth, campari, and gin, served ice cold with a lemon wedge, sufficiently novel and uplifting that you may ask for a refill.

Other popular lodges are the town's two five-star inns, the **Vila Inglesa** ($128 double), Rua Sen. Roberto Simonsenn 3500 (tel. 0122/63-1955), and the **Orotur Garden Hotel** ($133 double), on Rua 3 (tel. 0122/62-2833), both of which are expensive and have long been watering holes of an elite clientele from São Paulo. Prices for both hotels include all meals.

On the other end of the price spectrum are the **Cantinho de Portugal,** Rua Alexandre Sirim 127 (tel. 0122/62-1439), and the **Estoril,** Avenida Macedo Soares 241 (tel. 0122/63-1932).

Authorization to stay in the local youth hostel, the **Casa Azul,** may be obtained through the tourist office in the bus station.

Trout and fondue are the food specialties of the region. The **Só Quijo,** Avenida Macedo Soares 642 (tel. 63-1910), is an attractive restaurant in a colonial-style building, which in addition to the regional specialties, also serves crêpes and steaks.

Willy's Confeitaria, Avenida Macedo Soares 183 (tel. 63-1015), has an informal café atmosphere, and serves meals and desserts.

For French cuisine there is the **Casa D'Irene,** Rua Raul Mesquita 83 (tel. 63-1115), offering pâté maison, escargot, rabbit, and steak au poivre vert.

XI

ELSEWHERE IN BRAZIL

1. OURO PRETO
2. IGUAÇU FALLS
3. SALVADOR, BAHIA

Your vacation in Rio may be a dream come true. But what about the rest of Brazil? You've come all this distance, fallen in love with the Brazilians and their unique way of life, but, realistically, what are your chances of coming back to experience something of the rest of this magical continent-size nation? Among the great Brazilian cities, Rio is certainly *primus inter pares* (first among equals). But Rio's gorgeous beaches represent only a fraction of Brazil's 5,000-mile-long coastline. Brazilians themselves are often heard extolling not the well-known carioca beaches, but the unchartered strands of the *nordeste* (the legendary northeast), beginning with the region's gateway city of Salvador, Bahia. And Salvador's appeal, of course, goes way beyond its perpetual sunshine and beautiful beaches. This former colonial capital with the distinctly African flavor offers visitors a unique view of Brazilian culture, past and present. Another jewel of Brazil's golden era is Ouro Preto, one of several historic cities not far from Rio in the neighboring state of Minas Gerais. As for natural wonders, Brazil is hardly lacking in spectacular attractions, not the least of which are the Falls of Iguaçu in the south and the vast northern wilderness known as Amazonia, accessible to the visitor from the river city of Manaus.

HOW TO SEE MORE OF BRAZIL, CHEAPLY

Paradoxically, at least where foreign visitors are concerned, normally expensive air travel within Brazil can be surprisingly economical. The trick is to purchase a **VARIG Airline Air Pass** before you arrive in Brazil. VARIG is Brazil's flagship airline with the most flights to Brazil from both the U.S. and Canada. The airline offe s two categories of air pass. The two-week pass allows you to visit four additional Brazilian cities at a cost of $250. The three-week air pass, priced at $330, permits unlimited travel within the alloted time frame. The time does not begin to expire on either pass until its first use. The traveler who comes to Brazil for a month, armed with an air pass, can easily visit all the destinations described in this chapter, and still spend at least one glorious week in Rio de Janeiro. But remember, you can only buy the air pass outside of Brazil.

---

1. Ouro Preto

The title "Cultural Heritage of Mankind" was conferred on the city of Ouro Preto by UNESCO in 1980. Founded in 1711 as Vila Rica do Albequerque, Ouro Preto today contains the largest homogeneous collection of baroque architecture in Brazil. In a country oversaturated with baroque and colonial-era buildings, that's saying a lot. Ouro Preto is located 100 km (62 miles) from the city of Belo Horizonte which is an hour's flight from Rio.

THE HISTORICAL CITIES OF MINAS GERAIS

For the first 200 years, colonists in Brazil had confined their settlements to the country's coastal lands. They had looked on the mountainous interior as impassable and unihabitable. Late in the 17th century, however, word slowly drifted back to the coast that the pioneers and slave hunters, known as *bandeirantes,* had discovered gold in those inhospitable hills. Within a short time, the wealth that flowed from those early grub stakes attracted hordes of settlers to the virgin territory, and the rude camps of the prospectors were transformed almost overnight into the glittering pinnacles of baroque culture that are known today as the historical cities of Minas Gerais.

Along with Ouro Preto, the historical cities include Sabará, Mariana, Congnhas do Campo, Sao João del Rei, Tiradentes, and Diamentina. All are living tableaux of Brazil's "Cycle of Gold" which occurred throughout the 1700s, but touched the fringes of two other centuries as well, running from the 1690s to the early 1800s, by which time the auriferous flow from the mines had slowed to a trickle. The principal attractions of the historical cities are the scores of churches, residences, and commercial structures that have been preserved from those times, and the artistry with which the façades and interiors of those churches were decorated by a dozen great artists, most notable of whom were the sculptor Antônio Francisco Lisboa, called *Aleijadinho,* (The Little Cripple) and the painter Manuel da Costa Atraide.

Ouro Preto sits high in the mountains at an elevation of over 3,000 feet, so the climate is somewhat mild, with temperatures ranging from 40°F to 85°F. The highest point, at over 5,600 feet, is the landmark **Pico de Itacolomi.** There is no valley to speak of in Ouro Preto. Human structures occupy all the available spaces on the tightly packed hills, which are etched with a network of winding and narrow stone streets that follow the steep contours of the land across a dozen diminutive bridges over streams that empty from the surrounding heights, opening here and there into many small plazas, each of which is crowned with a graceful church.

WHAT TO SEE

Churches, churches, and more churches—each one packed with religious art and enriched by its own unique history and legend. Add to these the other historical buildings and museums, restaurants and inns, craft shops and events, and there's plenty to keep a visitor occupied and satisfied for days on end. The best way to see all the sights is in the company of a city guide. These uniformed guides, who are hired from their office on Praça Tiradentes 41 (tel. 551-1544, ext. 69), charge about $15 for four hours and are excellent sources of information on the art, history, and lore of the city. A map, stylized but useful, can also be purchased at the guide office for about $1, showing all the main streets and the placement of the principal sights.

To visit the first two churches, you will probably want to take a cab, as they are located on the fringes of town. Otherwise, unless health prohibits—the streets are often quite steep and the climbs can be arduous—most of the other places of interest are centered within walking distance of the main square, the Praça Tiradentes.

Capela Do Padre Faria

One of the early bandeirantes in the area, a Padre Faria, ordered a chapel to be built in 1701 in the vicinity of the earliest mines. The chapel, therefore, is located in the oldest section of the early settlement that predates the actual founding of the city. Towerless and rustic on the outside, the church is extremely ornate within, the main and two side altars both richly veneered in gold. The vestment cabinet is the oldest in the city, and the colors for the dome mural of the Coronation of Mary, painted in 1727, were all mixed from natural elements: the red from *sanguede-boi* (bull's blood), a kind of fruit; yellow from egg yolk; brown from a mixture of banana juice with the root of a local vine. Water damage has all but destroyed other ceiling panels in the chapel, a reality that underscores the terrible burden Brazil faces with maintaining its priceless art treasures in a country where resources for such projects are understandably scarce. Open 8 a.m. until noon daily, except Monday, when all the churches in Ouro Preto are closed.

The nearby **Rua Santa Rita** is Ouro Preto's oldest street, with its original paving stones called *pe-de-muleque,* the Brazilian term for peanut brittle. Some early slave houses can be seen along this street, which is still one of the poorest sections of the city. Of special interest are the roadside excavations where some of the earliest gold diggings in the city were made. They remain as cavities cut in the sides of embankments, overgrown with vegetation but otherwise unaltered.

Santa Efigênia

Built in 1723 entirely of granite from Mount Itacolomi, the church is also known as Our Lady of the Rosary, whose image (attributed to Aleijadinho) occupies a niche over the portal. Both Our

Lady of the Rosary and Saint Efigênia (a Christian Nubian princess) were patrons of the slaves, whose church this was. Legend has it that slave women hid purloined gold dust in their hair and then washed the mineral out in fonts at the church door, to provide a fund for artists who worked on the church. Open to visitors 8 a.m. to noon daily except Mondays.

Matriz De Nossa Senhora Da Conceição

This is Ouro Preto's largest church, dating from 1727. The church was designed by Manuel Francisco Lisboa, Aleijadinho's father, who also created the first altar on the right (one of eight side altars), beneath which his son Aleijadinho is buried. The church was not completed until the early 1800s, and the interior decor alternates between the carved wood of the baroque period and the later rococo style which made use of molded plaster. A side door in the church leads to the **Aleijadinho Museum,** which includes the artist's sculpture of São Francisco de Paula. The statue's head is of carved soapstone, and is painted. To this day it is not understood how Aleijadinho got the paint to adhere to the cold, smooth surface of the stone. The museum and church are open from 8 to 11:30 a.m. and from 1 to 5 p.m.

Igreja Do Pilar

This is the richest church in Ouro Preto, on the charming square in the middle of the city, dating from 1711. Over 1,000 pounds of gold, and nearly the equivalent in silver, add an almost blinding glitter to the carvings, much of which were the creation of Aleijadinho's father, his uncle (Antônio Francisco Pombal), and the artist's principal mentor, Francisco Xavier de Brito.

São Francisco De Assis

This church, located near the town's principal square, the Praça Tiradentes, is considered the jewel of Ouro Preto. It was designed by Aleijadinho and commissioned by the local military command in 1765. The façade, with its great medallion in soapstone, is one of the finest of Aleijadinho's works of this kind, carved entirely by his own hands without the assistance of his students or associates. The ceiling painting in the central nave is a rococo creation by Atraide.

Praça Tiradentes

This was the principal plaza of old Vila Rica, as it is Ouro Preto's main square today. On one end is the old Governor's Palace, at the other, the former Legislative Chambers and Jail. Both buildings currently house museums. Until well into the 19th century, the slave market and the public whipping post were both located in this square, which remains a picture of the past, with its stone pavement and border of colonial buildings. At the center of the square is a statue of Tiradentes, marking the spot where the republican martyr's severed head was displayed in a cage following his execution.

Museu De Mineralogia

A mineral museum containing some 20,000 pieces, uncut gems and minerals—precious and common—from the region, has been installed in what was the **Palácio do Governador** (Governor's Palace) in Minas Gerais from 1746 to 1897. The building was constructed in 1740 by Manuel Francisco Lisboa. In addition to the mineral collection, there is a gracious chapel in the palace that is worth visiting. Open daily from noon to 6 p.m.

Museu Dos Inconfidentes

The museum's exhibition rooms are filled with cultural artifacts of the colonial period, from arms to implements of torture used to punish the slaves, from plate and furnishings to the ubiquitous samples of religious art and liturgical paraphernalia. The two most important exhibits are the Aleijadinho room, with the articulated statue of St. George, which was mounted on horseback and used during public processions honoring the saint, and the monument to the *Inconfidentes,* an austere mausoleum containing the remains of many of the revolutionaries who, along with Tiradentes, failed to carry off an uprising against the Portuguese in 1789.

WHERE TO STAY

A number of the colonial-era dwellings have been converted into pousadas, inns of the bed-and-breakfast variety. One decision on choosing accommodations in Ouro Preto is whether to stay close to the center of town, within walking distance of many restaurants and other attractions, or in the outlying districts, where one's options include several fine inns and a resort-style hotel.

Formerly a state-run hotel, the **Grande Hotel de Ouro Preto,** Rua Senador Pocha Lagoa 164 (tel. 031/551-1488), has one of the best locations within the small city. Only a block from the central plaza, the Praça Tiradentes, and within easy reach of the largest number of shops and restaurants, the Grande Hotel, at only $37 per night double and $27 single, is a choice to be reckoned with. The Grande Hotel is the only modern structure in the city, designed by Oscar Niemeyer—principal architect of Brasília—and not one of his successes by any means. The hotel contains 17 rooms with baths, and the same number of duplex-style suites priced at $66 a night.

On the other end of the comfort spectrum, and across the street from the stunning Matriz de Nossa Senhora da Conçeicão, is the **Luxor Pousada,** Praca Antônio Dias 10 (tel. 031/551-2244). This inn occupies an old town house and has only 16 rooms, but they are first class all the way. The rooms are decorated in a colonial simplicity that is totally harmonious with Vila Rica tradition. All rooms have color TV, mini-bars, telephones, and separate baths. There is a small restaurant in the cellar, where guests also eat their breakfasts, under a beamed ceiling, surrounded by a foundation wall of stone. Rates are from $80 to $95 for a single, and from $90 to $105 for a double.

Unfortunately, I didn't get to visit the **Pousada te Galeria Panorama Barroco,** Rua Conselheiro Quitiliano 722 (tel. 031/

551-3366). But I was so impressed with the letter that owners David and Lucia Peterkin sent me, that I've decided to mention their small inn sight unseen. What impressed me was their commitment to the role of innkeepers, and the simple extras they offer with their rooms which demonstrate a genuine interest in the comfort of their guests. The inn has only six rooms in what the Peterkins describe as a renovated colonial house, where, they say, you will find "a comfortable bed, a substantial breakfast, a secure room, and a relaxed environment." The house is a ten-minute walk from the Praça Tiradentes, and at a level that provides a scenic view of the city from the veranda and rooms. There is also a telescope for stargazing and a library with editions in English on local flora and fauna, gems, history, and anthropology. Use of their washing machine is extra, as are excursions they will organize for sightseeing or gem buying in their four-wheel-drive land cruiser. Prices are in the $10 range per person.

The **Quinta dos Baroês,** Rua Pandia Cologera 474 (tel. 031/551-1056), is small but delightful, on a quiet lane which rises above the center of Ouro Preto in a nearby suburb. This old baronial country house has seven extremely well-appointed rooms, furnished and decorated in period pieces. There is also a small restaurant in the old cellar. The inn is a short cab ride (or long walk) from the center of Ouro Preto. For comfort, elegant surroundings, as well as peace and quiet, there are no better lodgings in the city. The rooms are priced at $25 to $30 for the standard, and $35 to $40 for the two deluxe accommodations.

The **Pouso do Chico Rey,** Rua Brigadeiro Musqueira 90 (tel. 031/551-1274), is another lovely little inn, this time on a side street, very near the Praça Tiradentes. There are three rooms and three apartments, the difference being that only the latter have baths. The several attractive public rooms at various levels give the inn a genuine "house" feeling. Breakfast is included in the price of the rooms, which range from $20 to $35.

A recent addition to Ouro Preto's inns, is the **Pousada Mondego,** Largo do Coimbra 38 (tel. 551-2040), directly across from the Igreja São Francisco de Assis and one block from Tiradente Square. Rooms with special views go for between $55 and $65 nightly, and those with balconies range from $60 to $72 per night, single or double.

The **Hotel da Estrada Real,** Rodovia dos Inconfidentes, km 87 (tel. 031/551-2112), is found about 8 km (5 miles) outside the city in the hills off the highway. This is the largest and fanciest hotel in Ouro Preto, in a beautifully landscaped resort-like setting on a scenic overlook. The hotel also has a fine restaurant, popular with guests and nonguests alike. Some of the 40 rooms are housed in separate bungalows at $71 a night. Rates for a standard room are $61 for a double, while deluxe rooms are priced at $76 for two. Special facilities include a large pool and a tennis court.

WHERE TO EAT

One of the most popular restaurants of Ouro Preto is the **Casa do Ouvidor,** Rua Direita 42 (tel. 551-2141), located on the second floor. There is always a good crowd dining here on any given day, a blend of locals and tourists. Most items on the à la carte menu range from $5 to $7. Brazilian drinks like caipirinhas are only about $1 each. Open daily from noon until midnight.

The **Casa de Pedra**, Rua Pandia Calogera 503 (tel. 551-2790), is a wine-and-cheese house, also serving fondue and other international dishes. This restaurant is directly across the street from the pousada Quinta dos Baroēs, whose own small restaurant is also open to the public.

The **Taberna Luxor,** in the Luxor Pousada has an excellent reputation.

Several other restaurants to consider are the **Restaurante da Estação,** Praça da Estação, in the old train station; **Taverna do Chafariz,** Rua São José 167 (tel. 551-2828); and the **Restaurante Vila Rica,** Praça Tiradentes 132 (tel. 551-2293)—all of which serve international dishes, as well as *comida Mineira,* the regional dishes of Minas Gerais, at prices in the $4 to $6 range.

---

2. Iguaçu Falls

Iguaçu Falls is the second most popular destination for North American travelers in Brazil after Rio de Janeiro. No wonder! The falls are truly one of the world's great natural phenomena, and are understandably the main attraction in Brazil's southern region.

THE RIVER IGUAÇU

Rising from an obscure spring on the outskirts of Curitiba, the Iguaçu River flows from the high coastal plateau inland, merging its waters with the mighty Rio Paraná. The Iguaçu winds along its westerly course for nearly 800 river miles. The final stretch of the river forms a border between Brazil and Argentina, cutting through the last great expanse of Atlantic rain forest that remains in South America. On both sides of the border, the forest—over 500,000 acres in all—has been converted to national park lands, providing a preserve for over 2,000 varieties of vegetation, and habitat for a large population of native fauna, including 400 bird species and innumerable reptiles and insects. About 11 km (7 miles) above its mouth (foz), the Iguaçu widens its bed to a span of some 3 km (2 miles), and here drops precipitously over a 200-foot-high cliff, forming an interconnected curtain of 275 cataracts.

THE BORDER TOWNS

By far the most appealing of the three border towns is **Foz do Iguaçu** on the Brazilian side. Over the past decade, Foz (as the town is called by locals) has grown in population from about 40,000 to 160,000 inhabitants, a boom resulting from the construction of the nearby Itaipú Dam, the world's largest hydroelectric power station. On the Paraguayan side is **Ciudad del Este,** a free port where Brazilians go to buy electronic appliances. **Puerto Iguazu** on the Argentinian side is a town very much in formation, given a boost by the inauguration of a new bridge linking Argentina with the Brazilian mainland.

WHEN TO GO

The Iguaçu Falls have a wet season and a dry season. The rains fall in the winter months, April through July, and so the volume of water crashing over the cliffs is greatest during that season, and the weather is mild, though it can be quite chilly in the vicinity of the falls themselves. During the autumn and summer months, the temperatures climb to their subtropical warmest, with humidity and mosquitos to match, and the water flow is cut by a third during the driest periods. In 1977, the falls dried up for the only time in recorded history. And in 1983, the flooding was so severe that much of the vegetation surrounding the cataracts, as well as a network of catwalks that allowed visitors a spectacular close-up view of the falls from numerous vantage points, were completely destroyed. They have since been rebuilt.

GETTING TO IGUAÇU

The falls are such a popular attraction—at least on the Brazilian side—that there is an international airport near Foz do Iguaçu receiving several daily 1¾-hour flights from Rio, via São Paulo, and from other points within Brazil, as well. Round-trip airfare from Rio, for those who do not have a VARIG air pass, is approximately $174.

CONSULATES AND VISITOR INFORMATION

In the city of Foz de Iguaçu, the **Argentine Consulate** maintains offices at Rua Dom Pedro I 28 (tel. 74-2877) and the **Paraguayan Consulate** at Rua Bartolomeo de Gusmao 480 (tel. 72-1169). The city of Foz also maintains a tourist information center, **FOZTUR,** at Rua Almirante Barroso 485, and a special three-digit *teletur* number, 139, for information, suggestions, and complaints.

THE FALLS: TWO DISTINCT VIEWS

There is a primary distinction between the Brazilian and Argentine vistas of the Iguaçu Falls. Since most of the cataracts are on the Argentine side, the Brazilian view is more sweeping, more panoramic. The system of catwalks and paths on the Argentine side provide the visitor with a powerfully intimate experience, as you follow the outline of the river wall, alternately walking from the edge of one cataract to another. Each view has its compelling validity; and so both must be experienced for one to claim to have really seen the Iguaçu Falls.

The Brazilian View

A clearly marked stairway opposite the famous Hotel das Cataratas leads to a mile-long path that accompanies the river upstream. This walk offers a spectacular view of the falls across the lower river, which has narrowed at this point to channel width. The high ground to the land side is matted with dense forest growth, and if you are lucky, you may sight a creature or two flitting through the underbrush. As you walk, a wider and wider horizon of crashing waters opens to view, until you reach the end of the trail near a tall elevator tower. The descent has been gradual, with many viewing stations along the way, but here you are actually below the first step of the Brazilian falls. A screened-in catwalk set on stone pillars leads, through clouds of boiling mists, to the very rim of a lower cataract, and the view here is a thoroughly breathtaking experience. Depending on the time of year, you can expect to be soaked or merely dampened while walking on this catwalk. During the steamy weather, the shower can be welcome and refreshing; otherwise, bring rain gear or rent an outfit from the enterprising vendors along the trail.

The Argentine Side

When visiting the Argentine National Park, using the services of a tour company makes considerable sense, especially if your time is limited. Rather than hassle the logistics as an individual, not the least of which is the border crossing, you can leave all these details to the tour guide. By all means carry your passport with you when crossing into either Paraguay or Argentina. Visas are not generally required for day trips into these particular border areas, but in the case of Argentina, this is not always so. Better check with an Argentine consulate before traveling to Iguaçu to avoid disappointment. Or consult with the consulate in Foz itself.

The entrance to the Argentine **Parque Nacional de Iquazu** is about 19 km (12 miles) beyond the town of Puerto Iguazu. A good place to begin your exploration, however, is several miles beyond the entrance at **Puerto Canoas,** which is serviced by park buses. Here a 1-km (half-mile) catwalk leads to the edge of the famous **Garganta do Diabo** (Devil's Throat)—the largest single waterfall in the world in terms of its volume of water-flow per second— which straddles the imaginary frontier line in the river between Brazil and Argentina. Along this walk, there are signs everywhere of the damage wrought by the devastating flood in 1983—the ruins of the original catwalk provide a particularly humbling reminder of nature's dark and angry side. Otherwise, on a given day, one is enveloped in the overwhelming beauty of the place, where so many strands of the great outdoors are woven into a single tableau. On one extreme, there is the serenity of the shallow river beneath your feet, gently flowing among the dozens of fragmented islets that sustain the catwalk. On the other, and just as near at hand, is the din of the falls, as those same quiet waters unleash their latent energy by spilling over the U-shaped chasm and crash on the rocks below. From the overlook at the Devil's Throat, the catwalk continues on for another 2½ km (1½ miles), back to the vicinity of the park's main parking lots, and here descends to the river bottom. Below there is a trail that takes you along the river's edge and across the several islands beneath the jungle canopy. Several pools beneath the more gentle falls are suitable for bathing, and meditating on the endless thundering echo of the cascading waters.

WHERE TO STAY

There are over 120 hotels of all categories in and around Foz do Iguaçu. The best known, and most in demand, is the **Hotel da**

Cataratas, located on the grounds of the Iguaçu National Park (tel. 0455/74-2666). This is the only hotel on the Brazilian side with a view of the falls—and a commanding view it is. The hotel is also a classic of colonial design. The main section is shaped like a squared-off U, in rosy-pink stucco and white trim. There is an elegant covered veranda along the front of the building, spanning the entrance. The 200 rooms are large, and fitted in heavy ranchhouse furnishings of the Brazilian mission period. The front rooms face the falls, and rear rooms overlook the manicured grounds which are all the more striking against the background of the encroaching rain forest. Both vistas are equally beautiful. All rooms offer heat or air conditioning, according to season. There is a swimming pool and some sports facilities on the grounds, where numerous animals can be seen walking about at their leisure, including *emas* or rheas, a close relative of the ostrich. Reservations are an absolute necessity, made as far in advance of arrival as possible. This can be done through any VARIG office, since the airline owns and operates the hotel. Rooms range from $77 to $107 for singles, and $85 to $128 for doubles, depending on front or rear view.

The best in-town hotel is the brand-new five-star **Hotel Internacional Foz,** Rua Alm. Barroso 345 (tel. 0455/74-4885). The building is a round high-rise tower, with all 211 rooms set spoke-like off circular corridors. The hotel has every facility, including restaurant, bar, and nightclub, as well as barbershop and beauty parlor, gift shops, and a sauna. An outdoor pool area is at ground level with a lawn for sunning and tent tops that shade a sitting area. The building is centrally located, but in a quiet corner of the town. Avenida Brasil, the town's principal avenue, is only a block away, and there you will find many shops and the offices of the major Brazilian airlines. The hotel is within walking distance of all restaurants and other in-town points of interest. The rooms are attractive with color TV, mini-bars, and full baths. Rates are $106 for a single, $130 for a double.

The **Lider Palace,** Avenida Juscelino Kubitschek 3146 (tel. 73-4281), is a brand-new, reasonably priced four-star hotel near the bridge leading to Ciudad del Este. The 111-room hotel welcomes you with a large comfortable lobby. The hotel has a lobby café (beef filet tips with farofa and a cold beer go for $4.25) and a large pool with patio area. Rooms are adequate in every way, though in no way fancy. Rates for singles begin at $24 and doubles at $28, while suites can be had for $43 nightly.

Fairly close to the entrance of the Iguaçu National Park, at Rodovia das Cataratas 17, is the **Hotel San Martin** (tel. 0455/74-3030). A massive central chalet with exposed interior beams dominates the hotel's structure and houses its public spaces, lobby, restaurant, disco, game room, and gift shops. The 142 rooms are modern and appealing, with all the usual amenities, from TV to full bath. The hotel's grounds, with swimming pool and outdoor barbecue area, do not overlook the river, but the left bank of the Iguaçu is within strolling distance here. Rooms are priced at $35 for singles, $39 for doubles.

Budget Hotels

The **Foz Presidente Hotel,** Rua Xavier da Silva 918 (tel. 0455/74-5515), is located around the corner from the Hotel Internacional. The Presidente is what Brazilians refer to as a "family hotel"—clean, well run, inexpensive, and no frills. There are currently 73 rooms, but an additional floor is being added to expand the number of accommodations. The rooms are of good size and airy, with TVs and *frigobars*. A large backyard area, surrounded by a high wall, has a pool and sitting area. Rooms, depending on size, range from $12 to $17 for a single, and $15 to $19 for a double.

Near the old, in-town bus station is a hotel in the budget range that is popular with European tourists, the **Luz Hotel,** Rua Alm. Barroso–Travessa B. (tel. 74-4998). Owner Pedro Grad Roth, a Brazilian of German extraction, prides himself in running a tight ship. Rooms are strictly no frills, but they are spotless and the showers work. Singles are $12, and doubles $15 nightly. Under the same ownership and similarly priced is the **Sun Hotel** (tel. 73-4343), Avenida Juscelino Kubitschek 1895, on the outskirts of town and not far from the interstate bus terminal.

Some 27 miles outside Foz do Iguaçu is the **Albergue da Juventude** (tel. 233-2746), a youth hostel located on the Fazenda Picui do Sul in São Miguel do Iguaçu. Two dorms on this farm can accommodate up to 30 women and 30 men for less than $2.50 a night. There are also two more-expensive "suites" available.

WHERE TO DINE

The favorite meal in Foz is churrasco (barbecued meat), and the town's newest and most elegant steakhouse is the **Bufalo Branco,** Rua Reboucas 550 (tel. 74-5115), at the corner of Rua Taroba. The service is warm and well polished and attentive to your smallest need. The salad course is buffet style, and I recommend trying the tender *palmito* (hearts of palm)—as much as you can load on your plate without embarrassment. The meats, available in many varieties and in quantities as large as you desire, are served French style at your table. All meats are raised locally, and the best among them to my taste were the slightly salty picanha with its band of fat, like a T-bone steak, and the buttery filet mignon. The price of this feast is from $6 to $10, depending on beverage consumption. Open daily from noon till 11 p.m.

For a change of pace from the town's ubiquitous barbecue fare, try the **Du Cheff Restaurante,** Rua Alm. Barroso 683, in the San Rafael Hotel, (tel. 74-3311). The Du Cheff is in the heart of Foz's downtown district, and is considered one of the better eateries in the city. I dined elegantly there on a *sopa do mar,* a seafood stew awash with large chunks of shell and fin fish ($6) and a plate of creamy fettuccine Alfredo ($5), with fresh fruit and ice cream for dessert ($1.50). Open daily from noon until there is no one left to serve.

One of the more appealing places, in which both to eat and simply relax in the downtown section of Foz, is the **Centro Gastronômico Rafain,** Avenida Brasil 157 (tel. 73-5599). The

Rafain family is well represented in both the local hotel and restaurant sectors, but the Centro Gastronômico has to be their flagship [20] ments: an interior dining room for sophisticated meals, several fast-food counters, and an outdoor café that remains open 24 hours a day. The restaurant is open from 11:30 a.m. until 3 p.m. for lunch, and from 6:30 p.m. until midnight for dinner. In addition to the à la carte menu, there is an above-average buffet served daily for about $7, offering two hot meat dishes, ten or more salad platters, rice and pasta, and half a dozen tasty desserts, not to mention numerous fruits and compotes. Outside, in separate stalls, there is a pizza stand, bake shop, ice-cream parlor, and a *pastel* counter selling those meat, shrimp, and cheese pies, all open 18 hours a day. The open-air café serves sandwiches, hamburgers, and draft beer around the clock.

The **Churrascaria Cabeça de Boi,** Avenida Brasil 1325 (tel. 74-1168), is a cavernous barbecue palace serving locally produced meats from the owner's fazenda (ranch). Service is buffet style, and you may return to the groaning board as often as your personal capacity will tolerate. In addition to pork, lamb, fowl, and half a dozen cuts of beef, there are many salads and side dishes, including a large baked *dourardo* to carve from. The golden-hued dourardo is fished from the Rio Parana, and is considered a delicacy of the region. The meal costs $6 a head, and the restaurant, which holds 500 diners and provides live-music entertainment, is open for lunch from 11:30 a.m. until 4 p.m., and for dinner from 6:30 until 11 p.m. The Cabeça de Boi closes only on Christmas day.

An unexpected novelty in dining here is the **Al Badiya,** Rua Alm. Barroso 893 (tel. 72-2026), an Arab restaurant that serves its Middle Eastern delights rodízio style. There is a large population of Arab descent in Foz, and if you're out for a drive around town, be sure to go past the very large and ornate mosque and cultural center that serves the Islamic community. The round-robin meal includes ten typical dishes, and you more than get your money's worth for the $6 asking price. Open daily for lunch from noon until 3 p.m. and for dinner from 7 p.m. until midnight.

3. Salvador, Bahia

Bahia was settled almost 100 years before the Puritans established their colony at Plymouth. Early Portuguese expeditionaries, plying the coast of Brazil, anchored in a spacious harbor on November 1, 1501, and christened it Bahia de Todos os Santos (All Saints Bay). In time the name was shortened by popular usage to simply Bahia, often referring to both the contemporary state and the city of Salvador, established on the right bank of the bay in 1549. The Portuguese, already hampered by their small numbers, nevertheless displayed a special distaste for physical labor when they began to inhabit their new empire. And so their dependency on slaves—both natives and Africans—to work their fields was even greater than their counterparts in the American colonies to the north. It did not take long under these conditions for the slaves to outnumber their masters, but neither element was so dominant in Bahia as to obscure the other. Both currents were strong, and they survive today as very separate realities in Salvador—the European descendants still representing power and privilege; the blacks, marginal in economic terms, but creators of a viable subsistence economy and a rich popular culture that has only been integrated commercially around its smoother edges.

Visually, Salvador today, reflects this division. On the 30-minute drive into town from the very modern airport, it is easy to observe the city's social organization. Along the outer rings are the squatters camps, called *invasões* (invasions), dwellings that are no more than hovels, filled with dark-skinned refugees from yet another cycle of droughts and failed harvests somewhere in the interior. The city's middle parts are suburbs of the working poor, tightly packed wood or brick bungalows, the streets and public spaces like bus stops, so exclusively occupied by blacks that you might as easily imagine you are in Nigeria as in Brazil. Even the details of the street scenes can be at times as patently African—for instance, when you see a file of turbaned women, balancing water cans and bundles on their heads, disappear from the main road down a winding dirt lane into their village. The inner city, on the other hand, suggests, not Africa, but Lisbon. Here the Portuguese masters of the colonial era built their mansions, their sturdy counting houses and massive fortifications, their scores of elaborately ornamented churches. And it is here today—as well as along the nearly 113 km (70 miles) of Salvador's shoreline—that their descendants have built their villas and their modern city, in the midst of an architectural preserve that includes over 20,000 structures built before 1800. Nowhere else in the Americas can you see, almost routinely, so many churches and other structures that date from the 1600s, and astoundingly, even the 1500s.

While the contrast between the city's two dominant and coexisting cultures may be stark in strict economic terms, the common ground they occupy is also great. In the areas of religion, food, music, art, and popular celebrations, both influences are strongly felt, and it is through these activities that the population of Salvador has achieved a kind of cultural synthesis, a common trunk that thrives despite the dissimilar roots that feed it. Catholicism and *candomblé* (an African-derived religion), the drum beat and the ballad, African street food and Iberian shellfish stews, folk art and fine art—all overlap their boundaries in Salvador, where, at its best, tolerance and compromise, not bigotry and confrontation, are the operative ingredients of the day-to-day social contract.

GETTING TO SALVADOR

Salvador is one of six Brazilian cities (along with Rio, São Paulo, Manaus, Belém, and Recife) that can be reached by direct flight on VARIG Airlines from the United States. Salvador-bound flights embark from Miami only. There are several direct flights daily from Rio to Salvador. The two cities are about 700 ground miles apart, and flying time is roughly an hour and a half, at a cost of approximately $250 round trip. There is ample bus service from Rio to Salvador, via both interior and coastal routes, a trip that will take a minimum of 24 hours and cost between $30 and $45, depending on whether you travel by express "sleeper," or on the local carrier.

SALVADOR'S GEOGRAPHY

Salvador's geographic layout is similar to Rio's, but also the mirror opposite. Both are cities built at the mouth and along the shores of immense bays. But while Rio occupies the lower bank of the estuary and curves around to the ocean beaches to the south, Salvador was built on the upper bank and has expanded up the northern seashore. Also, both cities combine coastal strips and high grounds. But in Salvador, the two levels—at least in the oldest part of town—are more distinct, forming a lower city of wharfs, warehouses, and commercial buildings, and an upper city which sits on a cliff 250 feet above the waterfront, connected to it by steep inclines called *ladeiras,* and by the **Elevador Lacerda,** a complex of municipal elevators that carries passengers quickly between the two levels. With only 1.5 million inhabitants, Salvador is also considerably smaller than Rio and easier to get around in. The beaches in Salvador, too, begin in the bay where, in most cases, swimming is not recommended, and stretch out for many miles along the ocean on a strip called the **orla.** The great arch of land that surrounds the bay, beyond Salvador's city limits, is called the **recôncavo,** and it was here that the plantation system first took root in Brazilian colonial times.

SALVADOR'S CLIMATE

Throughout the year, average temperatures hover between the 70s and the high 80s. Cool sea breezes ensure pleasant days even when the mercury climbs higher during the hottest summer days. Tropical rain storms are possible anytime of year in Salvador. Most typically, there will be a sudden and tempestuous downpour for an hour or so, and then the sun will return and reclaim all signs of moisture within minutes. On occasion—during the winter months—ocean squalls, like tropical monsoons, will close the city in for several days of gloomy, rainy weather. If there is one region in Brazil, however, where you can almost count on having some sun during your vacation there, it is the country's northeast—where Salvador serves as the gateway.

TOURIST INFORMATION

The state tourist board is called **Bahiatursa,** which has several information centers at key points throughout Salvador. Bahiatursa's main branch is in the Palácio Rio Branco (tel. 071/254-7000), off the Praça Tomé de Souza, adjacent to the Lacerda Municipal Elevator, open from 8 a.m. to 6 p.m. Other branches can be found at the airport (tel. 240-1244), which is open from 8 a.m. to 10 p.m.; and in the lower city at the Mercado Modelo, Praça Cairu (tel. 241-0242), open from 8 a.m. to 6 p.m. Bahiatursa can furnish you with

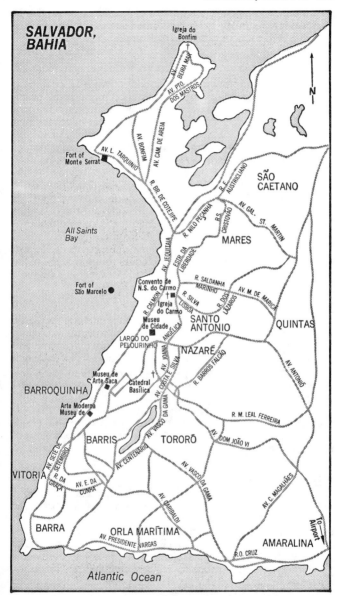

practical, up-to-the-minute information on such matters as available tours, English-language guides, cultural events, and so forth.

The agency also sells a map of the city for about $1, which is adequate to gain an overview of the urban layout. But, if you plan to do any serious exploration, buy a copy of the more detailed **Planta de Salvador,** put out by the Brazilian road guide company, Quatro Rodas; available at bookstores and newstands.

WHAT TO SEE

Salvador's most important sights and activities can be divided into five distinct groupings, each of which occupies a specific neighborhood or area within the city or on the bay, and represents either a full- or half-day excursion. First are the 30 miles of **beaches** along the orla. Second are the historical and religious sights, found primarily in the vicinity of the **Pelourinho,** the colonial district overlooking the bay from the edge of the cliff in the upper city. Third is the **Itapagipe Peninsula,** for a taste of the city's bayside ambience, including visits to **Bomfim,** the city's most important active church, and **Mont Serrat,** one of its oldest fortifications. Fourth is the neighborhood of **Barra,** between the orla and the city, with many medium-priced hotels and restaurants, and a center of café society and nightlife. Fifth is **Itaparica,** an incomparable island across the bay. There are, in addition, various events, points of interest, museums, and so forth scattered throughout other sections of the city.

Itaparica

All Saints Bay has a life of its own, independent of the hustle and bustle of the city. There are supposedly 34 islands in the bay, with Itaparica by far the most important. Itaparica is a summer and weekend colony for Salvadorans, serviced frequently by passenger and car ferries. But even on Itaparica one can see how different, and exquisitely so, life on the bay islands is from the urban intensity that is Salvador. On Itaparica you will find several villages, each with its complement of beaches, hotels, and restaurants. But a day trip is also strongly recommended for those on limited schedules who nevertheless have a yen to get out on the bay as well as to see something of life outside the city.

Bay Excursions

Several companies offer full- and half-day excursions aboard fully equipped schooners (written *escuna* in Portuguese) that cruise the bay and call at the islands. The ship **Bahia de Todos os Santos,** leaves from the Mercado Modelo pier. For fares and schedules contact the Companhia de Navegacão Bahiana directly on the dock, or make your booking through Bahiatursa.

Other companies that offer regular schooner excursions, for groups or private charter, are **L.R. Turismo,** Avenida 7 de Setembro 3959 (tel. 235-0981) and **Kontik-Franstur,** Praça da Inglaterra 2 (tel. 242-0433).

Many of the smaller *saveiro* sloops moored in the vicinity of the Mercado Modelo are also available for private rental. Arrangements are made directly with the skippers of these craft.

The Festivals of Bahia

Salvadorans celebrate often, and not only in private. Their best parties are public and take place in the streets, some even on the water. The feasting begins on New Year's Day with the impressive boat procession of the **Festa do Nossa Senhora do Bom Jesus dos Navigantes** (Our Lord Patron of Sailors). The third Sunday of January (and several days preceding it) is reserved for one of the city's most traditional celebrations, the **Festa do Nosso Senhor do Bomfim**. After barely a breather, one of the great popular spiritual manifestations of the year is orchestrated on February 2, the **Festa de Iemanjá**, goddess of the sea and principal mother figure in the pantheon of candomblé dieties. February also brings Carnival, celebrated in Salvador like nowhere else in Brazil. The celebration of Carnival in Salvador, moreover, has not been so thoroughly commercialized as in Rio. The spontaneous singing and dancing through the streets, behind sound trucks carrying live bands, is still more central to the event than the formal parades and competitions of the blocos and escolas de samba or the celebrations in private clubs. Festivals on a smaller scale occupy Salvadorans steadily for the remainder of the year.

LODGINGS

Hotel construction in Salvador has yet to catch up with the city's rising popularity as a destination for a new generation of international visitors, mostly originating from the demanding European and North American travel markets. One result is that hotel resources sometimes seem strained, and service can suffer. Standards in Salvador are not quite on a par with those of more tourist-sensitized Rio or more sophisticated São Paulo. One senses that Salvadorans are trying to adjust themselves to a new dimension in tourism, and that the necessary fine-tuning will follow this adjustment. All upper- and medium-bracket hotels listed here, unless noted to the contrary, furnish mini-bars, telephones, and TVs in their air-conditioned rooms.

The Upper Bracket

With the exception of the **Hotel da Bahia,** Praca 2 de Julho 2 (tel. 071/321-3699), all of Salvador's other luxury hotels are on the orla, the strip of suburban ocean beaches. The Hotel da Bahia is across from the Campo Grande park, mid-way between downtown and the neighborhood of Barra. The attractive ten-story Mediterranean-style building was completely renovated in 1984, and upgraded in the process to a five-star hotel. In addition to the attractive standard rooms, white in décor with dark-wood furnishings, the hotel has a variety of luxury rooms with large verandas, and two duplex suites, complete with wooden decks and private dip pools. The high-ceilinged lobby has stuffed leather chairs, several boutiques, and a travel agency. The large pool and patio on the second level overlook the park, where on occasion public fairs are staged, like the Spring Festival in early October with live music, craft and food stands. Standard and superior rooms, differing only in view, range from $54 to $60 for a single, and $64 to $78 for a double.

The **Salvador Praia Hotel,** Avenida Presidente Vargas 2338 (tel. 071/245-5033), is in Ondina, the first of the ocean beach neighborhoods, along a stretch of coast that is more rocky than sandy. Nevertheless, the Salvador Praia is blessed with a small private sand beach on its own grounds. The hotel has 164 rooms, painted in languid shades of café au lait, with polished wood furniture and original oil paintings. The bath is tiled in marble from floor to ceiling, with a stall shower, but no tub. Outside, overlooking the beach, is a large pool and sundeck area adjacent to an equally spacious shaded terrace. The hotel's breakfast room sparkles, and has some strange, but quite good, surreal art. Nightly rates are from $87 to $97 for a single, and $104 to $116 for a double.

A stone's throw from the Salvador Praia is the delightful **Bahia Othon Palace Hotel,** Avenida Presidente Vargas 2456 (tel. 071/247-1044). The Othon Palace lobby is one of grand conception, quite consciously a vaulted cathedral, but the lines are more square than curved, and the materials are thoroughly contemporary. Near the entrance, two floors are offset, with shops on each level. A succession of high arches deliberately creates the effect of a cloister yard and leads to the reception area. The building itself is brown-tinted, the two 12-story wings meeting in a V, a design that provides all 277 rooms with views of the sea. The pool area is built on a platform that slightly overhangs a rocky stretch of the shoreline, where the elevation is no more than 15 feet above the water. A trail leads to a nearby beach.

The rooms are very large, and the walls are decorated with tiles. The cabinetry and bed alike are curvaceous and shiny, like Oriental furniture. The headboards are rattan, and the floors of polished stone. Each room has a small balcony with teak floorboards, and lattice shutters. Blue-tile baths have tubs with shower curtains. The hotel's bright coffeeshop with blue-checkered cloth-covered tables overlooks the pool and serves a full lunch for about $6. Accommodations are classified in three categories—standard, deluxe, and super-deluxe—and are priced $70 to $77, $84 to $93, and $93 to $103 for singles and doubles respectively.

The **Enseada das Lajes,** Avenida Oceânica 511 (tel. 071/237-0095), is a former private villa nestled among the palms of a hill called the *Morro da Paciência,* and now converted into a small hotel of distinction by the same family that had once resided there. Each of the nine guest rooms has walls of polished red brick and wood plank floors, but no two rooms are furnished or decorated alike. Each is large, light, and contains several stunning antique pieces. One bathroom has a sunken tub and a separate shower with an outer curtain of lace. Venerable brass fixtures operate the plumbing. There is no lobby to speak of, but several large public spaces, including an atrium garden, and inviting lounge, and a glass-enclosed veranda restaurant with rattan tables and chairs, and a superb view of the sea. The hotel has a pool and patio, lovely grounds set on a sloping hillside, and access to several quiet, rocky coves on the shore below. Rooms are between $135 and $165.

Salvador's premier beach hotel, the **Meridien,** Rua Fonte do Boi 216 (tel. 071/248-8011), is the next luxury establishment along the beach, in Rio Vermelho, immediately following Paciência. The Meridien, with 277 rooms, is Salvador's largest hotel, and chic in the French mold, boasting of both a superior restaurant, the rooftop St. Honoré, and a popular discothèque, Regine's. All the hotel's rooms face the sea, since the tall high-rise building occupies the point of a small peninsula. The décor in the rooms is subtle—peach is the dominant shade—and the furnishings, like the maroon jug-shaped lamps, are modern and tasteful. Original art decorates the walls, and all rooms have small balconies with long views of neighboring beaches. Other facilities include a large pool and patio, sauna, and tennis courts. Rates begin at $76 for a single, while the least expensive double occupancy rooms start at $83.

About 24 km (15 miles) from downtown in Itapoã, the **Hotel Quatro Rodas,** Rua do Passárgada (tel. 071/249-9611), sits on 14 acres of beach land, thickly planted with coconut palms. The lobby and public rooms are large and elaborately decorated with plants and finely lacquered old farm equipment. There is a happy hour in the piano bar every night at 6 p.m. A small working watermill provides both theme and centerpiece for the hotel's restaurant. Outside there is a small natural lake on the grounds and boats for the guests to paddle. The beach itself, considered Salvador's best, is about a five-minute walk over a path that cuts beneath the palms. The 200 accommodations all look out on the sea over a landscape of dunes and beach vegetation. Standard rooms have twin beds, and deluxe accommodations have two large double beds. Rooms are spacious and clean-lined, with whitewashed walls and carpeted floors. Baths are also large and have tubs with showers. There are three tennis courts on the grounds, and a large swimming pool and sunning area. Rooms are $76 to $85 for standards, and $93 to $110 for deluxe.

The Middle Bracket

At the **Grande Hotel de Barra,** Avenida 7 de Setembro 3564 (tel. 071/247-6011), half of the hotel's 117 rooms are classified as standards and occupy an older building off the street. The deluxe rooms are in a newer building nearer the water, attached by glass-enclosed walkways to the hotel's older structures. The standard rooms are large, with enough space for several extra armchairs, and have giant baths, tiled in blue from floor to ceiling. The deluxe accommodations are newer and smaller, and they all have balconies with views of either the sea or a very private interior courtyard pool. Rates are $37 to $42 for the standard rooms, and $49 to $54 for the deluxe.

Nearby is the pleasant and sturdy **Praiamar,** Avenida 7 de Setembro 3577 (tel. 071/247-7011), with a nice diagonal view of the old Barra Fort. Rooms are of medium size, all very dayroom bright with bedspreads and other highlights in orange, and with solid furnishings. Along with green carpets and floral-patterned tiles in the baths, it sounds garrish, but the decorators somehow carry off their statement with good effect. A single room costs $49, and a double, $54.

The **Marazul,** Avenida 7 de Setembro 3937 (tel. 071/235-2110), is across the street from both the Porto da Barra beach and another old fort, the Forte de Santa Maria. The hotel is relatively new, with 125 rooms in a nine-story modern building of glass and molded concrete. A terrace at mezzanine level with a small but stylish pool on a raised teak deck, overhangs the street, but looks through the tops of palms to the water beyond. The rooms are no-nonsense modern, with large double beds, built-in hardwood furniture, all in light earth tones (except for the dark-brown blackout curtains). The baths are fully tiled, and the ceiling is a single recessed light. Rooms prices are the same as the Praiamar, $49 single and $54 double.

The **Bahia Park Hotel,** Praça Augusto Sévero in Rio Vermelho (tel. 071/248-6588), has 56 rooms, each with its own large stenciled number on the door. Shades of brown dominate the décor in the rooms. The bedboard is unusual—detached from the bed, it hangs from the wall. The rooms' stark design and use of abstract paintings is appealing, and the baths have marble sinks, tile floors, and large stall showers. The rooftop terrace is very simpatico; it only has a dip pool, but a spectacular view of Rio Vermelho and its environs. One major defect of the Bahia Park is that roughly half the rooms in effect have no windows, because the glass is covered by a metallic façade fixed to the building's front, creating not only an intrusive feature, but one that is totally unnecessary architecturally or functionally. Standard rooms are $36 to $42, and the deluxe room is $60. The hotel does not charge the 10% service fee.

On the downtown side of the Avenida 7 de Setembro at no. 2209 is the **Hotel Bahia do Sol** (tel. 071/247-7211), between Barra and Campo Grande, along the so-called Vitoria Corredor. The building has wooden shutter shades, a feature so typical of apartment buildings in the tropics. The shades shut out the light, but allow ventilation, a nice feature for people who like to sleep without air conditioning. The walls of the 90 rooms are papered, while bright heavy-textured fabric is used for the bedspreads. The furniture is modular, constructed of hardwood, with white Formica surfaces. The baths are large with attractive turquoise-colored tile walls, seashell pedestal sinks, and mirrors framed in wood. Off the lobby is an atrium garden and a restaurant bar set in the rear of the building, distant from the street. Rooms cost between $38 and $42 a night.

The next-door **Vila Velha,** Avenida 7 de Setembro 1971 (tel. 071/247-8722), is an older hotel, but well maintained and newly redecorated. The rooms are mid-sized but have large baths with powder-blue tiles and marble-topped sinks. The rooms don't face the front or back, but the sides of the buildings, and all have good lateral views. Rates are the same as at the Bahia do Sol, between $38 and $42 a night.

Budget Range

There are several inexpensive beach hotels on the orla, along the city's outer strands. Two that are run by the same management as the Bahia Park in Rio Vermelho are the **Hotel Itapoã,** Rua Dias Gomes 04 (tel. 071/249-9988), and **Hotel Praia Dourada,** Rua Dias Gomes 10 (tel. 071/249-9639), both in Praia Placaford.

Students and impecunious writers favor the cheaper hotels—by no means flea bags—that are located in the old city, like the **Hotel Pelourinho,** at Rue Alfredo de Brito 20, in the Largo do Pelourinho (tel. 071/242-4144), and those off the inner-city plazas, like the Praça Anchieta and the Terreiro de Jesus.

EATING IN SALVADOR

Bahian food is the most unique and varied of all regional cooking in Brazil. The use of many spices and herbs along with coconut milk and an African palm oil called **dendé** make it so. The cuisine of Bahia owes much to African tradition and to the improvisational abilities of the early slaves, whose choice of ingredients were limited to a catch from the sea or the master's unwanted leftovers. Out of this adversity has come a great school of cooking.

Many a restaurant meal in Salvador will begin with **casquinha de siri,** a concoction of white crabmeat mixed with dendé, onions, and tomatoes, and served in its own shell with a sauce, and topped with sprinkles of grated parmesan cheese. **Moquecas,** fish or shellfish stews cooked in earthern pots, are the city's culinary emblem. Moquecas should be made with the freshest ingredients from the sea, and are flavored by hot chiles and dendé, but are seldom overly spicy right from the kitchen. **Molho de pimenta,** a hot sauce of chile paste and dendé is always present on the table, and can be added according to taste for those who savor truly "hot" food. Cooked with coconut milk instead of dendé, a moqueca becomes an **ensopada.**

Bahians have two favorite chicken dishes, the first a stew called **xim xim** (pronounced "shing shing"), with ingredients that vary from cook to cook. The preparation can include ground peanuts, coconut, mint, fish, or squash, but the sauce is always thick, and the chicken well stewed and flavorful. **Galinha do molho pardo** is a freshly killed chicken served in a brown gravy from its own blood. This dish is a popular offering to the gods in candomblé rituals, where animal sacrifice is a central element in the liturgy. From here the dishes become even more exotic, like **efó,** beef tongue and shrimp stew, and **sarapatel,** a pork dish in which innards like tripe and other unmentionables are stewed in the pig's blood. Bahian-style **feijoada,** with red instead of black beans, should also not be overlooked.

As is usual throughout all Brazil, side dishes also play an important role in every Bahian meal. Commonly served as accompaniments are rice, **Farofa de dendé** (manioc flour fried in palm oil), and **vatapá,** a very tasty porridge made primarily from bread, ground cashews and peanuts, dried shrimp, dendé, and the usual flavorings.

Bahian desserts are rich and much in demand. The most delicate are **quindim** and **papo de anjo,** egg yolk custards, the first with coconut, served doused in sticky syrup. **Cocadas** are coconut candies, white or dark depending on whether regular or burnt brown sugar is used in their preparation.

Street food is sold everywhere in Salvador by Bahianas, women in traditional costume—wide skirts and lacey white blouses, turban-headed and bejeweled. These vendors once had to be sanctioned by their respective candomblé temples, where as devotees the young women were initiated into the culinary secrets of the sect. They learned how to make those bean-cake fritters, called **acarajé,** which you will see boiling in oil on their improvised braziers. A dried bean called *fradinho,* similar to a black-eyed pea, ground and mixed with dendé is the basic recipe. Salvadorans have as many opinions about who makes the perfect acarajés as New Yorkers have about where to buy the best pizza. You can eat the acarajé by itself, or have it served stuffed with vatapá and shrimp and seasoned with hot pepper sauce. Some Salvadorans hold that the best acarajés are sold on the Praça de Santana, across from the Ad Libitum bar. The perfect beverage with this snack is **caldo de cana,** freshly squeezed sugarcane juice, which is also sold at this same location.

Since Bahian food is bound to represent a whole new taste for many visitors, it would be wise to sample the fare first at the **Casa da Gamboa,** Rua da Gamboa de Cima 51 (tel. 245-9777), where you will be assured of fine ingredients and fastidious preparation. This whitewashed old town house on a hill would be a perfect setting for any meal in Salvador, but ask to be seated near a window looking out over the bay, if possible. Order the moqueca of your choice, and the xim xim too, if in company, along with vatapá, rice, and farofa, and then settle back with an apéritif, say a fruit *batida* (freshly squeezed mango, passion fruit, or maracujá) with cachaça cane brandy. Sample as many desserts as you have appetite for, and one or more of proprietor Dona Conceição's homemade liquors. If you decide you've enjoyed the experience, you will have many other opportunities in the city to satisfy and widen your newly acquired tastes. Depending on your selections and bar bill, the meal will cost you between $10 and $15 per person. The Casa da Gamboa is open for lunch from noon until 3 p.m., and for dinner from 7:30 p.m. until midnight; closed Sundays.

Your next Bahian meal then should be at the **SENAC,** an acronym for Serviço de Educação Nacional de Artes Culinarias, the state-run restaurant school where young chefs get their training. The SENAC occupies a grand old building at Largo do Pelourinho 13/19 (tel. 321-5502), and serves its meals buffet style in a formal atmosphere, a reproduction of a dining room of state. More than a dozen regional dishes are kept hot in steam trays on a central table, and guests can serve themselves at will. There is a separate table with over 20 desserts, including sweets and fresh fruit. Here you can sample the more exotic offerings, like efó or sarapatel, relatively risk-free in small doses. Drinks are served by waiters and are charged separately. After the meal, which costs about $6 per person, you can stay for the folklore show staged outdoors in the yard behind the building. SENAC is open for lunch from noon to 3 p.m., and for dinner from 7 to 10:30 p.m. Patrons may order the seia, coffee, or hot chocolate with the sweets alone for $2 between 5 and 8 p.m.

There's a small French restaurant in Ondina, the **Chaillot,** Avenida Presidente Vargas 3305 (tel. 237-4621), in a renovated house facing the sea from across the main avenue of the orla, that just may be the best restaurant in the city. Owner Caio Mario Gatti moved the family business from Petropólis, outside of Rio, to the Bahian capital a few years back. Caio, a quiet bear of a man, creates the dishes and supervises the cooking in his restaurant, and judging from the results, he is not one to rest on his reputation or past laurels. As you sit in the zany bar at an open window being refreshed by cool sea breezes, on zebra-striped banquettes before tables that look like sawed-off temple columns, Caio may suggest a round of *cajú amigos.* This batida is made with the juice and pulp of the cashew fruit, with a healthy dose of cachaça, only available when that delectable fruit is in season during the Brazilian springtime. To dine, you descend a set of stairs into the dining room, and begin the meal with *boca de carangueijo,* the forelegs of the mangrove crab, fried in batter and dipped in fresh mayonnaise. The *moqueca de badejo,* a local fish similiar to sea bass, is likely to be the most delicate fish stew you will sample in Salvador. A second course of *filet molho de roquefort* (filet mignon in roquefort sauce) is equally superb. For dessert, melt-in-your-mouth *mousse de côco*—coconut mousse, what else! Entrees are less than $10 each, remarkably reasonable for meals of truly gourmet quality. Open daily for lunch from noon to 3 p.m., and for dinner from 8 p.m. to midnight, later on weekends.

The **Restaurante Bargaço,** Rua P. Quadra 43 (tel. 231-3900), in Jardim Armação (after Pituba beach on the orla), began as a simple neighborhood fish house. Today the restaurant can boast the most chic clientele in the city. Upper-class Salvadorans from Cabinet Minister on down dine regularly on the fine seafood at the Bargaço. Most of the tables are on an outdoor covered patio. For appetizers there are generous portions of crab and lobster meat, grilled shrimp, and raw oysters, at about $7 a platter. The principal entrees are several varieties of esopadas, mariscadas, and fish stews simmered in coconut milk, which arrive at the table still bubbling and cost an average of $13. The Bargaço is on a back street in the vicinity of the city's Convention Center complex, and it's not easy to find on your own. But most cab drivers will certainly know how to get there. Open daily for lunch and dinner at the usual hours.

A less pretentious seafood restaurant, and just as good, is the popular seaside **Marisco.** Rua Euricles de Matos 123, in Paciência. Lobster dishes are $9, and shrimp $6.50. Fresh fish, sautéed, baked, or grilled in a variety of styles costs from $4 to $9 a serving. Octopus stew runs $7, and the crab Créole is $5. Caipirinhas and batidas cost between 50¢ and 75¢ a drink. You sit on a veranda at a table covered with a rumpled cloth and begin the meal with a heaping mound of crab's legs fried in batter and plenty of cold beer. But the ensopada is the real treat, a clay pot filled to overflowing with a stew of fish, clams, octopus, shrimp, and crabmeat, for about $12. Open all week from 11:30 a.m. to 3 p.m. for lunch, and from 7 p.m. to midnight for dinner.

For French cooking and one of the best views of both town and sea in Salvador, there is the rooftop **St. Honoré,** in the Meridien Hotel, Rua Fonte do Boi 216 (tel. 248-8011). While not quite on a scale of conception or performance with the equivalent category of restaurant in Rio or São Paulo, the St. Honoré comes close enough, and it has an atmosphere that is refreshingly relaxed, rather than stiffly formal as is commonly the case where French service is imposed. Surprisingly, the St. Honoré is not that expensive, so if you want to treat yourself to some genuine designer food as a break from *comida baiana,* this is a recommended spot to consider. Open for dinner only, from 7 p.m. to midnight, and later when attending the weekend set.

A Few Nightspots

Off the narrow alleys of the *Pelorinho* is the French-owned "in" spot **Banzo,** Largo Jose de Alencar 6, a bar and restaurant on the second floor (no telephone). Here's where international castaways spend their wastrel days in Salvador. Out along the beachfront, there are several possibilities for nightlife, including the **Bon Vivant** (tel. 245-2056), a combined bar and art gallery in the Itapoa section of the seashore, with a stunning view from the terrace. In the summertime, the beach of Stella Maris is generally a popular nightspot, usually in the specific vicinity of **Padang, Padang,** "next to the abandoned hotel," and known for its well-chilled beer, natural foods, and fresh fruit juices.

MANAUS

Manaus is the capital of the state of **Amazonas,** built up from an obscure river village only at the end of the last century as a result of the rubber boom. Amazonas has a sparse population of perhaps 1.2 million inhabitants, and yet represents some 20% of Brazil's national territory. After the fall of the Brazilian rubber market immediately prior to World War I, Manaus foundered for half a century. To revive the city, Manaus was designated a free port by the Brazilian government in 1967, and since then government policy has encouraged the growth in the city of extensive assembly plants by major multinational firms, primarily in the consumer electronics field.

Manaus grew up on the hilly left bank of the Rio Negro, which is carved by an endless chain of creeks called *igarapés,* where water enters or recedes depending on the time of year. In July the river is at its highest, and December, its lowest, a difference of as much as 35 feet most years, sometimes more. Floating houses and stilt dwellings are the adaptations made by those who live near the riverbank in response to flood season. And while the city is some 1,000 water miles from the Atlantic, its general elevation is only 20 feet above sea level. With few historic buildings and a pattern of hodgepodge industrial development over the past 20 years, Manaus is not what you would call a pretty city. What Manaus does have in its favor is its location on the great river, and—despite the hive-like activity of its port and industrial suburbs—an eerie sense of isolation from the mainstream of civilization. Manaus is hot and humid. The year-round mean temperature is 85°F, September through November being the hottest months.

A stay of two or three days in Manaus is sufficient to see the city and a few of the better-known sights on the river, like the truly impressive "meeting of the waters," where the different colored Rio Solimoẽs and Rio Negro run parallel before mixing into the muddy brown of the Amazon. Manaus, of course, is also the major port of entry for visitors who wish to travel extensively on the river, taking advantage of the dozens of excursions and adventure tours that originate from the city, and which are usually booked long in advance of arrival through specialty travel agents at home.

---

1. Where to Stay

Manaus does not have an abundance of good hotels, and because of the generally higher cost of living in the city, expect to pay more here than for hotels of comparable quality in other Brazilian cities. Unless otherwise noted, all rooms listed here are air-conditioned, and are equipped with TVs and mini-bars, and have breakfast included in the daily rate.

THE DELUXE BRACKET

By far the best address in Manaus—and one of the most luxurious resorts in all Brazil—is the **Hotel Tropical,** Estrada da Ponta Negra (tel. 092/238-5757). For those who wish to be in the Amazon, but remain insulated from its rough edges, the Hotel Tropical provides the perfect environment. The hotel even organizes all its own tours, including several options for overnights in the forest at the Tropical's very own first-class floating lodge. Located near the airport, approximately a half hour ride from the city, the Tropical sits on the bank of the Rio Negro, with its own access to one of Manaus' most popular beaches, and on acres of private, beautifully landscaped grounds that contain a small zoo, a playground, an enormous central courtyard with swimming pool, and tennis courts. Everything about the Tropical is voluptuous, including the somewhat oversized fazenda-style furnishings. Several of the public spaces are genuinely elegant, including the very masculine bar in polished hardwood and leather, several lounges and seating areas off the lobby, and a formal restaurant, which serves a succulent and very traditional feijoada, with all the trimmings including *batida* cocktails and black bean broth, every Saturday.

Perhaps because the Tropical is a star property belonging to VARIG Airlines, it is among the best maintained hotels in all Brazil and always heavily booked. So make your reservations far in advance. The hotel has one of the most sophisticated communications systems in the world, but it can function at only 30% of capacity because, as hotel managers will tell you while nearly pulling out their hair, the city will only cede 45 phone lines to the hotel. As a result, guests do on occasion experience delays when dialing out.

The Tropical has 559 rooms, with a total of 620 projected for 1991–92, and many planned additions and improvements to the public spaces and outdoor and sporting areas. The rooms are being redecorated, leading away from the colonial style to a more modern décor. Baths have bright tiles painted with floral motifs, and contain separate tub and stall shower. The standard and deluxe rooms differ only in their location within the hotel. Rates for single occupancy range from $100 to $115, and for doubles, from $135 to $158.

THE UPPER BRACKET

Away from the river, about 15 minutes from the city, in Adrianopolis, one of its most affluent suburbs, is the **Da Vinci Hotel,** Rua Belo Horizonte 240-A (tel. 092/233-6800). The 116-room Da Vinci is a hotel, not a plush resort like the Tropical, but it still provides elegant digs in Manaus.

There are four categories of rooms, distinguished by location, size and, to some degree, furnishings. The least expensive standard room does not suffer a decline in either comfort or the tastefulness of its décor. The room has a double bed, armchair, and deep-brown carpeted floors, and is of high-quality workmanship in its furnishings and finish. The regular deluxe room adds a balcony with plenty of elbow room, covered by a sloping tile roof, and sports two modern rocking chairs. A large set of double doors—part louvered slats, part mullioned window panes—separates the room from the balcony. The deluxe room also contains a couch, and all rooms display dried floral arrangements that have been fashioned into unique wall hangings.

A lovely sunken lobby is imaginatively divided into several discreet seating environments, each with individually styled armchairs, love seats, and tables—all of rattan and cane. Borders of living plants and vases of dried flowers, grasses, and leaves complete the effect. Both the bar and the restaurant off the lobby convey an air of sophistication, and outside there is a large pool area with two dozen patio tables with chairs shaded by umbrellas. The standard rooms cost $60 to $71, or $70 to $81 if they face the pool. The regular deluxe rooms run $80 to $97, while an extra-large executive deluxe room is priced from $89 to $105.

Right in town, close to both the free-port shopping district and the floating dock and market is the 171-room **Hotel Amazonas,** Praça Adelberto Valle (tel. 092/234-7679). Deluxe accommodations at the Amazonas are high-ceilinged rooms with good-sized balconies offering views of the active waterfront and the Rio Negro. The standard rooms are smaller and face the rear with views over the back commercial streets. All the rooms are furnished with cabinetry and surfaces in modern, straight-lined designs, with two single beds in the deluxe rooms and a double bed in the standards. The hotel has a large second-floor restaurant with voluminous black columns, and heavy handmade, country-style tables and chairs, and a small courtyard pool with a hardwood deck and separate bar. Standard single and double rooms rent for $52 to $66, and deluxe rooms are priced from $66 to $79.

The **Imperial Hotel,** Avenida Getúlio Vargas 227 (tel. 092/233-8711), is a ten-story apartment-style building with 100 rooms, located on one of Manaus' principal avenues. Rooms are of good size, approximately 12 feet by 15 feet, and comfortably furnished, some with large double beds, a couch and a lace-covered table with chairs; while others have two single beds and an armchair. The hotel's second-floor restaurant is a pleasant room where food is served both à la carte and buffet style, and there is live music on Friday and Saturday nights. Behind the hotel is a mid-size backyard, with a pool and a tile deck. Rates begin at $90 to $99 for standards, and are $106 to $124 for deluxe accommodations.

THE MIDDLE BRACKET

The best of the middle-bracket hotels is the **Lord,** Rua Macílio Dias 217 (tel. 092/234-9741), though it has a few serious flaws, some of which are being corrected by the gradual renovation of the accommodations. The six-story building with a pseudo-modern façade occupies a corner (with Rua Quintino Bocaiúva) on an active commercial street closed to traffic, and recently converted to a pedestrian shopping mall. Many consumer shops selling crafts and electronic goods line the street. Rooms on the upper floors look out over the surrounding rooftops and are pleasant enough, though the individual air conditioners make a terrible noise, forcing you to open the windows at night, which is not necessarily unpleasant. The hotel is well situated, quite near the central section of the waterfront, and has a reasonably spacious lobby—something lacking in most hotels of its class in Manaus. Standard rooms have no TVs, and cost from $45 to $50; deluxe rooms cost from $54 to $63.

A block from the Lord is a street with several of the city's older medium-priced hotels. The **Hotel International,** Rua Dr. Moreira 168 (tel. 092/234-1315), is the best of the lot. The deluxe rooms in the 39-room hotel are large and breezy, when the windows are open. All rooms are also equipped with individual air conditioners. The rooms contain two good-sized beds, and the floors are carpeted. Baths are tiled with decorative *azuleijos.* The furnishings are definitely well used, but not in bad shape by any means. Rates start at $38 to $46 for the standard rooms, and at $40 to $53 for the deluxe.

In the heart of downtown Manaus, the **Sombra Palace,** Avenida 7 de Setembro 1325 (tel. 234-8777), can provide you with a very nice three-star room in the $30 range. The relatively new 43-room hotel has a well-constructed and well-maintained appearance. Rooms are spacious, with uniquely patterned parquet floors, and modern, yet homey furnishings. Standard rooms go for $27 single, and $33 double, while deluxe accommodations are priced at $33 and $39 for singles and doubles, respectively. The 90-room **Hotel Mónaco,** Rua Silva Ramos 20 (tel. 232-5211), is close to the Amazonas State tourism office, EMANTUR, on the city's downtown fringe, but still easily within walking distance of the more central parts of Manaus in the vicinity of the Duty Free Zone. The Mónaco has recently undergone a major renovation, and the newly decorated rooms are greatly improved. Nightly rates are $27 to $34 for singles, and $34 to $40 for doubles. The hotel building itself is very attractive, and houses a fine restaurant, the Mirante (see "Where to Eat"), and also serves as headquarters for **Rio Amazonas Turismo** (tel. 234-7308), a reliable tour agency operating actively throughout the Amazon.

BUDGET HOTELS

The **Kyoto Plaza Hotel,** Rua Dr. Moreira 232 (tel. 092/232-6552), with 15 rooms, is more of a *pensão* than a hotel. Rooms are small without windows, but otherwise adequate. Some rooms have single beds, others doubles, and all are air-conditioned. Rates are $12 for one person, $21 for two, and $27 for three a night.

The **Hotel Dona Joana,** Rua dos Andrades 553 (tel. 233-7553), has several plain but spacious air-conditioned suites with balconies that go for $17 a night, including breakfast. Standard rooms for $14 a night are smaller, but all have double beds, bathrooms, and Amazon River views. A simple open-air restaurant occupies the fourth floor, and can be reached only by stairs because the 62-room Dona Joana has no elevators. The food served there, especially hot meals, is good, plentiful, and cheap. The hotel is spotless, has a pleasant, well-chilled lobby (not to be gainsaid in a city where the mean temperature is 86°F), and is a good bargain for the budget traveler in pricey Manaus. The same can be said of the nearby **Hotel Rio Branco**, Rua dos Andrades 484 (tel. 233-4019), its style and layout resembling a boarding house more than a hotel. The Rio Branco sits on a street that runs parallel to the river, a few blocks in, and somewhat upstream from Manaus's famous floating pier. In all, the hotel has 36 rooms, with air-conditioned units priced at $9 nightly, those with fans at $7, and those with neither, $4 to $5. Only the more expensive rooms have bathrooms, while breakfast is included in all rentals.

2. Where to Eat

The regional food in Manaus derives to a large extent from traditional Indian cookery. Such dishes as *pato no tucupí* (duck in fermented manioc sauce) and *taçaca* (the strongly flavored tapioca porridge served in a gourd, primarily as a street food) are readily available throughout the city. But the mainstay of the local diet is fish—*pirarucú, tambaquí,* and *tucunaré* are the most popular, but the list only begins with these. Despite the high cost of living in Manaus, restaurant food is not appreciably more expensive than elsewhere in Brazil.

One very popular fish restaurant, and one of the most expensive in Manaus, is the **Caçarola,** Rua Maures 188 (tel. 233-3021), located on the outskirts of town in a modest suburb. The Caçarola has the atmosphere of a neighborhood outdoor café, nothing fancy; indeed, the chairs and tables are a bit rickety. But the restaurant has won its reputation on the basis of its kitchen, not its décor. All the typical fish dishes are served, in a variety of presentations, and the steak is also excellent. Most of the à la carte entrees cost between $10 and $15. Open daily for lunch and dinner, the restaurant takes a break between 3 and 6 p.m.

The **Mirante,** Rua Silva Ramos 20 (tel. 232-5211, ext. 273), overlooks Manaus from the 13th floor of the Hotel Mónaco, and definitely provides the best public rooftop view of the city. Food at the Mirante, open daily for lunch from noon to 3 p.m. and dinner from 7 p.m. till 1 a.m., is excellent and moderately priced, with most entrees in the $6 to $8 range. Good bets are the *caldeirada* (fish stew), made with *tambaquí* and served with rice and *pirão,* as well as the tasty and imaginative *frango cubano,* a tempura of chicken breast, banana, tomato, palmito, onion, and pineapple. With its small swimming pool, the Mirante is a weekend meeting place, and many shutterbugs show up to record the magnificent Amazon sunset. Visible from the deck of the Mirante, across the Praça do Congresso, is the tall building housing the exclusive **Ideal Club,** Avenida Eduardo Ribeiro (no telephone). The club restaurant, known as **VIP's** (tel. 232-7004), serves a buffet lunch ($5) Monday through Saturday, and offers sophisticated à la carte dining with live music Thursday through Saturday nights.

A restaurant in the nearby Educandos neighborhood that actually overlooks the river is the **Panorama,** Boulevard Rio Negro 199 (tel. 232-3177). The Panorama is a popular institution in Manaus where you can eat very well for between $4 and $6 a meal. Especially recommended are the appetizer of *bolinhos de peixe* (fish cakes, at $1.25), the *farofa de tambaquí* (chunks of fresh fish fried in farina flour, at $4), and several rounds of *caipirinhas* (80¢ each). For dessert, try the delicious cream of *cupuacu*—a favorite local fruit prepared like a custard ($1). Open every day from 11 a.m. till 3p.m. and from 6pm till midnight.

Manaus has two branches of the **Fiorentina** restaurant. The first occupies an attractive brick and timber open-air lean-to on a busy intersection in the Adrianapolis neighborhood, at Rua Recife 900 (tel. 232-3334). The other, the original Fiorentina, is downtown at Praça Roosevelt 44 (tel. 232-1295), and more popularly known as the Praça da Policia because of the presence there of a military police barracks. The food at both locales is Italian, offering pizzas for around $3, pasta dishes for $2 to $3, and meat plates for around $5. House specialties include Amazonian fish platters from $4–$6.50. Hours are from 11 a.m. till 11 p.m. daily.

Many of Manaus' favorite restaurants are located outside the city, along various suburban access roads. The **Palhoça,** Estrada da Ponta Negra (tel. 238-3831), is such a place. A large, open-sided shed with a straw roof, the Palhoça serves a good mixed-grill barbecue for about $5.

Two restaurants in an area called Parque 10 are worthy of note. The **La Barca,** Rua Recife 684 (tel. 236-8544), is a white stucco building trimmed in dark hardwood, open on three sides, that looks like the veranda of a hacienda. The tables are attractively set for elegant dining, and the menu is extensive, listing over 100 plates, including many *iscas* (side dishes and appetizers). Best of all, meals are reasonably priced from $5 to $10. Open Monday through Saturday for lunch and dinner, but on Sunday for lunch only.

The **Timoneiro,** Rua Paraiba 07 (tel. 236-1679), is also in Parque 10. For native décor, this is the most attractive restaurant in Manaus. The large space is saturated with authentic artifacts of the Amazon Indian cultures, as well as taxidermic oddities like mummified alligators, strange fish, tortoise shells, and jaguar pelts. Bird cages in the parking lot are filled with chatty parrots and aryaras. Specialties here are tambaquí barbecue, tucunaré stew, and filet of pirarucú. International platters are also available. Fresh fruits of the Amazon are recommended for dessert, especially the cupuaçu, tucuma, pupunha, and graviola. The liquor made from graviola is strong and smooth and makes an excellent apéritif. Prices are very reasonable, from $4.50 to $6 for most dishes. Open for dinner seven days a week, and for lunch only on weekends, when live music is also featured.

Strictly for local color, try the immense **Bar e Restaurante Central Natália,** Rua Barroso 237 (tel. 233-8058), at the corner of Rua Saldanha Marinho. This is a very unfancy, untouristed dining spot with live music—organ when I went there—Monday through Saturday. The Natália is open daily from 11 a.m. to midnight—later on weekends—and claims to serve a "delicious" feijoada at Saturday lunch.

---

3. Nightlife

Nightspots come and go with great rapidity in Manaus, but as long as the *lambada* craze continues, you will probably still find **Brega e Chique** going strong at Estrada Ponta Negra 5006. This club has been about the most popular *danceteria* in Manaus since 1989. Super-crowded and very animated is the **Conciente Bar** (tel. 232-1425), open after 5 p.m. Monday through Saturday, and not winding down until dawn on the weekends. On the fringes of the city's redlight district, the streets surrounding the Conciente are a dangerous place to walk late at night. To get there by cab from the Hotel Amazonas in the heart of the Duty Free Zone costs about $2 —off the meter. On some nights two musicians play guitar while singing old standards and current hits, and dozens of couples squeeze onto the Conciente's small dance floor, with dozens more sitting around small tables, drinking beer and keeping up a steady din of chatter, adding to the very agreeable bistro-style atmosphere.

Every Sunday evening on the **Praça da Saudade,** near the Hotel Mónaco, there is an outdoor fair with impromptu beer gardens mounted under tent tops, crafts booths, children's rides and lots of tempting food stands. Also extremely popular on the weekends, I am told, is **Paulo's Bar,** Rua Nelson Batista Sales 102 (tel. 244-.2479), in the suburb of Conjunto Preto. I was impressed by the size of the house, its large veranda, and its generally festive air and appearance.

---

4. The Sights and the River

One of the most popular nonriver sights in Manaus is the old **Teatro Amazonas,** an opera house that was opened in 1896, a cultural by-product of the city's newfound rubber wealth. The building is a synthesis of various styles, including baroque, neoclassical, and art nouveau. The structure beneath the façade is of cast iron which, along with all the other building and finishing materials, was imported from Europe. Renovations on both the exterior and interior of the theater have recently been completed at a cost of $8 million, and opera has been scheduled once again for performance within the walls of the Teatro Amazonas for the first time in decades.

Near the theater is the **Praça do Congresso,** a popular zone for evening promenades.

The **Municipal Market** at dockside is an impressive cast-iron building, similar to the Belém market.

INPA (Instituto Nacional de Pesquisas da Amazônia), the National Institute of Amazonian Research on the Estrada do Aleixo 1756, (tel. 236-5860), is a government research facility outside Manaus that is worth visiting. It is necessary to enter through the main gate and get permission from the security police. Once inside the forested grounds, you immediately hear the music of the jungle, since the many trees provide a kind of urban refuge for great numbers of birds. INPA is also like a large college campus, with many buildings where scientists pursue the various branches of naturalistic studies relevant to gaining a greater understanding of the Amazon. You can see many different animals here as well, like the manatee and the *ariranha,* a very funny and animated Amazonian otter. Don't be surprised at the large numbers of Americans you see within the grounds. They are here serving on staff, sharing their ecological training in exchange for a rare opportunity for practical study in the world's largest remaining forest reserve.

While at INPA, try to arrange a brief tour of the sawmill belonging to the Centro de Pesquisa de Productos Florestais (Center For the Study of Forest Products) on the same grounds. Civil engineer Murilo Suano, head of the mill, not only showed me around but also presented me with a dozen *amostras*—block-size pieces of exotic hardwoods—as souvenirs. One sample, true to its name—purple heart—was indeed beet purple in color; another wood was positively canary yellow; and many others were dense and dark, resembling mahogany or ebony. Samples of as many as 70 species of Amazonian woods can be purchased at INPA, packed in well-made boxes with hinged tops, when available, for approximately $50 a box. Murilo explained that mill workers cut the samples during rare periods of down time, in between their more significant experiments, and consequently demand for the sample boxes far outstrips the supply.

NATURAL HISTORY AND INDIAN CRAFTS

A very small, but infinitely worthwhile museum has recently opened on the outskirts of Manaus. The **Museu de Ciéncias Naturais** (tel. 244-2799) is located in the Conjunto Preto section of the Aleixo suburb. Within a single, stucco white exhibition hall, hundreds of stuffed fish and mammals, mounted butterflies and insects, are displayed in handsomely constructed cases. The taxidermy is first rate, and the effect dramatic and spellbinding as you confront at such close quarters the enormity and stone age appearance of some of these Amazonian specimens, especially the fish and the beetles. The seven-foot-long *pirarucu* is truly a sight to behold. In the center of the pavilion is a large fish tank, where many live species may also be seen through observation windows that line the walls. For anyone with the slightest interest in the natural history of the Amazon region, I can not recommend too highly a visit to this thoroughly fascinating institution.

As if the collection of river and forest specimens were not enough, the Japanese director of the museum has also created a gift shop that sells the very best examples of Brazilian handicrafts I have ever seen gathered in a single locale in that country. Many of the crafts, in particular the baskets and bark drawings, are the products of still healthy Indian economies, the work of tribal artisans who continue to dwell in remote areas far from contact with the modern world. Prices at the gift shop are reasonable if not cheap, and marked in dollars. The museum is open every day except Monday from 9 a.m. till 5:30 p.m., and the entrance fee is less than a dollar.

Another excellent source of Indian and artist crafts is the **ARPP-AM,** Avenida Adolfo Dulk 165 (tel. 244-2246), in the Parque Acariquara section of Aleixo. ARPP stands for Associacao dos Artesaos de Arte Primitiva e Popular, which is a league of artisans who work in primitive and popular media. The Association is currently led by the brothers Andrade, Rogério, and Cláudio, and the address listed here is that of the suburban studio where Cláudio—a highly talented woodcarver—does his work. When I visited the studio, Cláudio showed me an album with photographs of Association members' work, much of it quite appealing and unique. But the Association also maintains contact with large numbers of tribal artisans, and offers for sale numerous objects of Indian workmanship, especially baskets, utensils, and masks. The best place to see the Association's stock of crafts is not at Cláudio's studio, but on the floating pier in Manaus where they set up a stand whenever a cruise ship comes to port.

A RIVER DAY TRIP

The eight-hour river excursion organized by **Amazon Explorers,** Rua Quintino Bocaiuva 189 (tel. 092/232-3052), came highly recommended. I boarded the double-decker boat around 8 a.m. from the floating pier. (This pier is a considerable engineering accomplishment in itself, for it must not only accommodate many sizes of ships and boats, but also accompany the rise and fall of the river's seasonal water levels.) The company's excursion boat has a top deck, part of which is open to the sun, the other part covered by a permanent roof, with canvas side flaps for nighttime and inclement weather. Down below, there is a bar and gallery, four heads, and a souvenir stand selling T-shirts, hats, and suntan lotion.

As the boat glides from its slip, you get your first view of the city from the water. Most of the buildings sit on the high ground, well back from the river embankments. Since the river was low when I made the trip, I could see the outlines of the creeks and the highwater marks on the pilings and stone retaining walls. The stilt houses *(palafitas)* stand like circus clowns on stilts high above the water. Boats are everywhere on the move, mostly canoes, some propelled by paddles, others by outboard motors. There are also the *barcos regionais,* the typically long and narrow barges with superstructures covering the entire deck. Like so many *Merrimacks,* these floating houses of the river traders seem to ride right on the surface of the water.

For the first few miles as you head down stream, you pass a half-dozen giant platforms moored in midstream—floating gas stations. The shore is lined with saw mills; millions of board feet of sawed lumber stockpiled on land, millions more uncut in the form of saw logs floating in the river on the edges of the banks. Roughly an hour later you begin to pick up the silty coloring of the Rio Solimoēs, as it joins the dark Rio Negro and flows alongside without mixing, as if each river still occupied its own separate channel: the "living" river and the "dead" river. This "meeting of the waters" stretches on for several miles until the rivers have finally melded into the yellowish Amazon. But here you reverse course and begin to run up the Solimoēs, hoping to sight a few dolphins, and sure enough —as if responding to a predetermined script—the rose- and gray-colored *botos* begin to surface and submerge as they accompany the lazy perambulation of the slow-moving boat.

The vegetation that's visible along the banks of the Solimoēs as you sail on for almost two hours is all secondary growth. It can even be said to be sparse in places. You pass no settlements, but there are scattered farms at decent intervals at the edges of the shore. At each of these homesteads, a system of wooden pipes can be seen running from the water and disappearing over the embankment. These are the hollow branches of the *imbambeira,* a deciduous tree, linked together to make a conduit for carrying water to the fields and houses. For any real experience of the dense jungle, it would be necessary to travel many more hours above Manaus you are told by your guide.

At a clearing where there is a single residence, you make your first stop. Past the dwelling, past a small garden plot where scrawny chickens are scratching the ground, past a few banana and mango trees, you follow a wooden boardwalk into the forest to a platform built over an *igapó,* a creek bed that is permanently flooded. Growing in the water are the giant lily pads, the *Victória Régia,* today very much a symbol of the Amazon despite their being named to honor an English monarch. That crackling sound you hear beneath the lilies is the gnawing of piranhas and other small fish who feed on the plants and give them their perforated appearance. Here several hundred yards beyond the riverbank, the jungle begins to reappear. Wildlife is abundant, especially birds and butterflies. But you can see small alligators as you approach the platform, especially if you are quick of eye, as they slide off the mud banks into the safety of the water. Kingfishers dive for fish. Many other birds—blues, yellows, reds—dart among the branches, or bounce along the water's edge as they feed, in what must be a particular treat for bird fanciers familiar with the names and habits of the various species. Flocks of black birds (called *anuns)* flit through the bulrushes and swamp cane as we retrace our steps to the river. When domesticated, they are said to talk as well as parrots.

For your second stop, you visit a small village, populated by migrants from the northeast. A *caboclo* (rural Brazilian) demonstrates how to tap a rubber tree. He tells you that he goes out at night with a head lantern like a miner's hat and taps all his trees. Then in the morning he gathers up the latex, which is rendered slowly in a little smokehouse over a fire using only green wood. When the substance coagulates, it is joined into large balls called *pelas,* which are collected by boat at riverside, along with the other produce like cacão, mandioca, and fruits grown by the little community. The caboclo is also an artisan, and some people buy his model canoes, delicately carved from rosewood. Others buy petrified piranhas or native-style jewelry. You'll walk into the village, a cluster of little wood buildings, including a diminutive clapboard chapel, to look at the cacão trees. The flowers grow almost stemless right from the trunk and mature into a large green fruit with a funny shape, like a pleated balloon. You'll also see the *castanheira* with its coconut-size *ouriço,* which when opened expels anywhere from 25 to 30 Brazil nuts.

From here you begin your return trip. Lunch is served on the boat, a delicious home-cooked fish stew and a variety of side dishes. You can drink little cocktails of Amazon fruit juices with cachaça. A while later, you stop at a swimming spot and everyone takes a cooling dip in the river, with much giggling and guffawing about the danger of piranhas. In fact, the fierce little fish seldom attacks humans, you are told, but a cow unfortunate enough to fall from a floating pen during the flood season can be consumed in seconds. You are back in Manaus by 3 p.m. The cost of the excursion is about $30 per person.

Informal Day Trips

Below the market, on any given day, there are dozens of boats tied up along the shore (or at the piers when the water is high) whose owners will take you on the river and cover pretty much the same attractions as the large companies. No lunch is served on these boats, and there is no deck to walk around on, but you also are not required to follow any formal program. The skipper will take you wherever you want to go—and may even have a few suggestions of his own. His fee should be no more than half of what the excursion boats charge.

Bugs

There are many small, flying insects that will penetrate the otherwise hermetic security of even the city's finest hotels. Come to the Amazon prepared to tolerate a certain amount of insect annoyance. If you are prone to allergic reactions from insect bites, bring plenty of repellent or other appropriate medications. To lessen the impact of insects, most overnight river excursions are on sites along the Rio Negro, where the relatively antiseptic ecological conditions keep the bug population to a minimum. The flora is also less disturbed along the Rio Negro, while the Solimoẽs is known for its fishing.

Overnight River Trips

Dozens of tour operators in Manaus, like Rio Amazonas Turismo (tel. 234-7308), offer overnights in the jungle, usually at special "lodges" or "villages," located three to six hours from the city, up the Rio Negro. Typically, these excursion packages offer one or two nights in comfortable accommodations, occasionally with hammocks for beds and a variety of daytime and evening programs. These include walks into the jungle, canoe trips up streams and creeks, and an alligator hunt, where flashlights are used to "freeze" the reptiles, which are then captured and released unharmed. A package of three days and two nights runs about $300 per person, and two days and one night, around $175. Cheaper overnights are also available through numerous other tour operators in Manaus. These generally involve accommodations that are considerably more rustic than those offered by operators on the upper end of the market.

ECOLOGICAL SAFARI

One of the more interesting excursions out of Manaus for the ecologically minded traveler, but suitable for the general public as well, is a seven-day river tour aboard an 80-foot boat called the *Tuna*. The *Tuna* has every comfort, including ten first-class, double-occupancy air-conditioned cabins, each with private bath. Other features include a well-equipped kitchen, dining room, lounge, bar, and a library well stocked with titles about the Amazon's ecosystem. The *Tuna* cruises far up the Rio Negro, making calls at several research stations, where there are scientific lectures and videotape presentations. The safari costs $805 per person. A mini-safari of four days is also available for $435.

More Jungle Tours

Other options for jungle overnights roughly in the same price range as the Ariau Tower are the **Amazon Lodge** and the **Amazon Village**, both reachable in Manaus at Rua Leonardo Malcher 734, (tel. 232-1454). The Lodge complex floats in the middle of Lake Juma, and is the more rustic of the two. The Village, slightly more pricey, provides the most deluxe digs available for a sojourn in the jungle.

Now if it's real—or close-to-real—adventure you're after, a relatively new excursion package has come on the travel market, known as **Nature Safaris** (which, along with the above locales, may be booked in the States through Brazil Nuts—800/553-9959). Nature Safaris can take you deep into the Amazon on an eight-day trek they call **Humboldt's Track,** named for the great German naturalist who explored this region from 1799 to 1804. You first embark from Manaus on a three-hour flight over the rain forest to the interior Amazon city of Gabriel da Cachoeira. From there you travel, sometimes by motorized canoe, others by four-wheel-drive vehicle, to small villages and up obscure channels along the trail Humboldt followed, crossing the Equator and visiting the three-nation border of Brazil, Colombia, and Venezuela on the way. The cost of this excursion is $700, plus $180 additional airfare, and requires both pre- and post-night stays in Manaus.

METRIC CONVERSIONS

Like almost every country in the world (the major exception is the United States), Rio uses the metric system of weights and measures. Thus you may find the following information useful. I suggest that you become familiar with the rough equivalents given below, or you can use the formulas if you need more exact conversions.

LENGTH

1 millimeter = 0.04 inches (*or* less than ¹⁄₁₆ inch)
1 centimeter = 0.39 inches (*or* just under ½ inch)
1 meter   = 1.09 yards (*or* about 39 inches)
1 kilometer = 0.62 mile (*or* about ⅔ mile)

To convert kilometers to miles, take the number of kilometers and multiply by .62 (for example, 25km × .62 = 15.5 miles).

To convert miles to kilometers, take the number of miles and multiply by 1.61 (for example, 50 miles × 1.61 = 80.5 km).

CAPACITY

1 liter = 33.92 ounces
        = 1.06 quarts
        = 0.26 gallons

To convert liters to gallons, take the number of liters and multiply by .26 (for example, 50 l × .26 = 13 gal).

To convert gallons to liters, take the number of gallons and multiply by 3.79 (for example, 10 gal × 3.79 = 37.9 l).

WEIGHT

1 gram   = 0.04 ounce (*or* about a paperclip's weight)
1 kilogram = 2.2 pounds

To convert kilograms to pounds, take the number of kilos and multiply by 2.2 (for example, 75kg × 2.2 = 165 lbs).

To convert pounds to kilograms, take the number of pounds and multiply by .45 (for example, 90 lb × .45 = 40.5kg).

AREA

1 hectare ($100m^2$) = 2.47 acres

To convert hectares to acres, take the number of hectares and multiply by 2.47 (for example, 20ha × 2.47 = 49.4 acres).

To convert acres to hectares, take the number of acres and multiply by .41 (for example, 40 acres × .41 = 16.4 ha).

TEMPERATURE

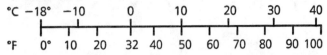

To convert degrees C to degrees F, multiply degrees C by 9, divide by 5, then add 32 (for example 9/5 × 20°C + 32 = 68°F).

To convert degrees F to degrees C, subtract 32 from degrees F, then multiply by 5, and divide by 9 (for example, 85°F − 32 × 5/9 = 29°C).

INDEX

GENERAL INFORMATION

SIGHTS AND ATTRACTIONS

Rio

Day-Trip and Excursion Areas

Iguaçu Falls

Manaus

Ouro Preto

Salvador

ACCOMMODATIONS

Rio

Day-Trip and Excursion Areas

KEY TO ABBREVIATIONS: *B* = Budget; *D* = Deluxe; *FC* = First Class ("Upper Bracket"); *M* = Moderately priced

RESTAURANTS

R i o

KEY TO ABBREVIATIONS: B = Budget; E = Expensive ("Upper Bracket"); M = Moderately priced

Day-Trip and Excursion Areas

NOW, SAVE MONEY ON ALL YOUR TRAVELS!
Join Frommer's™ Dollarwise® Travel Club

Saving money while traveling is never a simple matter, which is why the **Dollarwise Travel Club** was formed 31 years ago. Developed in response to requests from Frommer's Travel Guide readers, the Club provides cost-cutting travel strategies, up-to-date travel information, and a sense of community for value-conscious travelers from all over the world.

In keeping with the money-saving concept, the annual membership fee is low—$18 for U.S. residents or $20 for residents of Canada, Mexico, and other countries—and is immediately exceeded by the value of your benefits, which include:

1. Any TWO books listed on the following pages.
2. Plus any ONE Frommer's City Guide.
3. A subscription to our quarterly newspaper, *The Dollarwise Traveler*.
4. A membership card that entitles you to purchase through the Club all Frommer's publications for 33% to 50% off their retail price.

The eight-page *Dollarwise Traveler* tells you about the latest developments in good-value travel worldwide and includes the following columns: **Hospitality Exchange** (for those offering and seeking hospitality in cities all over the world); **Share-a-Trip** (for those looking for travel companions to share costs); and **Readers Ask . . . Readers Reply** (for those with travel questions that other members can answer).

Aside from the Frommer's Guides and the Gault Millau Guides, you can also choose from our Special Editions. These include such titles as *California with Kids* (a compendium of the best of California's accommodations, restaurants, and sightseeing attractions appropriate for those traveling with toddlers through teens); *Candy Apple: New York with Kids* (a spirited guide to the Big Apple by a savvy New York grandmother that's perfect for both visitors and residents); *Caribbean Hideaways* (the 100 most romantic places to stay in the Islands, all rated on ambience, food, sports opportunities, and price); *Honeymoon Destinations* (a guide to planning and choosing just the right destination from hundreds of possibilities in the U.S., Mexico, and the Caribbean); *Marilyn Wood's Wonderful Weekends* (a selection of the best mini-vacations within a 200-mile radius of New York City, including descriptions of country inns and other accommodations, restaurants, picnic spots, sights, and activities); and *Paris Rendez-Vous* (a delightful guide to the best places to meet in Paris whether for power breakfasts or dancing till dawn).

To join this Club, simply send the appropriate membership fee with your name and address to: Frommer's Dollarwise Travel Club, 15 Columbus Circle, New York, NY 10023. Remember to specify which single city guide and which two other guides you wish to receive in your initial package of member's benefits. Or tear out the next page, check off your choices, and send the page to us with your membership fee.

FROMMER'S CITY GUIDES

(Pocket-size guides to sightseeing and tourist accommodations and facilities in all price ranges.)

☐ Amsterdam/Holland	$8.95	☐ Montréal/Québec City	$8.95
☐ Athens	$8.95	☐ New Orleans	$8.95
☐ Atlanta	$8.95	☐ New York	$8.95
☐ Atlantic City/Cape May	$8.95	☐ Orlando	$8.95
☐ Barcelona	$7.95	☐ Paris	$8.95
☐ Belgium	$7.95	☐ Philadelphia	$8.95
☐ Boston	$8.95	☐ Rio	$8.95
☐ Cancún/Cozumel/Yucatán	$8.95	☐ Rome	$8.95
☐ Chicago	$8.95	☐ Salt Lake City	$8.95
☐ Denver/Boulder/Colorado		☐ San Diego	$8.95
Springs	$7.95	☐ San Francisco	$8.95
☐ Dublin/Ireland	$8.95	☐ Santa Fe/Taos/Albuquerque	$8.95
☐ Hawaii	$8.95	☐ Seattle/Portland	$7.95
☐ Hong Kong	$7.95	☐ Sydney	$8.95
☐ Las Vegas	$8.95	☐ Tampa/St. Petersburg	$8.95
☐ Lisbon/Madrid/Costa del Sol.	$8.95	☐ Tokyo	$7.95
☐ London	$8.95	☐ Toronto	$8.95
☐ Los Angeles	$8.95	☐ Vancouver/Victoria	$7.95
☐ Mexico City/Acapulco	$8.95	☐ Washington, D.C.	$8.95
☐ Minneapolis/St. Paul	$8.95		

SPECIAL EDITIONS

☐ Beat the High Cost of Travel	$6.95	☐ Motorist's Phrase Book (Fr/Ger/Sp)	$4.95
☐ Bed & Breakfast—N. America	$11.95	☐ Paris Rendez-Vous	$10.95
☐ California with Kids	$14.95	☐ Swap and Go (Home Exchanging)	$10.95
☐ Caribbean Hideaways	$14.95	☐ The Candy Apple (NY with Kids)	$12.95
☐ Manhattan's Outdoor		☐ Travel Diary and Record Book	$5.95
Sculpture	$15.95		

☐ Honeymoon Destinations (US, Mex & Carib) $14.95

☐ Where to Stay USA (From $3 to $30 a night) $10.95

☐ Marilyn Wood's Wonderful Weekends (CT, DE, MA, NH, NJ, NY, PA, RI, VT) $11.95

☐ The New World of Travel (Annual sourcebook by Arthur Frommer for savvy travelers) . . $16.95

GAULT MILLAU

(The only guides that distinguish the truly superlative from the merely overrated.)

☐ The Best of Chicago	$15.95	☐ The Best of Los Angeles	$16.95
☐ The Best of France	$16.95	☐ The Best of New England	$15.95
☐ The Best of Hong Kong	$16.95	☐ The Best of New York	$16.95
☐ The Best of Italy	$16.95	☐ The Best of Paris	$16.95
☐ The Best of London	$16.95	☐ The Best of San Francisco	$16.95
	☐ The Best of Washington, D.C.	$16.95	

ORDER NOW!

In U.S. include $2 shipping UPS for 1st book; $1 ea. add'l book. Outside U.S. $3 and $1, respectively.

Allow four to six weeks for delivery in U.S., longer outside U.S.

Enclosed is my check or money order for $_____

NAME _____

ADDRESS _____

CITY _____ STATE _____ ZIP ____

0690